SALTWATER

GAIL SOLIWODA CASSILLY

Editor: Richard Weiss
Book Designer: Ben Pierce

Bluebird Publishing Co.
8220 Exchange Way
St. Louis, MO 63144
www.Bluebirdbookpub.com

for
Max and Daisy

SALTWATER

PREFACE

I t's bedtime and I'm cozily retired from disturbance – my pillows precisely fluffed, my feather comforter pulled high, my eyes lazily focused on my nightly reading – when suddenly, *Wham!* The full-body weight of an idea tumbles from the sky and crash-lands onto my waterbed and me, waves everywhere. The disruptive idea is accompanied by a booming voice, no nighttime lullaby sweetness: it commands, "*Write the story!*" Bizarrely obedient, I rise to search for pen and paper and just like that, I start to write.

My wide-eyed response warrants the first-aid of a disclaimer: I am a sculptor by trade, accustomed to communicating in tactile shapes. If I am to obey the command to now shape with words, I will need to fall back more heavily on the trusty broad and cushioned bed of artistic liberty. After all, everyone knows that artists are beings entitled to excessive amounts of liberty and a lion's share of forgiveness, permitting them to pull off capers and dodge bullets like ole' time born-in-the-saddle bandits. But, even claiming this entitlement as my own, I am wary regarding the particular challenge of words – so tiny, so weightless compared to dirtying my hands with wet and heavy malleable clay. Can words be equally satisfying and giving? My written language may, quite naturally, ooze moist, kinetic, exaggerated, fleshy, squishy words, pounded words, gashed words, painted words. Words that stretch and compress until they are transformed into the shapely body of a remembered whole.

As the whole of the story comes to life it will inevitably be colored in with splashes of the following:

1: A child's tendency towards random, out of context memories – images reformatted to establish meaning for a young and inexperienced mind.

2: The rusting of memory over the passing of time. With such lapses, however, comes the clarity to discern from a great physical and emotional distance exactly what remains memorable in mind and heart. What to share.

3: Subjectivity. These white pages will be infused with the blood-red life of my own perspective. I may sever limbs, repositioning them awkwardly and questionably, as I explore the proper means for portraying individuals, memories, and the truth as my eyes have come to see it and my mind has come to know it. Indeed, I may take great artistic liberty in the polychrome rendering of the start to the finish, the before and the after, the then and the now.

And, as for now, onto the untold stories: beautiful shiny gems and crushing sorrows.

BOOK ONE

CHAPTER 1. THE START

I slithered out between my mother's taut exhausted legs, exiting the warm womb of oblivion, to find myself detached and breathing on my own in Erie, Pennsylvania. It happened in a hospital room on the east side of town in the wee sleepy, early morning hours of November 29, 1947. Despite the disheveling hour, I appeared groomed with a Dairy Queen tuft of a curl on top my head, enough to earn a pink bow right then and there. In addition to the bow, with no more than my first bawling cry, I acquired a nationality, a religion, a family, and a place – just like that. Beginnings come with far more than one cord attached, and when you stay long enough in one place to grow from 20 inches to 66 inches, as I did, you might wake one day and find yourself bound *and* defined by the *somewhere* of your birth – even against your will.

The Erie, Pa. where I landed was heavily populated by skis: Poplaski, Dombrowski, Chludzinski, Lipinski, Bronaskowski, Zielewski, Dylewski, Pinski, Pelowski, Weunski – more snowless skis than you could dream of. My birth certificate didn't come with a ski, but I was still a full-fledged member of the club: "The 100% Polish Through and Through as Far Back as You Dare Go Club."

I was born into the family name of Soliwoda. In Polish the "w" is pronounced like a "v" (*voda*), but in Erie, Pa. the "w" was pronounced just like a plain ole' "w" (*woda*) -rhyming with the likes of *wotta*. So… pronounce Saul – eh – wotta and you've got it, or at least, the American version of it. I grew up thinking that my family name, precisely translated, meant "saltwater." Gail Joan Saltwater. But upon more recent inquiry, I was led on a rather untranslatable Polish journey of "No…not exactly…. but…yes, water is voda/woda….and there's a salt connection in soli…. or…perhaps it means more the act of someone pouring salt into water… but it could be…" The more I asked, the less I understood. Maybe Polish translations varied according to region, or maybe I was baptized into a joke. Don't know, but in Erie, Pa. we stood for saltwater.

For the most part, I regretted not being a ski like most people; Soliwoda, believe it or not, was harder to pronounce for many than the previously mentioned ski names. Erieites were accustomed to the multitude of skis – the voda/woda was more foreign sounding, more questionable as to origin and belonging. Occasionally, someone would interpret my name in a wildly exotic manner, like being Indian or African. When that happened I loved the name without reserve. Thoughts of such origins sprouted fantasies in the depths of my Polish Catholic being and hazily doodled lines formed mapping out an escape route from the common, yet tainted, place of my birth. You see, I *had* to escape from the place of it for in my young eyes and mind, tragedy and befuddled logic had conspired to turn my birthplace into nothing but a thick cloud of suffocating loss.

....

When I study Ben and Irene, my parents, through photos of the years prior to their marriage and prior to me, they radiate images as far away from loss as possible: they practically glow, even in black and white. They are young. They are not the "them" I know, older and in living color. I don't know if I am glimpsing the real of each of them in black and white, or a for-the-camera-only flicker of a performance of real. If a picture is truly worth a thousand words, then I suspect that a picture can, likewise, conceal a thousand words; after all, how much can the snap of the shutter and a flash of the flash really show? Their youth is, perhaps, the greatest and the most irrefutable revelation offered. As their child, it simply astounds me.

There's Ben: Propped against a car door, legs crossed, arms dangling loose, head cocked, teasing smile, eyes hooded but penetrating, high pompadour, medium brown colored hair: James Dean! Well, a Polish version, perhaps. The nose is a dead giveaway. The pose is pure cocky, attractive, and sexy; it's saying, "Hey, it's me, *Hard-to-Get*." Despite his limited years, he appears sure of himself and in control. I recognize those things about him and they serve to convince me that he is, indeed, my father. And there are those eyes: *his* eyes. They are sweet and tempting with their lids drooping over ever so slightly. They call such a pair "bedroom eyes." He has the most gorgeous bedroom eyes.

There's Irene: Model thin, strikingly attractive, long wavy hair coiled in a curl at the ends and medium in color like Ben's, a tilted smile, coy eyes arched with super tweezed eyebrows – everything about her coquettish and seductive, including her outfit. She wears the overall look of an accomplished hunter, the look of a woman who knows that she can track and bag any man she wants. She wears the look like a weapon. Even in group photos, arm in arm with her girlfriends, her eyes are secretly whispering to the camera: "Hey there, focus on me…only me."

These photos of each of them capture beauty and bravado, framing a seemingly idyllic blink of time void of the trappings and insecurity of getting there: youth at its best, without youth at its worst.

My mother shared with me the fact that when it came to my dad she was, beyond a doubt, the pursuer and he the pursued. They met through her close gal pal Vickey Kocon and double-dated with her and her main squeeze Stanley Kulesa. Ben made it pretty clear from the start that he wasn't seriously interested in her – cute…yes, but too young to bother with. Ben was born in 1919 and Irene was born in 1923; that difference of four years seemed to matter to him, providing a mathematical excuse for his chilly shoulder. He implied rather bluntly that: 1. She was out of her league (which she wasn't) and 2. She didn't stand a chance with him (which she did). Her haughty response to his assumptions held the perfect air of, "Don't really care." And, with that, the match was made: Mr. Hard-To-Get would marry Ms. I-Can-Get-Any-Man-I-Want. It was as clear as a pair of stars twinkling above Erie, Pa.

Naturally, this astrological discovery took some time to identify itself; they did not immediately recognize that their contrary positions aligned them like puzzle pieces cut to tuck into a fit. They did not immediately welcome the pasting over of singular photos ripe with independence and availability, with that of a twosome depicting smitten and taken. But… their separateness soon morphed into a *BenandIrene*, rolling so smoothly off the tongues of those they knew that you would've thought it had been so forever.

BenandIrene had a long engagement, more than three years. Irene was only 18 years old when she became engaged; by then she had already known Bernard Joseph Soliwoda for over two years. Maybe that's why she appeared too young for him when they first met. She would have barely been 16 compared to his adultish 20. Their engagement was a long distance one for 22 months while Ben actively served in the Navy overseas in Hawaii. Rummaging through the basement one time, I came across a banded packet of romantic cards sent from my dad to my mom during their overseas separation. I presume that letters were enclosed, but only the cards remained – cards syrupy with love and longing, hope and promise, and signed simply. "All My Love, Ben." Twenty-two months of separation is a cruel eternity for young lovers – hell, twenty-two hours is often more than a young romance can bear. It's hard to imagine the torturous nights and meaningless days that crawled along at a snail's pace; time pausing to tick from second to second, everything virtually standing still in terms of the heart. Aren't we lucky that time continues to move even when it seems not to, even when we cannot.

....

Before moving on to their wedding and beyond, before fully entering the phase of their togetherness, there are separate things to tell.

Irene was the eldest child of Alex and Stefania Poplaski, the first of four and the overall shining star of the clan, despite the permanent stain of having been conceived out of wedlock. She was intelligent as well as pretty, managing to skip a year of grade school at St. Hedwig's and making her parents proud. Jean, her sister, could best be described as painfully shy, nervous and twitchy, lacking in confidence, and seemingly resentful. Jean's name is actually listed as Francis on her birth certificate – a Catholic saint name, male and all, required for Baptism, perhaps – but we always knew her as Aunt Jean. To add to Jean's identity dilemma, my grandmother's naturalization papers list Jean/Francis as Genieve, which may or may not be the Polish translation of Jean. Follow? I'll just call her Jean.

Alex, Jr., Uncle Al to me (his parents and sibs called him Junior), was intellectually challenged, short-changed in some basic but unnamable way. It was obvious. He rarely talked to his nieces and nephews and his silent presence was embarrassingly awkward and disconcerting. As my uncle, I figured that it was his duty to act the grown-up, but he never quite fit the part, leaving the full burden of polite conversation squarely on my tiny shoulders, being that I always wanted to please. Uncle Al lived with my grandmother for what seemed like forever and their mother/son bickering had that very same feel to it. My mother was the unhappy heir of the Uncle Al parenting plan once my grandmother died: only one of many reasons why my mother seethed with frustration towards the family she was born into. Charlie, the youngest child, was born mentally retarded – that was the precise term used at the time. I don't know the details of his condition since his name was rarely spoken, but I do know that it was severe enough to warrant placing him in an institution once he grew to be too problematic to care for at home. He was sent to Polk State Hospital, a two-hour drive from Erie, Pa. My stranger-of-an-uncle lived out the rest of his life in that institution, dying in 1960 at age 29. I don't recall my mother ever speaking of him.

Being Polish did not appear to be a point of pride for my mother, at least not in my eyes as I grew up around her. She took personal offense at stereotypical Polish jokes, showing zero tolerance for the, apparently, too-close-to-home mockery of her own. I sensed early on that her Polish ancestry was something she would have preferred to blot-out; no "POLISH AND PROUD OF IT!" threatened to roar from her pretty painted lips. But I didn't know if the crux of the issue was related specifically to her "being Polish," or to some cloud of embarrassment and shame over life within the Poplaski household. I suspect the latter, as she had a trunk full of issues with the ways and means of her parents. She coped by keeping her emphasis on being American, *only* American. She had her own way of running away.

I guess I inherited the escape gene from her.

In our own household I got tangled up in the roots of her homegrown discontent. It was unavoidable because it was who she was and who she was was how she mothered. And it didn't help one bit that, still at a tender age, I developed the chronic disease of Feeling Too Much. Privately, I set about interpreting the deluge of my sensitivities with only the library of a child's mind for reference, translating and cataloguing my mother's personal vibes into: embarrassment, inferiority, shame, and last, but not least, stupidity. I guessed, for whatever reason, that all the vibes had Polish family origins and I never guessed beyond that. I knew no beyond that.

And so it was, without any clear understanding, I, a dutiful child, said to myself and to no one else: *"These are my vibes, too, for I am her daughter: This is Me."*

Dad was the middle son of Anthony and Mary Soliwoda. He was couched between my Uncle Stanley who acted like he knew everything, and Uncle Chet (Chester), my dimpled godfather who could do no wrong in my eyes. He lived with his family on the ground level of a two-family flat on East 21st Street that they owned. The east side of town was the Polish side of town. The whole of the east side looked pretty much the same to me, but my dad's parents believed that they lived in the "better" part of the east side, as opposed to East 4th St., the lower part where my mother and her family lived. That supposed distinction was cause enough for a prickly rash to erupt and linger between my paternal and maternal grandparents.

Ben's friends thought of him as a fun-loving sort of guy disposed to joking and yucking it up. My mom claimed that movie going with him could be an embarrassment because he was prone to releasing mighty chuckles at times when no one else managed a titter. Ben had an easy-going way about him, a persona far different from that of his regimented, stone-faced mother, and just maybe because of her.

He joined the Navy in 1942 during World War II and quickly shipped out overseas to Oahu. In Hawaii he was stationed at the Pearl Harbor Navy Yard, working as a mechanic in the shipping yard. He arrived after the deadly attack; nonetheless, he got a Certificate of Honorable Service. I found it. It reads:

This is to certify that during the Second World War
Bernard J. Soliwoda
was employed by the United States Navy at the
PEARL HARBOR NAVY YARD
for a period of 34 months
Where his services contributed to the mission of that Pacific Naval
Base in support of the UNITED STATES FLEET
For his faithful work and his contribution to the winning of the war
he is awarded this Certificate of Honorable Service to the United
States Government.

This might not be as impressive as a shiny polished medal dangling from a ribbon, *but still*, my dad clearly contributed to winning the war. He was a doer. It says so right here. Go Dad!

....

The East 21st St. Polish boy marries the East 4th St. Polish girl in living color.

There's Ben and Irene: She, in a long white satin dress swirling out onto the ground in choreographed semi-circles, a dainty bouquet of white and lavender flowers in the grasp of her ivory hand, a lacey veil cresting her precise brown curls, and a face all but lost to the rosiest of cheeks and a manicured smile. He, in a dark fitted tuxedo and white bow tie, the jewelry of a wedding band glittering golden on a slender finger, the bedroom eyes at their bluest, wide awake, and victoriously proud.

The church-blessed photo was taken on April 10, 1944, commencing the first day of their life together as man and wife. Before God they vowed togetherness through the best and worst of times, though their minds envisioned only on the best.

Ben was home on leave from duty when they pronounced their vows. Two weeks after the wedding, they departed together for Pearl Harbor; Ben returned to his mechanic's work and Irene became employed doing clerical work on the base. They weren't destined, however, to enjoy the luxury of being a footloose twosome for long. I don't know if pregnancy was the game plan, or if they hadn't fully mastered the cycle of timely restraint called for in Catholic lovemaking, but planned or not their first child, Karen Jean Soliwoda, was born in Oahu on March 23, 1946. She was christened with an island name, as well: Leilani. My mother was the first to admit that she felt totally unprepared to have a child, that she was unskilled and unknowledgeable in every possible way, that she might not be ready for…but her plumped up belly of nine months presented no alternative, crowning her ready. Little baby Karen came out needy and howling for a mother, ready or not.

Irene's first problem was an immediate one: breast-feeding. True to her own prediction, she failed miserably at it. Her breasts generated famine. She compensated by bottling up papaya juice to hush up and fill up wailing Leilani. To this day – wearing a long-suffering smirk – my sister claims that the deprivation of mother's milk and the substitution of papaya juice was tantamount to physical neglect, providing a legitimate excuse for any and all of life's challenges. Having failed to unearth any clear data on her hypothesis, the Papaya Juice Theory rests with a question mark. It may well have, however, had plenty to do with the relentlessly fussy and colicky nature of her early months.

A peek at the proud Papa: he stands shirtless and tan, holding his overly-swaddled little daughter, raising her up like a grand prize winner hoists a trophy. In male fashion, he is oblivious to the juice/milk/breast crisis plaguing his wife and driving her to tears. He's grinning like a corndog goofball!

With the ending of Ben's official tour of duty, the threesome headed back to Erie, Pa., returning with a clutter of baby paraphernalia and a three-month-old daughter. They settled into the second story flat above Mary and Anthony Soliwoda. Ben found work with General Electric – just like his father and stepfather had – and Irene transitioned into the fulltime post of housewife and mother. Karen's role of "precious one and only" soon altered, as well. Nine months after their return, Irene was once again pregnant. Yep, me this time, the one with the DQ curl on top of her head. From all accounts my early baby days went without trauma or fuss compared to Karen's. She was the test baby, the lets try-it-and-see-if-it-works baby. No papaya juice for me.

Five decades after my appearance, for the occasion of my 50th birthday, my mother penned a letter ripe with remembering:

> "It was a very cold, snowy night when your dad called
> for a taxi to take us to Hamot Hospital. This was the <u>only</u>
> time, out of three births, that Daddy actually took Mommy to the
> hospital, and it was the only easy and quick delivery with no
> complications. Your dad's first words – 'Look at her hair!'
> You had olive skin and brown hair curly and thick enough for the
> nurse to form a curl and tie a pink bow around it. You were
> so easy to take care of – a perfect baby!"

Even at 50, my hunger for parental praise and approval hadn't been sated. I craved it constantly, like chocolate. The writing of "Daddy" and "Mommy," with their sing-songie "ddy" and "mmy" endings, lullabied sweetly in my ears, nearly curling me fetal upon reading them.

In the same letter, she wrote about my fearlessness.

> "A perfect example of your fearless side was the day you
> nearly gave me a heart attack. I had been to visit your dad in the
> hospital and your grandmother had put both of you down for a nap.
> Later, as I got out of the car, I heard, 'Hi Mommy' and there you
> were, both legs hanging over the window ledge of the 2nd floor flat we
> lived in. I think that day stands out like no other. You were three."

Now I wonder why my dad was in the hospital? And, I wonder why I don't feel so fearless anymore? I am, in fact, quite fearful right now – fearful of confronting the memories and words needed to flesh out this story, fearful of the price of honesty and the toll of remembering. Browsing through photos provides a much softer path to recall, posed and selective snapshots revealing the best glued and tabbed into albums for the sole purpose of looking back. But...sometimes, in your browsing, you inadvertently page across a photo that turns your mouth dry and knots your heart, all in a split second – a photo that should never have made it into a family album. A photo that doesn't belong anywhere.

CHAPTER 2. GREENGARDEN BLVD.

While I was dangling my legs out the window of the second story flat, my dad was busy constructing our own brand spanking new house. He was doing this on evenings and days off work. I suspect he had friends who helped out, and certainly he subcontracted this and that, but still, if you ask me, it was a mighty ambitious undertaking while holding down a fulltime job.

My parents ventured beyond the Polish side of town, heading west and buying an acre of land that came to be known as 3304 Greengarden Boulevard. The area was transitioning from country wilderness into residential suburb. Though the move was little more than five miles from our familiar east side turf, it felt like hundreds. It felt like we were leaving Poland. My mother opened her arms wide to embrace the move. She welcomed it as a bona fide escape from her conflicted past.

All the front and back yards in this west-side part of town appeared humongous to me. Many were flanked on both sides by undeveloped forested lots with a wild and woolly look about them. I was sure that we were building smack dab into the middle of adventure. The homes being erected were ranch style brick, way different than the two-story frame and brick variety crammed in tight rows along east side streets. The ranch homes were awash in land, allowing sun and clouds to drape themselves around them and pour graciously in on all four sides. Our home was being constructed in bricks the color of my hair, blonde bricks – a groovy out of the ordinary color for brick. But groovier than the color of brick was the boulevard: an island of manicured green dividing the wide newly paved road for no apparent reason other than to call itself a boulevard. We felt rich just looking at it!

My dad's modest two-bedroom layout was smaller than some and larger than others. It fit somewhere dead center, which was where we wanted to be, where we wanted to belong. Alongside the house, he built a garage accessed by a long gravel driveway that would one day turn to concrete and pave us in for good. My dad set about doing things the right way, guiding us up the ladder one rung at a time to becoming a modern all-American family. We ventured beyond our elders, all of whom had emigrated from Poland and planted themselves in America for our future benefit. Uprooting their settled efforts, we transplanted anew for the very same benefit.

It wasn't long before we discovered that we had unknowingly swapped Polish territory for Italian territory. Nearly every family building around us seemed to be Italian: Luciano, D'Aurora, DeDad, DeLoretto, Amendola. No skis to be found, just the woda/voda of us as conspicuous as could be in our Italian neck of the woods. This supposed American melting pot of a suburb was filled with spaghetti and meatballs, emitting smells my nose strayed towards, defecting early on from my pork and sauerkraut upbringing. My parents accepted the tomato red of the neighborhood in stride. After all, Polish jokes and Italian jokes are totally interchangeable. They became best of friends with two of the Italian couples directly across the street, I mean, the boulevard. An easy chumminess formed on both sides of the boulevard – it was as if Greengarden Blvd. was its own nationality. You would think that the Polish neighborhoods would have offered up the same kind of chumminess, even more so, but somehow they didn't. There, everyone seemed slightly guarded, slyly protective of their rectangular turf and the hard-earned possessions housed upon it. It felt as if no one was sure that they wanted to be a part of what they *were* a part of. But…none of that mattered anymore. That neighborhood was history to us. We belonged somewhere else.

Right around the time my dad was building our house, he redesigned our lives in another way, as well, by joining the fire department. This decision ignited sparks of disharmony between my mother and her mother-in-law: my mother being against it and my grandma for it. Grandma nudged her son towards the green color of financial security, while my mother nudged her husband away from the fiery color of danger. I don't know if Grandma won out with the heft of her formidable will, or if Dad took manly charge and decided to do what *he* wanted to do, despite the problematic female divide, but the flames around the decision-making process were extinguished when he became a full-fledged member of the Erie Fire Department.

His job was both glamorous and thrilling to me: the uniform, the shiny red truck, and the firehouse itself where all the uniformed men congregated, mostly in backslapping jovial spirits. A firehouse visit was an earned family perk: slipping our feet into giant idled boots, wrapping our thighs around the cold, slippery brass pole connecting the upper sleep level to the ground awake level, and mounting the awesome beast of the truck itself. Holy cow! What more could a kid ask for? I gawked in fascination at the vast assortment of matching firefighting clothing and boots lined up in marching order rows. The display was impressive, but the items looked rather hollow and useless without the bulk and skill of their inhabitants – kind of like bodies without souls. The empty shells stood ready 24/7, waiting for manly bodies to slide down the pole, hop inside, and ignite their purpose. Then…off to the rescue…lights flashing and sirens blazing, just like in the movies.

Those boots that I loved to step into – almost up to my neck it seemed – weren't the only, or the first, boots to have captured my youthful and vivid imagination.

....

Anthony Soliwoda, Dad's dad, was born in Poland in 1895. He had thirteen brothers and sisters, including three sets of twins, some of whom died at birth. At the time I touched ground, Grandpa was dwelling in the bottom level of the two-family flat with his wife, Mary, and his mother, known as Bobka, and my parents and sister were living above them. From what I could tell – when I was old enough to surmise anything whatsoever – Bobka appeared to be close to a million years old. Due to one leg being significantly shorter than the other, she clopped around with a customized black boot on one foot; meaning, a painted block of wood fastened to the bottom of it to level out her tiny, tilting frame. She dressed almost religiously in full-scale black, buttoned up to the neck and all the way down to the black painted block. Her boot, with its clumsy sound and appearance, is what I remember about her most, but another pair outdid even Bobka's noisy boot in my memory.

Anthony was a handsome man with a full head of silver gray hair combed straight back in mafia-like strokes. His three-clip suspenders yanked his pants upwards at two points in front and one point in back, dead center. Though he was only in his 50's when I buddied around with him, I thought that he, like his mother, was ancient. Physically, that is all I remember about him, *except* for his hulking black work boots, which housed his toes, and his black metal, trailer-shaped lunch box, which housed his work-a-day lunch. As a tyke of about four, his boots provided my first opportunity for employment – a kind of " work for food" type of deal. After a long day of work at the General Electric plant, Grandpa returned through the back door of the house, making his way to the kitchen table, plopping himself down onto a vinyl-covered chair, and groaning in relief like the old man he was. I'd be waiting for him, ready for my job to begin. I knew the drill. Leaning back into the chair, he extended the first of his big black boots towards me. I sat on the floor with my chubby legs spread to embrace the bulk of the dusty black leather and began the formidable task of unlacing the super-sized boot…loosening… loosening…until the worn black tongue of it could be peeled back from a damp, grayish white sock. Next, came a required series of twists and pulls to soften it all up for removal and retirement to its nighttime spot in the corner of the kitchen. The wiggling…twisting…pulling…grunting… carried on until the boot and I both toppled, marking the end of phase one of the operation. Phase two was a repeat of phase one on the remaining laced up boot. You can reread the phase if you feel the need to experience the full scope of my child labor.

Grandpa wore a mischievous smile during my battle with the boots, delighting in my struggle and doing absolutely nothing to make my chore any easier, which was fine with me. I exhibited a feisty stubbornness when it came to phase one and two, preferring to handle the job my way. Phase three, on the other hand, required something more akin to devotion.

It started with the peeling off of each sweaty ripe sock to free the flesh of his aching feet to bask on the cool kitchen lino. As instructed, I stretched a damp sock lengthwise and gave it a candy cane twist or two. Then, I threaded and worked the rope-like sock between each of his clotted toes, pulling back and forth with gusto, until the gunk of the factory workday fell away. I could just about hear his toes squeal with relief as they took to curling and uncurling with reeking delight. Some toe gunk clung to the sock, some disappeared into the cracks of the linoleum floor, and some stuck to me. Grandpa's toes were like wiggly wormy pets to me: *His* boots held my heart.

And as for my paycheck, his lunchbox provided it. The box itself seemed every bit as old as my ancient Grandpa, as well as being similarly dinged and dented. It, too, could've been born right around 1895. Quite different from the smell of his boots, socks, and feet, his lunchbox held the odor of a long sealed refrigerator, or a moldy kitchen – a kitchen that had wax paper, baloney, sausage, horseradish, ripe bananas, stale cookies, and a whole lot more baked onto its walls day after day for a thousand years or so, give or take a few. Smelling it did not require opening it; it reeked of eau de lunchbox inside and out. Tucked in there, along with the mighty smell, was my pay, a remnant of something or other saved: a trio of orange slices, a quarter of banana, a corner of sandwich…And, if I was super-duper lucky, I might be permitted to eke out the last few drops of tepid coffee from the rich silver lining of his submarine like thermos bottle. I had to be so verrrrrry careful with the thermos, though, for its insides were as fragile as they were shiny. In some ways I was like that thermos bottle: I was shiny with sweat and pride after my hard work, and he needed me on a daily basis. Being so little, I guess I was pretty fragile, as well.

One day our routine got messed up.

I did my part, but when it came time for my paycheck his lunchbox didn't click and clang open; instead, he reached deep into his pocket, pulled out a silver dollar, and placed it into my damp pink palm. I didn't have a clue what it was, but I got the certain feeling that it was something special. A few days later my grandpa dropped dead of a heart attack, right on his very own floor. He was fifty-seven years old. The scent of "eau de lunchbox" vanished from his kingdom and from my life.

....

"Salty" was Dad's nickname among firemen and non-firemen friends alike – even his brothers called him Salty. I've explained the origins – well, sort of – but in case you forgot, Salty came from the Soliwoda/ saltwater translation muddle. When I heard his comrades at the firehouse speak his nickname, it sounded seasoned with just the right pinch of camaraderie and affection. He was like a spice.

Since long work shifts extended day into night and night into day, Salty was often called upon to spend nights at the firehouse. Fires had a knack for being brutally insensitive to personal convenience and family affairs. Days and nights of extended hours on the clock were compensated for by added days off to balance things out fair and square. Within the firehouse, the men co-existed like a second family: they ate there, slept there, worked there, and during lag time, they played there – mostly cards. If you were to drive by the firehouse on a warm weather day, you'd find the big garage door heaved open and you'd witness authentic vignettes of their life together: men sitting in chairs tilted back precariously, feet propped up, lazily watching the traffic go by while puffing on cigars; or, men circled around a table shuffling cards fast and furious, chomping out their ploys on pulverized, slobby cigar stubs. Passers-by honked and waved at the reassuring sight of time off from disaster. No one begrudged these men playtime, for everyone knew they weren't goof-offs. They were men in waiting, waiting for the next siren to signal catastrophe, interrupting their calm and the calm of some very unfortunate others. When it screamed at them, shrill and unforgiving, they bolted into action with breathtaking speed and flawless execution – a moment of calm flushed away and a moment of urgency upon them. They were prepared for extremes.

Food was taken as seriously as fires. The comrades took turns buying groceries and preparing meals for those entrenched for the long shift ahead. Salty had the reputation of being among the best, if not the very best, of the firehouse cooks. He was a meat man…pork, kielbasa, meatballs, liver, kiszka (blood sausage)… Sometimes, he cooked up fancy gruesome things like thymus and pancreas – usually referred to under the more appetizing label of "sweetbreads." As his *first* family, *these* goodies were more often prepared for us, lucky us. It was during these delicacy meat meals that I learned to lean on ketchup – my buddy Heinz.

On bone-chilling winter days, when Dad returned home from long night shifts in the dawning light, the entire household would be nestled cozily in sleep. Before retiring to his bedroom to snuggle in the toasty warmth of his wife – before even removing his cumbersome coat – he crept into the bedroom that Karen and I shared, as sneaky as a trained mouse. My ears perked up at the hint of his tiptoeing steps, but I pretended to be asleep, while dread and delight rushed through me simultaneously. Slowly, he lifted the bottom corner of my blanket and placed his big, dry ice hands all over my tiny curled feet. Squirming giggles and half-hearted grumbles squealed out of me while he chuckled devilishly and shushed me back to sleep – as if *I* were to blame for his disruptive shenanigans! The reason that dread so often accompanied my delight had nothing to do with my dad's chilly hands finding my toes: I was (kind of, sort of) a chronic bed-wetter. What I feared/dreaded was his hand coming into contact with the damp, oddly sweet smelling puddle upon which I slept. Such a discovery could lead to punishment piled on top of the self-inflicted punishment of boiling embarrassment that torched me so regularly. As my heart raced at the sound of his approach, the best I could do was scurry to stretch my feet as far away from the damning evidence as possible. Alerting myself to his approach was the trickiest maneuver, given that I couldn't wake up in time to go to the bathroom in the first place. Sometimes, his well-equipped Polish nose caught me "wet handed" all on its own, leaving me shamed and miserable because I was more than certain that I had destroyed the joy of his return home – and that was, yet, another punishment to add to the heap.

....

Remember when I said my dad was doing things the *right* way? Well, no man is perfect. He made a serious error in shortchanging our fine new home of bedrooms. My parents occupied the main bedroom and Karen and I occupied the remaining one. Where would Tim go?

They were at it again.

Child three, Timothy James Soliwoda, arrived on November 23, 1951. Space was nipped and tucked here and there to accommodate the little prince, but the tightening was nothing compared to the joy of a boy child – certainly not from my parent's perspective. Our small family den took on a dual identity. In the daytime it held its place as a comfy TV den, but at nighttime, with only a few forceful tugs on the sofa bed, it unfurled into Tim's very own bedroom. This part-time room was a lousy deal for my brother, so after several years among us he herded himself and his possessions down into the basement, creating somewhat of a loner's boy pad and holing up there like a turtle under its self designed shell. He had good reason to want to escape us – us being my sister and I. My brother was so scarce at times that some of my friends teased that he was a figment of my imagination.

The picture that pops repeatedly into my head when I think of my brother as a little boy is one of him as a slight and scrawny, tow-headed kid of six being swallowed up in an over-sized pair of red swim trunks dotted with a yellow do-nothing pattern splashed about them. I think it took him nearly a decade to grow into those trunks. He's goofy cute at that age because his grin exposes two Bugs Bunny-ish front teeth that all but squawk, "What's up Doc?" It took him awhile to grow into his teeth, as well. During these growing up years, Tim occupied himself with demonic boyish pastimes. Roaming and inspecting the backyard, he captured a variety of unfortunate insects in assorted glass jars for mandatory participation in bug wars: a survival of the fittest spectacle. With a wicked glint in his eyes and fiendish glee plastered all over his Bugs Bunny grin, he upped the mayhem by vigorously shaking the jar and/or adding water to the bug mix. Despite my distaste and disinterest, Tim was forever scouting me out to share, "Hey Ya, look at this!" then, as if making a milkshake, jiggling the jar for all his skinny arms were worth. Tim started calling me "Ya" when he was a tiny tot; it was the half version of the full "YaYa" he assigned to me when he found it too difficult to pronounce "Gail." I could never understand how one led to the other, but the other is the one that stuck for him.

Peddling back in my mind to capture a young version of Karen, I see her as a foot taller than I, standing territorially over me with a long, slender intelligent face far superior in appearance to the oblivious, plump pumpkin look about me. Only 18 months separated us in age, but somehow those months gave her an air of confidence, poise even, like an anointed one, like a boss. In the early years of her self-appointed authority my brother and I complied in relatively docile fashion to her dictates. Revolt came with age.

We played a rather weird game: Church – Catholic Church, specifically. Our props amounted to vestments made out of old sheets with religious symbols drawn in magic markers, a makeshift chalice, and other homemade odds and ends needed to effectively dramatize Mass and the sacred mysteries that transpired therein. Karen, of course, played the role of priest and Tim and I played the role of congregants, sinners. We followed her priestly orders with nothing less than blind faith and devotion. And it wasn't easy, particularly at Communion time. Hosts for Tim and me amounted to circles cut out of paper – usually lined school paper with a bit of writing on one side. The priest, however, got a super-size host made from the soft white insides of a slice of Wonder Bread rolled into a dense bread ball and then flattened and trimmed into a giant holy host. Could I ever become a priest, I wondered? Communion hosts were stationed on the tongue until dissolved; waiting for paper hosts to dissolve without chewing was time consuming, as well as yucky. Dare I admit that when the priest's eyes were closed in prayer, I would, if I could, dislodge the pulp from the roof of my mouth and sacrilegiously chew it up, or more sacrilegiously spit it out in my hand. I also wondered if Italian kids played this kind of heavy-duty game? We tended to keep the game to ourselves, as if it were a Polish family secret.

In order to keep ourselves in good enough standing to receive any kind of Communion host we were obliged to play the Confession Game as well. Yes, Karen was the confessor and Tim and I were, you guessed it, the sinners. We used our bedroom door to form a partition, placing a chair on either side of it, for the pouring out of sins was a dark and secret affair. I don't recall what sort of lies I rattled off to confess as sins, but I do recall the penance she dispensed as being hefty: a decade of the Rosary, twenty Our Fathers, fifteen Acts of Contrition… And I was expected to execute my penance right then and there, on my knees in front of my bed turned altar rail. As penitents, it required a mighty stretch of the imagination to consider such a game fun, but under the direction of our pious leader, we were instructed to enjoy it.

My sister and I shared a room –16 years of forced union and sisterly bickering. Our twin beds were placed as far apart as our small room would allow, and an invisible barrier right down the middle divided the one and only closet. The two sides of the room and the closet clearly defined themselves as belonging to either "Karen the Neat" or "Gail the Slob." Karen's half of the closet was lined with hangers hung with pressed blouses, skirts, school uniforms…and my side was relatively sparse because everything that should have been on hangers was rolled in a dirty ball and stashed under my bed for the sake of tidiness. The clothes ball remained hidden until my mother would come along – without warning – and erupt like a lunatic version of Mt. Vesuvius, forcing me down on my belly to retrieve all the items that had been conveniently stored out-of-sight, out-of-mind. Frankly, I just didn't see the virtue in, or the need for, such compulsive organization – though my sister's need for it came in handy. Thanks to her tidy inclinations, I found myself with access to clean pressed clothes whenever I needed them. My unauthorized bouts of borrowing reliably resulted in screaming matches when discovered, and the screaming reliably resulted in my mother storming in to join the ruckus. The punishment was reliable, as well: a trip down to the basement for a prolonged visit with the tedious trio of washing machine, dryer, and ironing board – a drag of a dull time for one with an artistic temperament.

Back to games.

Across the boulevard, Karen and I had our Italian girlfriends, Leslie and Adrian, to play with. The moms gathered in one or other of our Greengarden kitchens to drink coffee and yap a blue streak, while we played in the basement, in the garage, or out in the yard. The Italian moms were vivacious beyond measure, laughing boisterously and gesturing dramatically – their idea of whispering was a big fat joke. With our friends we played the traditional game of House. The game held staring roles for the husband and wife, but quite honestly, the kids' roles were the most fun: you could cry, suck your thumb, sit on laps, talk baby talk, wear diapers, and regress freely, all for the sake of the performance. Misbehaving was encouraged when you played a kid, however, you risked incurring the wrath of an overzealous Dad who might spontaneously pull off his belt and attempt to administer a few swift licks – also for the sake of performance – and not even get in trouble for it. House was a reality game. If you were lucky, the Mom would come on stage in the nick of time and come to your defense, halting the Dad's arm before the belt struck. Then, the two of them would duke it out in words rather than whooping you with a belt. This was the desirable outcome for it offered an occasion to use adult vocabulary, the kind we had learned by listening in on real life games. But, in order to get away with adding such adult vocabulary to our game, we had to be certain that we were well out of hearing range of the hens clucking in the kitchen.

It's quite ironic that by the time a game like House starts to morph into real, real life, the players seem to develop a desire to play just like kids.

In the summertime we were more inclined to drop priest and parent roles and play our plain ole' selves. Our summer play was physical and raucous often centering on our inflatable mini swimming pool. Oh, how I loved that pool! Calling it a pool is like calling one single flower head a botanical garden. But to me it was vast, cool, and clear – a bright yellow blow-up donut resembling a giant inner tube with a sheet of tough green plastic attached to the inside. Its yellow ring was patterned with red and green fish, adding a "for real" sense of depth to the water. The actual depth was about a foot, before we started splashing and sloshing the water out all over the place. Normally the pool was set up in front of the garage on our new concrete driveway. I have no idea why it didn't dawn on either of my parents to set it up on the cushiony green lawn, insuring a safer and softer landing for our running, belly flopping dives. Perhaps, they were concerned with protecting the lawn. This mini-pool of ours couldn't have been more than six-feet in diameter, yet Karen, Leslie, Adrian, and I all paddled around in there as if it was Lake Erie, itself. We weren't guarded, as the danger of drowning with so little water and so many bodies seemed detached from threat. The danger of a concussion ranked considerably higher, thanks to the combination of hard concrete and slippery wet plastic. No one seemed concerned about that; drowning was the big fear for Lake Erieites.

The only thing that could better one of our little girl pool parties was Dad happening upon it. He came home for lunch occasionally, driving up with a roar in something far less grand in size and color than a fire truck. He came behind the wheel of a beer delivery truck. On his firefighting days off, Salty had a part-time job delivering beer. In those days, you couldn't buy beer in a grocery store or even in a state liquor store. You had to go to a licensed beer distributor to buy it, or have it delivered like many locals did. The delivery of beer was more anticipated in many homes than the delivery of milk. At the sight of a pool party in his driveway, he hopped out of the truck, grabbed the hose, and sprayed us wildly while we shrieked with glass-shattering delight. After blasting us without mercy, his eyes gleamed with vicious little boy delight – resembling Tim's – as he dashed into the kitchen, leaving us no chance to retaliate and keep the moment wonderfully alive and wet.

If my mother expected him she'd have lunch ready for him. If not he prepared a fried baloney sandwich – his finest specialty, if you asked me. Taking out the black cast iron skillet, he heated it up, added a dollop of butter, and laid in an over-lapping circular pattern of baloney slices. For a minute or two the slices stayed that way…then they began to pucker up, buckle, and shrink from the heat. I loved to watch the flat thick slices of baloney blacken and bubble themselves into sputtering greasy configurations (think Henry Moore reclining figures). Dad took three or four baloney shapes, stacked them onto a slice of rye bread, and doused them with my pal Heinz. He made the best Dad Sandwich in the whole wide world! But, there was yet more pleasure in his lunch stops than hosing and fried baloney. The absolute best came after lunch.

Before heading off to serve the thirsty masses with his truckload of beer cases, Dad piled us into the back of the truck and proceeded to drive forward and backward...forward and backward...up and down the driveway... screeching and braking....purposefully causing us to tumble and topple about the bottles like a flock of baby drunks. It was MORE than glorious! Upon lifting us out and steadying our wobbly feet, he reached into his jingle-jangling pockets and pulled out nickels, placing one in the palm of each sweaty, excited little hand stretched before him. The beer man was as good as a candy man any day.

With money in hand, Karen and I nagged my mother to allow us to cross over the giant boulevard and walk down the block to Teresa's Delicatessen – an Italian Delicatessen. Teresa and her husband Ben sold bits of everything, but our eyes were only interested in the rows of penny candies spread out, irresistibly, at kid's level across a long and low sandwich counter. This set-up was cruel punishment for kids lacking penny-power. Trooping in with shoelaces untied and limbs flying, we lined the counter to spend exaaaaaggerated minutes surveying each and every penny goodie before coughing up our nickels. Either Teresa or Ben stood guard over us because, as kids do, we tried to paw every offering – as if a touch held flavor and provided more for our money. With looks of exasperation, they tried to hurry us along, scolding us if we snuck a touch. But they liked us well enough. We were, after all, customers – just not Italian ones.

A little later down the road, I managed to turn this perfectly nice delicatessen into an occasion for sin. My mother had come to consider me capable of running grocery errands: a loaf of bread, a quart of milk, or some other form of boring that I could identify and manage to carry home all by myself. When I went to Teresa's solo, I spent leisurely time cruising the narrow aisles and studying every can and wrapper with grave curiosity and greedy desire. Passing the ice cream freezer nearly drove me berserk...by the time I got to the candy counter, where the cash register stood by, the devil all but owned me. I started by snitching pennies from my mother's grocery change to feed my desire for candy; then, I advanced to nickels and dimes. I turned into a thief: a little Polish thief brazenly operating in the full light of day on the boulevard. I stole from my own mother. Along with sinning the inevitable occurred – after all, my mother *could* count.

Returning home after one of my store-capades, I headed straight down to my basement hideout to enjoy my contraband: a bag of Sugar Babies. Sugar Babies demanded a particularly secure place to chew because the caramel filling took long minutes to swallow down and pick out from between your teeth. To fully savor the sloppy juices of the crime, privacy was essential. So, there I was munching deep into pleasure and caramel goo when a God-awful "**Gaaaiiiilllll!**" sounded in my ears. My mother bounded down the steps, a store receipt clenched in her pumping fist. Caramel juice dribbled out of the corner of my mouth and a sticky wad of candy turned hard and unswallowable in my panicked mouth. BUSTED!

Honest to God, you would have thought that I had robbed a bank! She went off like stick of dynamite, exploding with a barrage of burning criminal accusations against me. I became so terrified by her fury that I turned equally hysterical, but in a sobbing, crumpled up way. Off to my room I was sent, to await Dad's return from work and the belt of punishment. Mom controlled the verbal end of things and Dad the physical. Worse than the guilt of betraying my mother's trust, and far worse than the belt, was the humiliation of having my father exposed to the bitter truth about the apple of his eye. An over-the-knee spanking was piddley-ass stuff in comparison. But, that wasn't the end of it. Additionally, I was sentenced to my room for the entire night, and no supper. I heard everyone clattering, munching, and chatting around the kitchen table, and then I heard them giggling around the TV set. They sounded so painfully complete without me. They were better off without me. I didn't deserve to exist among them. Sprawled out on my bed with red-rimmed eyes aimed at my bedroom door I cried out, "I'm sorry (sob sob), I'm sorry (sob sob)" over and over. The door didn't budge, and neither did my parents. I was served, and rightly so, nothing but a cold plate of silence in the darkest moment of my young life.

My sickeningly vivid recollection of this scene after fifty some years, tells me that – given the nature of the crime – I may have clung to guilt more tightly than many a child. And shame hung on tighter than that. It was shame that pretzel-knotted my insides and slumped my shoulders; it was *shame* that shrunk me. Having first been exposed to it just under the skin of my mother, I now bore its mark visibly on my own.

Time for confession. Where was Karen when I needed her?

After everything my father had done to advance our family's cause, there I was making a rotten mess of life on beautiful Greengarden Blvd.

CHAPTER 3. EASTER SUNDAY

Though official west-siders now, we regularly ventured back to our east side roots to visit our grandparents. Holidays amounted to double duty on the east side of town: an early meal at the Poplaski's, and a later meal at the Smieciuich's. Dad's mom remarried into that mouthful of a name after Grandpa Anthony's sudden death. At her house the Soliwoda name got tucked away with the silver and china.

Religious holidays were comprised of prayer, outfits, and food, each battling for top honor. Easter called for a new bonnet, a new or hand-me-down newish spring coat, and shiny patent leather shoe, things that would show well at church, even in the event of a cold and flurried Easter, which Erie, Pa. was known to produce. The inside of Blessed Sacrament Church, our new parish church, resembled a fashion parade of pastels on Easter Sunday. You could barely recognize some congregants: winter dull and grayish looking creatures resurrected from head to toe in the hopes of baby egg blue, cotton-candy pink, and Peeps yellow. The overpowering distraction of shiny buttons and crisp bows made it nearly impossible to pray.

After the church/clothing tradition came the traditional drive to Alex and Stephanie's (Stefania had turned into Stephanie) for a holiday meal guaranteed to delight – the food anyway. Grandpa Poplaski was a great cook, a natural. Better, even than his awesome Easter spread, however, was what he dished up during mushroom-picking season, when he ventured out into the damp, musty woods to collect baskets filled with fleshy assortments. He cooked up batches of his pickings in a skillet, along with browned ground pork and beef, fried onions, crumbled bacon, and showers of salt and pepper. You could never have too much of this goulash-like mushroom concoction. Planning a sleepover timed to mushroom picking time was high on my list of priorities. Such a sleepover allowed me the pleasure of sneaking downstairs in the creepy dark of night, opening the refrigerator, and plunging my greedy fingers squarely into the goulash pot for one more mouth-stuffing nibble. Standing in the refrigerator's dim light, I ate off my fingers like a half-starved night animal ripe with prowling and rummaging and instincts. Stealing the goulash made it taste even better, despite the cold slop of it in my paw. There was, however, a disturbing element to my refrigerator capers. When the refrigerator insides lit up, there shone my grandpa's choppers floating in a Libby jar identical to the jars he used to can mushrooms. His teeth glared at me with a yellowed pearly stare, rather than talking to me like they usually did. Grandpa's dentures *saw* what I was up to; I was certain. The very first time I discovered his refrigerated teeth a sickening thought ran through my mind: maybe the rest of him was dead! To me his choppers seemed important, vital – like a heart or a lung might be – something you couldn't be okay without. But Grandpa himself delivered flesh and blood proof that I was wrong when I came upon him one evening walking and talking toothless, though his sweet face had disappeared into a shapeless mush toppled into the purple pit of a shriveled mouth.

When Grandpa Alex had his teeth in, all warmed up and clicked into position, he was an attractive man. His meticulous dressing habit backed up his pleasant appearance, though he was well shy of any impressive height. His sloppy English took a slice out of his groomed appearance, but, to my ears, he sounded and looked just dandy. I understood him perfectly. Grandma's body, on the other hand, was framed in short, soft, and chubby. Attractive was not a word you would use to describe her, but neither was unpleasant – except for the two bulbous moles on her face that sprouted a whisker or more from dead center. They scared me. Fearful that they might stick to my fresh and tender flesh, I tried to avoid direct contact with them. Since my grandmother wasn't big on physical affection, it wasn't that hard to do. Removal of these pea-sized eruptions would have improved her overall appearance considerably, but she saw no reason to concern herself with them. Vanity was not in her, her vocabulary, or her wardrobe. Compared to her "Dapper Dan" husband, she resembled a "Messy Bessie" wife. This mess about her, coupled with a relentlessly jovial spirit towards her grandchildren, was downright lovable in my book.

As for Easter, when we arrived at the Poplaski's to celebrate the Resurrection of Christ from the dead, the scene looked like this: Grandma would be busy barking irritable orders to Grandpa in Polish, my mom and Aunt Jean would be busy setting the vast table, the guys would be busy drinking in earnest, and the kids would be busy avoiding all of the above. Aunt Jean came with a husband and three sons. In some skin-crawly kind of way her husband, my uncle, scared me. It had something to do with his wet glistening lips, the continually bobbing Adams's apple on his skinny neck, the way he dropped his head and raised only his buggy eyes to stare at me, and his whiskey breath. We weren't close to this cluster of our cousins anymore than our mothers were close as sisters. Oh yeah, there was the blood bond and all that stuff, but its flow was pretty thin. When we plopped our bodies down and tucked our knees under the familial lap of Grandma's table, however, we connected, almost miraculously, like a closely-knit family for a brief moment in time. A sacred Polish tradition was responsible for the fleeting sensation.

With everyone seated and quiet, my grandmother would raise a large communion-like wafer called Oplateki. Breaking off a piece, she then passed it to the next person, and that person passed it on to the next person until each of us held a piece of wafer in our hands. We then consumed our morsel of wafer at the same time. The ritual gesture moved through us like a reconciliation of sorts: a wafer thin band-aid to mend whatever had been bruised, or might yet be bruised. It provided a gentle nudge towards the dumping of simmering resentments. (We purchased the Oplateki from the Polish parish church, St. Hedwig's. It was usually rectangular in shape and embossed with a religious scene or religious symbols. It came in the holiday colors of pink or blue, as well as plain white.)

When the conciliatory gesture passed, there wasn't the trace of a pause before the digging in began with animal-like abandon. We tumbled right back to earth and reverted into our self-serving selves, rendering the forgive-and-forget reconciliation digested and passed on through. As the drinking proceeded, arguments sloshed over between any mix of adults and for any mix of reasons, or no reason at all other than the spontaneous combustion of alcohol and sharp words. The mood turned sour on the spot, insuring the abrupt departure of Jean's family, or ours, or both, for reasons no one ever remembered. We hopped in the car and continued our Easter parade, heading towards East 21st St. to visit and eat, more, with my dad's side of the family. It was usually an indigestion filled drive.

By the time we arrived at Dad's stomping grounds the party was well underway. The special occasion smells of pierogi, ponczki, and Polish kielbasa filled the kitchen and paternal relatives tightly populated the small maze of box-shaped rooms. The house was standardly crammed with knitted afghans, crocheted doilies, and embroidered this-and-thats, all layered upon each other and then over the backs of chairs or couches, or laid out flat on end table tops and loaded with knick-knacks. The furniture was dressed out in matching outfits. And the couches, covered in clear plastic, looked as if they had yet to be unwrapped, or as if they might yet be returned. The plastic protection was far from inviting; no one enjoyed having their butts and thigh backs stuck and puckered.

A card game was usually taking place in one room of the house, Uncle Stanley and Uncle Chet deep into it when Salty, the middle brother, pressed and pestered to jump in, regardless of who was ahead. My dad had an insatiable appetite for cards: he could count 'em and deal 'em night or day. Whenever he sniffed out a game he wanted in. My new Grandpa John, a happy-go-lucky sort with the stand-up buzz of a crew cut, didn't involve himself with cards. His English was…sparse and mangled might define it…so he worked the crowd amiably with not much more than a good-natured grin. And Grandma, a woman with a no-frills demeanor, despite all the doilies, flitted between her cooking post in the kitchen and her guard post over the whiskey bottle stowed in the dining room china cabinet – the one from which she tendered shots measured out with exaggerated precision and tallied them in her head.

During my earliest of years, her physical appearance raised goose bumps of terror in me: her solid frame, broad padded shoulders, and no nonsense stance; her iron gray hair strictly parted and waved ever so cautiously; her wire rim glasses and razor thin lips slashed, on occasion, with lipstick – a gash more than a stroke of beauty. I suppose you'd call her kind and loving towards her grandchildren, but her physical demeanor posed her like a scary question mark. The only tender spot about her that I took note of was her apparent fondness for pets. While living in the flat above her, there was often a quacky, web-footed duck in the back yard penned up alongside her tiny vegetable garden, which was alongside her garage. Ducks aren't the most playful pets for a kid, but I embraced them wholeheartedly, deficiencies and all. I personally named each and every duck that came our way – and there were quite a few. I don't know exactly how old I was before I discovered the ghastly link between our holiday Czarnina – a murky brown colored, vinegar flavored soup with homemade kluski noodles and prunes afloat – and the disappearance of our resident duck. Even with a platter of steaming duck meat sitting conspicuously alongside the Czarnina soup pot, how could I possibly imagine the barbaric connection? Though Czarnina was commonly referred to as "duck blood soup," it never dawned on me that it could be *my* duck's blood! Surely the outside chopping block was colored with beets.

While the adults carried on with their version of Easter, we kids gathered with a fresh batch of our cousins, laying claim to a room where we could deal out our own sort of entertainment. My cousin LeRoy, the one and only child of Uncle Chet and Aunt Doris, was insanely funny in my eyes, a real hoot. Though he was a few years older than I, we hit it off in a soul-mate kind of way; in fact, he, too, turned out to be an artist. We shared more than a kindred pulse from the get-go. As ringleader, LeRoy called the shots to our favorite holiday game: mischievously tormenting and teasing cousins Dennis and Cynthia, the offspring of Uncle Stanley and Aunt Virginia. Our methods weren't hardcore abusive, just relentlessly unkind. Picking on the two of them livened things up for us, helping to pass the dragging time of our blah holiday gathering. Dennis and Cynthia, did absolutely nothing to deserve our wicked attentions, poor cousins! Though my conscience was naturally inclined towards the underdog, I clicked it off - I wanted to stay cool with cousin LeRoy.

Driving home from a torturously long day of visiting relatives, our bodies suffered equally from the pleasure and pain of being over-stuffed on double helpings of Polish sausage. We felt over-heated and thin-skinned, just like the sausage. But, when our car turned into the driveway of 3304 Greengarden Blvd., it was like coasting up to a cooling oasis. At the sight of it we slipped into another gear, another us: the us I believed to be the *real* us, the one that would last forever.

Forever vanished, however, with the arrival of yet another Easter Sunday, one that never quite resurrected itself.

The plan was for the same ole' same ole' with the Poplaski visit first. My dad had to work the Saturday night leading into this particular Easter dawn, but he hoped to catch enough winks to be bushy-tailed enough to enjoy feasting on Grandpa's finely simmered Polish kielbasa – the sausage he loved to gob over with spicy beet horseradish. As kids, our hype focused on the hordes of Easter candy we planned to amass parading between relatives. Mom usually bought an Easter present for Dad and labeled it as from his little chicks. For the Easter of March 29th, 1959 we wrapped up a tie and matching handkerchief - something shiny and pressed to spiff up his holiday suit. I don't know if Dad hid a gift for Mom, but I was certain that he had stashed dozens of foil wrapped treats for his three chicks, staging a hunt that was every bit as much fun as the candy was sweet.

It just so happened that Easter weekend fell upon my turn at an overnight with my grandparents, a rotation that Karen and I took regularly. I was only eleven at the time, but I was capable of performing like a hopping bunny when it came to helping out with holiday preparations so they loved having me. And I served as a buffer to their bickering, as well. While there, I slept upstairs in the bedroom with the twin beds overlooking Grandma's beloved garden. It was Grandma's room but we shared it like actual twins. Grandpa slept alone in the bigish front bedroom designed for the two of them, but not working out that way for I'm not sure why. I liked having Grandma in the bed next to me, even though wettish gurgles and snorts erupted from her nearly all night long.

In the dark early morning hours well before Easter dawn, sounding in between Grandma's ruckus came the ringing of the telephone. I heard Grandpa lumber out of bed and shuffle down the stairs to answer the call. First his voice was muffled sounding, then a squeal of sound broke loose from him - a high-pitched, wheezing, shrill, whimpering buzz. It was inconceivable to me, but it sounded like Grandpa was *crying!* By now, Grandma was awake, muttering to herself and making her way down the stairs towards Grandpa and the one and only telephone. I don't know why, but through the commotion I pretended to be asleep. Grandma spoke in Polish, surely translating to: "*What's wrong?*" Grandpa responded with two words in English: "Salty's dead."

Dar...k   *BLANK*   *Limb less*   *Darker*   nothing

darkest   stomach pains   *brain Explooosions*
Ears... Hot   Brea*t*h *stalled*
heart......heart???

Why would Grandpa **say** *such* a thing? DRUNK! He **must** be drunk!
How *stupid* to be drunk in the middle of the night! *What about Easter?*
What about the sausage? Dad's sausage! **What about the sausage?**
The words. I heard the words, the two words, spoken side-by-side like
they should never be. Ever.

blank   all   over   then......what?   What?   WHAT?
Salty's dead!   **What????**   **Daaaaddy!!!**

Other sounds. Grandma huffing up the steps, entering the bedroom,
leaning over and whispering raggedly to me that my dad was hurt...in
an accident...but...everything would be all right. "Go back to sleep,"
she said. "We'll be back soon." I said nothing in the middle-of-the-night
dark...I saw nothing of her though my eyes were wide open to her. "Go
back to sleep," she had said...they would be back soon...everything
would be all right. I pretended that I hadn't heard the two cursed words
out of Grandpa's mouth. I acted like I believed *her* words. I acted like she
hadn't just stood right over me and lied. With maddening desperation
I clung to the promise of **hurt** and **all right**. I wanted *her* words to be
God's truth, not **his**. Drunk! Grandpa was drunk and confused. Maybe he
simply *misunderstood* the English words spoken on the other end of the
phone line. He could've misunderstood!
When the front door slammed shut behind them, I jumped high in
terror from the cold bang of it, though I knew it was coming. They drove
off into the night heading for the west side of town, my side of town.
White/black electric specks flickered, sprayed, and streaked before my
eyes, in my eyes, in the whole room...little whizzing spots....jumping
and darting...jumping and darting...catching me up in their startling
chaos and momentarily erasing the fateful words that had triggered them.
I stayed with them, losing myself to their dance of craziness. Dad had had
an on the job accident once before: a scary accident, but an *okay* one in
the end. The specks darted about spastically in hope.

The "other" accident took place a few years earlier, on the day he didn't
return home from work when he should have. My mother's jitteriness

tingled all over me as she repeatedly peered out into the thickening darkness, hoping for a flicker of him coming from any which way. *Where was he?* He was never late without calling. I hated the taste of whatever was stirring in the pit of my stomach, and in the pit of our house. As if everything were just honky-dory, Mom told me in a brittle voice to go about my business and play, get out from underfoot. Long, long minutes later earth quaking vibrations rumbled up the driveway and strobe lighting bounced crazily off the walls and windows like Martian lightning bugs gone spastic. The living room lit up like a dance hall, but the sound around us registered more like 100% dread. Accompanying the noise and light, was the vision of a monster fire truck snuggled tight along side our house. I tell you…no one *really* wants to see a fire truck unannounced and flashing in their very own driveway…even kids who are nuts about trucks.

I circled my mother like a pesky kitten, but she shooed me away, ordering me to my room, though I deserved no punishment. I trembled in my sneakers. Two firemen dressed in full gear presented themselves at the front door and explained to my mother in calming tones that Salty had been in an accident. "He's alright," one quickly added, "just injured." Behind the crack in my bedroom door I wobbled in terror. Injured?

The accident occurred like this.

When the alarm sounded its call to arms, the firemen wiggled themselves into their gear and hopped aboard the ready truck in a handful of speedy seconds. As my dad ran to leap on the rear running board of the truck, grabbing hold of the pole provided for such maneuvers, the truck revved up and accelerated forward with a jolt. Apparently, before he could secure either grip or footing, the truck swooped into a sharp turn onto the street, whipping him off like a rag doll and flinging him towards the side of the road. The roll and tumble of it all broke his leg and bruised him up. My mother, I suspect, was more relieved at his injuries than she was upset, after all, a leg's a leg, he could hobble home on it. In fact, it was only minutes before a fire department ambulance, also, appeared in our red crammed driveway. Out poured Dad supported by two firemen half lifting him up the stairs and guiding him into his own house. A grimace was plastered on his face and a big cast on his leg, but no sign of crutches. Peeking steadily from behind my door, and breathing a little softer, I watched curiously as Dad transformed a pair of dining room chairs into temporary crutches: cumbersome, but serving to get him where he needed to go.

This sort of nerve-wracking episode was precisely the type of thing my mother had fretted over when she took a stand against the firm wishes of her mother-in-law and voted against Dad joining the Erie Fire Department. Money simply wasn't worth the priceless toll of fear.

Having Dad around the house came to brighten the accident. Traditionally, the daytime house was categorized as the domain of the rest of the family: my mother's rules and our schedules. But, now…well, gosh…someone must have painted a sign outside our door saying, "Party Time!" because revelers poured in day and night. Salty had lots of friends - firehouse news traveled fast. Comrades, neighbors, relatives, all popped in to wish him well. This spree of visitors required the stocking up of salty snacks: chips, pretzels, nuts, pepperoni and cheese slices, and the like – nibbles that went well with cold beer and whiskey. The basement refrigerator was weighted down with frosty long neck bottles of beer ready to be uncapped and guzzled away. Rising to the occasion and the festive air surrounding it, I offered up my services. As soon as his pals came through the door, I rounded up their drink orders, prepared them accordingly, and served them. Most orders were simple and manly: a shot of whiskey (usually Seagram's 7) paired up with a bottle of beer. Placing one shot and one beer on a small tray, I gingerly made my way to guest #1, then I mimicked the routine until every order was filled to satisfaction. As if belonging to some sort of booze brotherhood, each and every guy picked up the shot of whiskey, cocked his head back, downed it in one swift gulp, and let out an exaggerated "Aaahh" – or made a whistling, sucking noise through his front teeth, like Dad did. Following the hot gulp came a long swig of cold beer to chase the whiskey burn away. I tell you, these guys knew a thing or two about dousing flames! Dad's buddies thought that I was the "darn cutest little bartender" they'd ever seen, and when I noted the pride glistening all over Dad's face, I blushed hot pink in and out. There was little time, however, to gloat, for round two came up fast, just like the volume in the house. Raucous laughter and man-silly yuckity-yucks inflated balloons ready to pop. Only intermittent cigar puffing could tame the crowd while clouding up the air. Waltzing through the stinky haze of cigar smoke and sweet booze with a tray in my hand made it feel like an honest-to-goodness Catholic holiday.

....

Even after decades of remembering, I don't quite know how to describe the endless hours that followed my grandparents' abrupt departure in the dark hours of Easter Sunday: the static time I spent abandoned and drifting in the bog of that twin bed waiting for I don't know what...the dawn to come?...the two words to vanish from my ears? I tried to yank them out, but it was too late, they had passed through the canal and fixed themselves deep inside like a killer bug. The words weren't going anywhere – not ever! My mind's misery finally sprung into hot tears, then ceaseless sobs. I begged and pleaded: "*NO, NO not Daddy....please oh please oh please...NOT Daddy!*" My pleading was directed to God; there was no one else around. Was *He*, even? My body seemed to flip outside-in and downside-up; my stomach felt squished and wrecked. Gripping hold of the bulk of my own body wherever I could grab, I squeezed myself together to keep from breaking. I curled up and took to rocking...to rocking the endless night away.

The Catholic Church had repeatedly drilled into us that God could do *anything*... "soooo...**fix** him damn it!" What was the tiny matter of breath and heartbeat to an all-powerful God? I would *make* God fix him! WE would bargain it out. I would offer up my entire self in exchange. "*Fix him, damn it, fix him!*" I couldn't shut up my head or my demands. Deals spilled out of me...deals upgraded with desperation. *Anything! Everything!* My invisible bargaining partner stayed mum through it all. My everything wasn't good enough. My gambling chips were duds.

After the longest and blackest night of my life, the dawn finally broke with a feeble offering of light. I ventured out of bed, crumpled and bent like a battered and withered woman, and wandered through the thick emptiness of small rooms. It was Easter Sunday morning, March 29, 1959, and my dad was dead. I wondered when, and if, someone would return for me, someone would remember me. In a robot daze I did what I was trained to do: I stripped off my pj's, dressed into my Easter outfit, and made my way down the block and around the corner to St. Hedwig's Church for Easter Mass. I recall nothing of the pastel colored crowd, but I do remember approaching the communion rail, tilting my head back, and extending my tongue to receive Holy Communion, while hot tears streamed down my cheeks and dribbled into the corners of my mouth.

Back at the house, time continued to abuse me with its wait.

When my grandparents finally returned, they entered with wretched looking faces prepared to tell me the news – the truth this time. Before they could utter one sorry word, I fessed up and told them that I had heard Grandpa's words, the two words. They looked stricken dumb, and the news that I attended mass by myself threw them for a second loop. I was the only one in the family who satisfied my religious obligation that Easter Sunday of 1959. After wiping at their red veiny eyes and honking their stuffy noses, they confessed to me all they could of my father's death.

This is what I made of it.

Around 2 a.m. an alarm shattered the still of the firehouse, rousing the troops and scurrying them into trained action. In only a wisp of time the fire truck sped off heading to a two-story east side flat. Heavy black smoke was pouring out of the second story when the team arrived. It appeared fortunate that no one was home at the time, but as a crew worked on extinguishing the fire, my dad clambered up a ladder and crawled through a second floor window to do a search, just in case. He discovered a three year old – Debbie was her name – hiding under a bed, terrified and choking from the thick mesh of smoke surrounding her. Swooping her up and cradling her, he managed to pass her out the window and into the safe arms of another fireman. Dad went back in to search further. Here is where the muddle begins and monster questions remain hanging unanswered.

Having successfully doused the fire's danger, the men piled back onto the truck and headed back to the firehouse. But, they left my dad *in* there – they *left* Salty in the flat! They left *without* him! They - fatally - assumed that everyone was onboard and accounted for. Discovering his absence along the way back to the firehouse, they swung the rig around and headed back, sure to find him sitting on a curb chomping on a cigar stump, a smart-ass comment plastered on his tongue. The curbs were bare. Searching through the soaked and sooty remains of the flat, they found him on the second floor slumped over a bed, respirator on, but not breathing…not breathing at all. Even with all their skill and training, they couldn't coax air into him. They couldn't save one of their own. Sure, they turned the rig around, but too late – they were *too, too* late! You just can't rescue when you're *too late*.

Salty suffocated to death by the time his comrades found him.

Salty breathless.

Salty motionless.

Daddy dead.

Two weeks earlier Dad celebrated his 40th birthday. Aging over.

So, how could my dad suffocate with a respirator on? Did it break or what? Did he lose his way in the blinding smoke, maybe fall and hit his head? Did he have a heart attack? How on earth could they *leave* him?... *forget* him? Firemen had a buddy system, a one-on-one pairing assuring that someone had your back. I know for a fact that Dad's buddy was working that night. Where the hell was he? What a jerk! **Fire him!!!** And why the hell was a child *alone* in there, anyway? For Christ's sake, *where were her parents???* **Arrest them!!!** *God,* I hate *them...* I hate *them all!*

....

My grandparents drove me home. My seven-year-old brother greeted me at the back door with his Bugs Bunny front teeth set in a bizarre smirk. With casual matter-of-factness he said, "Hey Ya, guess who died?" "Shut-up!" I replied and stormed right by him. I failed miserably in interpreting his manner as just another expression of numbing confusion and panic, his sad little pathetic way of pretending that he wasn't knocked off his feet, that his brain wasn't fried, that his heart hadn't fallen off a cliff. Not a speck of me was capable of seeing through his defenses. That big sister failure on my part is set vividly in my mind and has never stopped scratching at my heart. On that dreadful Easter day, and for several days after, everyone seemed to think that Tim was best off parked in front of the TV, silent consensus that cartoons provided the sort of comfort needed by a seven-year old boy whose father was never coming home.

After passing my brother by, I moved through the den and into the hallway, coming face to face with the bedroom door to my mother's room closed tight in a forever kind of way. Inside, I could hear the highs and lows of jumbled words; I could hear choppy, wailing noises rising to an unsettling pitch and collapsing into cold and frightening quiet. I wished my ears could drop dead on the spot. Theresa and Mary, my mom's Italian friends from across the boulevard, were in the bedroom with my mom. Mom was a wreck and I was not permitted to see her; I was only permitted to hear her god-awful heartbreak bouncing off the walls. It sounded like an entire family dying: parents, kids, house, garage, driveway, and all. And that's exactly what it was.

Hiding out with Karen in our own bedroom, we sprawled on our beds like senseless zombie girls feeling nothing and everything: nothing and everything the same. Not knowing what to do with ourselves, we stayed glued there closed off tight and out of sight from the people going in and out off my mother's room. I don't know what we said to each other, if anything; I don't remember how we survived the rest of the day and night. I don't know how it came to an end. What I do remember is the following morning, Monday morning, and the phone call I got from a grade school friend telling me that her mom would pick me up for the school roller skating party at one o'clock in the afternoon. "I can't go," I said into the phone. Nothing more. She pestered to know why because she knew that I'd wanted to go, so I tacked on what I could to shut her up and get her off the phone, "My mom won't let me." Three words would have told the truth, but I didn't know how to say, "My dad died." The truth of it somehow embarrassed me.

Dad was laid out at Slomski's Funeral Parlor, right around the corner from his childhood home. There he lay – not cracking a joke – for three whole days. Three days amounted to standard funeral parlor stay. We, the survivors, were the first ones permitted to view Salty "laid out" in his casket. Each of us was swamped with our own tangle of longing and dread as we marched heavy-legged into the hushed and floral scented parlor room. I crept up to the open box of his coffin and peered in. He didn't look like Dad, Salty, the Candy Man, the Beer Delivery Man, the Fireman, but I recognized his holiday suit, and…oh my gosh!…our Easter presents: the new tie knotted around his neck and the matching handkerchief tucked in the breast pocket. How'd he get his present? We sure hadn't gotten ours!

The skin of his face was tight and shiny, grayish and chilled; the sides of his neck and jaw were bloated – looking like when he puffed hard to add some air to our little swimming pool. Dad looked inflated and deflated at the same time, making no sense at all. Someone told me that a bloated face was a sign of suffocation. Of course, I didn't know if that was true or not, but at least it was an answer: one lousy answer. To sum up the sight of him, it looked as if someone had sucked my warm, fun-loving dad right out of the cold shell of him dressed up in his brown and gray twilly suit, and whisked him away in the dead of night – to heaven, I hope. Staring both hard and softly at him, there was absolutely no doubt in my mind that he was 100% drained of Salty before we ever got there, and we were the first ones there. I swear, his buddies could've hung up the little that was left of him on a hook, right alongside the other firefighting shells of uniforms lined up back at the firehouse. He would have fit right in: pure useless without being dressed out in life.

One finger was wrapped in his wedding ring, while his rosary beads bound both hands, decades of Hail Mary's advancing nowhere. Staring at my dad in his coffin for three eight to ten hour days, I found myself waiting for an eye to peek open and wink at me, one eye to tell me that he knew I was right there with him, that he knew he was not alone. I prayed for that wink more than anything; even though he had left *me* alone just to save Debbie, a three-year-old *total stranger*.

Somebody snapped a close up photo of my dad in his casket, all bloated and dead. For years I thumbed across that photo in a family album. How did that photo make it into an album of all smiles? One day it disappeared.

Oh, how the crowds poured in! Nuns came, priests came, entire classes of kids from Blessed Sacrament School came, friends, relatives, and all the firemen in Erie, Pa. came. The funeral parlor was packed tight day and night. Stuttering about for normal sounding words, we were obliged to talk to everyone - even strangers, even firemen. I was miserably self-conscious inside and out *Everyone was sorry…everyone was praying for us…everyone hugged and patted my head… everyone called Dad a hero.* A roundish pale looking priest leaned in my ear at one point to inform me that my dad was, in fact, **blessed** to have died on Easter Sunday. He said that Dad was *lucky* because anyone who died on the feast of the Resurrection would automatically go straight up to heaven, bypassing any do-over time in purgatory, and certainly hell. He made it sound as if Dad had won the lottery! And, weren't we fortunate! *What an idiot! What a holy jerk! What a crazy man! I hated his breath in my ear! I hated him!*

More and more frequently such feelings of fury began to strike at me, but I choked them back, trying hard to swallow away the bitter and foreign taste of them. But all I really managed to do was blend them into homemade bombs wired with super sensitive fuses and stored for future defense.

Boy, was it awkward having all my friends and classmates – boyfriends included – come to visit me and my dead dad. There were friends that I used to blabber a blue streak with, but now…? What brought them to Slomski's Funeral Parlor was so outrageous that it oozed silence. I felt like a leper. I knew of no other Erie, Pa. father dying and leaving his young family to fend for themselves, leaving them fatherless. I was certain that, as far as kids were concerned, we were the first and the only ones in town to face such a life.

Quite a few firemen must have downed a whiskey or two before they dared to show their sorry-ass faces at the funeral parlor. Weirdly, their presence seemed to lighten the mood and bring comfort, despite their despicable behavior. We hadn't yet severed ourselves from thinking of them as family - the shock of their betrayal hadn't fully sunk in. At moments the mood almost turned festive, as Salty jokes and yarns rolled out to crack people up and release some of the boiling pressure in the room. I welcomed the change in mood – I was sure that Dad did, too. He'd be partying right along with us if he could just get himself up out of that box.

Then...I thought they never would, but three days passed...the casket lid was lowered...Dad was shut.

CHAPTER 4. BLESSED SACRAMENT

Blessed Sacrament was the name of our parish church and school. I suppose the name referred to the Sacraments of the Catholic Church: Baptism, Confirmation, Holy Eucharist (Communion), Penance (Confession), Matrimony, Holy Orders, and Extreme Unction (Sacrament of the Dying). The first four of the Sacraments were bestowed upon me in Blessed Sacrament Church, itself. Number five found me in St. Louis, Mo.; number six is still for boys only; and number seven is closing in on me each and every day. The only thing I know for certain about number seven, other than its certainty, is that I have no intention of it catching me in Erie, Pa.

Looking back at my Record of Progress (report card) from kindergarten (1952-1953) the following is noted: "left handed...retells stories and rhymes well...uses good judgment...a good rester....gives good attention....promoted to first grade." I was promoted steadily year after year, and I am proud to add that, even after many decades, I have retained the bulk of my kindergarten accomplishments. For whatever reason my mother hung onto all of my Record of Progress reports through eighth grade, and, more curiously, so did I. There are A's in Art all over the place, but a D in Conduct popped up the first half of third grade (a bit of a surprise from a kid always eager to please). That D surely earned me a verbal session with Mom and a physical session with Dad because the grade promptly changed to B in the second half of the school year. Effort – an actual grade category – mostly ranked C-ish, but it notched up towards B-ish over time. Basically, you'd call me a So and So kind of student. Subjects like History and Geography tended to bring me down: too much nit-picky factual info on the dead past and too much searching in vain to find the speck of a foreign place on a spinning globe. It was most unfortunate for me that my, relatively acceptable, ho-hum grades were negatively shaded by my sister's consistently excellent shining grades. If she would've relaxed her effort just a smidgen, I would've looked and felt a lot better about the business of school. Fortunately, brother Tim added relief to my side of the grade spectrum: the worse he performed, the more my performance was tolerated. Having a brother was finally paying off.

Along with my academic tribulations came the hint of a lisp. It sounded mostly with my R's and S's: "I wanna wed car without a woof" and "Tho what?" Feeling like punishment, I was given private speech lessons with some lady-teacher-type-specialist. The two of us met in the miniscule, windowless school bookstore, sitting among piles of textbooks, composition notebooks, pencils, rulers…with a single light bulb dangling over our heads and bumping hers when she stood. This lady-specialist forced me to exercise my tongue in ridiculously unnatural positions, doing everything she could to elicit a "red" instead of a "wed" and a "really" instead of a "weally." Boy, the two of us looked and sounded soooo stupid in there! Anyhow, this lady-specialist met with only limited success. To this day, "woof " and "wed" spill out of me whenever I'm excited, naturally high, and pleased with myself.

As well as correcting my speech, my teachers were obsessed with converting me from a leftie to a rightie - so much about me needed correction. But, as far as relinquishing my left hand, I put my foot down and held my ground: my left hand dominance remains intact. I tried to hang on to myself as best I could at Blessed Sacrament School. I tried to stay upbeat, despite grades that carried the chilly feel of stupid, a lisp, and a dominant left hand.

Karen had a leadership position in grade school, as well as at home; her friends referred to her as "Judge." She appeared overly grown up in my mind; taking things like studying ridiculously to heart. I took recess to heart. Maybe that papaya juice had given baby Karen's brain cells an academic boost right off the bat.

The territory I took to mastering was the playground, a large square patch of ground behind the school building devoted solely to running and screeching. As for games, we engaged in old-fashioned and reliable standards like tag and skipping rope, but we could always count on an outbreak of hands on physical and verbal battling, which quite reliably produced teary faces and snot dripping noses, to steal our attention away. Recess was viewed as an essential escape from the prison of a stuffy classroom packed with boxy little desks to cage us lined up in orderly rows.

In third grade, my recess transitioned from a time of playful rowdiness to a time of romance: Larry Markowski and I were going steady. On my finger was a ring plumped with fuzzy angora yarn to fatten it for a fit. I can't remember where Larry got the ring; it was more than the candy store variety and it clearly symbolized that he was mine and I was his. More exciting than the ring, however, was the *ski* at the end of Markowski, meaning that when we married I would inherit it for myself. Larry and I spent our entire recess standing close and holding hands, blind to the games being played and deaf to the noise of the unfortunate others charging around like wild animals unfamiliar with love. The particular beauty and strength of our relationship was that it extended beyond the playground, beyond love, even. There were tons of art projects to be tackled in school, and it just so happened that Larry and I were considered to be the best artists hands down within our grade level. We worked together on top of everything else. The truth is that he may have been a tinsey bit better than I, being that he tended towards tidy draftsmanship and I tended towards loosey-goosey. Each and every classroom came equipped with a long and narrow stretch of bulletin board set high above the blackboards, and one or two rectangular blocks along the sidewalls. The challenge was to keep the boards decked out according to seasons, holidays, special events, or study topics. Students were assigned turns at the task, but some kids had feet for hands, causing the bulletin boards to resemble flaming garbage. As a class we took pride in our displays – it was a competitive thing among neighboring classrooms. Larry and I were the bulletin board fire fighters. We doused the garbage, rescuing our teacher and our class reputation. I tell ya, the two of us could whip up some creative dynamite out of nothing more than a pack of colored construction paper and right-handed scissors – everyone "oohhing" and "aahhing" at our creation. Clearly, we would have no trouble making a living for ourselves, and our children would be talented beyond belief.

Larry was slender, cute, and topped with a well-combed head of blonde hair. His voice and giggle out came surprisingly high-pitched, girlish in a way. As an only child his clothes were not of the hand-me-down variety that I knew so well. He dressed in spiffy new duds with a splash of western flair and bolo style. Being that Larry's voice and body leaned towards the delicate, he tended to hang out with girls more than boys. Lacking that sort of delicacy myself, I was more the pants wearer in the relationship. I didn't care who wore them, I was crazy-nuts-in-love with him in an absolute third grade kind of way. But…I learned the hard side of love at an early age. Despite a ring and what I thought was mutual all-consuming young love, our romance hit the rocks and failed to advance to fourth grade. When my back was turned, my destiny was kidnapped right off the playground in the full light of day: some horrible, conniving, jealous, petty, ugly, stupid, cheating, creepy little third grade girl made her move and snatched up my Larry, ski and all. Such a low and brutal move.

Larry and I pretty much lost track of each other once we graduated into different high schools; after graduation he headed off to college. I knew nothing more of him until I heard the news. While playing baseball he was hit in the head by a fast sailing ball. He was rushed to the emergency room. It appeared as if he had only suffered a concussion, but more soon appeared. Larry died from that misguided missile of a ball. Sweet and talented Larry, the only child of his parents, my third grade love, dead at 19. At his funeral parlor viewing I placed a red rose on the ever-slender body of my first true love. I couldn't stand to look at his parents, their grief so raw and naked.

About 17 years ago, while attending a Blessed Sacrament Grade School reunion, I was chatting among my grown-up classmates – most recognizable by nametag alone – when I saw them walk in: Larry's parents. Though aged over decades, our eyes flickered with an instant recognition. We gravitated towards each other in a way that we were incapable of doing at Larry's funeral. Their appearance brought tears to my eyes: how *much* they still loved and remembered their son. As they focused their own glistening eyes upon me, I felt like precious treasure flown in from afar to cradle in their hands. My worth amounted to being touchable. They could hold me – a warm piece of their son's past and their heart's love.

....

We Soliwoda kids, like most kids, walked to and from grade school every day. Our house was between 32nd and 34th and the school was on 26th and Greengarden, only about a half-mile hike each way, but the stretch seemed a heck of a lot longer. Heading home each day we arrived at the foot of a small hill right around 31st – had there been such a street – that we perceived to be as high as a mountain. Huffing and puffing, loaded down with heavy book bags and clumsy lunch boxes, we dreaded the grueling ascent, resorting to a one-step-at-a-time mentality to conquer it. Cresting the mountaintop, the oasis sign of Teresa's Delicatessen appeared before us: salvation close at hand – our doorstep was a mere four houses away.

I rushed through my homework to get in extra playtime before supper. Douglas, a fourth grade classmate who lived a few blocks away, often came calling for me. Off we'd head towards the big low-branched cherry tree across the boulevard. When it came to climbing, I was as brave as the most foolish boy. Douglas's habit was to urge me up ahead of him. His apparent concern for my safety (catching me in case I fell) led me to think that he had a crush on me, until, in one of those light bulb brain moments, I realized that his concern was directed entirely up my wide-legged shorts. His peeking interest didn't trouble me much, other than leaving me a tad confused over the exact purpose of it, but I had another neighborhood playmate whose peeking heavy-duty ruffled me.

In the house to the north of us lived a slightly older boy who was single-mindedly keen on playing doctor. Given his great interest in health, he offered me free regular check-ups. You would think that even a dimwit could've drawn a connection between Douglas's peeks and Dr. Jeff's physicals, but I just didn't associate trees with doctors. I played along with Dr. Jeff because I didn't want any trouble with a boy whose back yard touched mine. I was kind of sort of afraid not to play doctor with him – I mean, him with me. Besides, Jeffrey was a real smooth talker. (He became a radio broadcaster later in life.) Not only did he make the game sound perfectly normal, he made it appear downright necessary. The physical involved me removing my panties to insure a thorough exam. Then the doc gave me a close up visual once over requiring lots of position switches rewarded with soft and soothing praise, "You're doing great! You may be my best patient ever!" Dr. Jeff liked me so much that he offered me an internship (of sorts), volunteering his own naked body for me to study on, but my rosy cheeks shook out a decline. I thought that patients should be patients and doctors should be doctors. Besides, I had no idea what it I might find behind the lumpy zipper of Dr. Jeff's dungarees. Due to something like patient/doctor confidentiality, Dr. Jeff insisted that our game remain secret, just between us. The secrecy stuck in my throat a little like the stolen Sugar Babies I had swallowed in the very same spot of the basement where my physicals were taking place: the Devil's workshop.

Despite my tomboy inclinations, I had plenty of girlfriends in grade school: Peggy, Carol, Heather, and Dee, to name a few. Peggy and Carol were my closest pals: one Polish, one Italian, both Catholic. Sleepovers at their houses offered up a lot more fun and equal satisfaction than playing doctor with a rather bossy neighbor boy. I found it curiously satisfying to observe up close and personal just how other families lived out life behind closed doors on the west side of town. Sleepovers provided me with occasions to compare parents, language, food, rules, and possessions. My best girlfriend stories, however, occur in high school, so I'll hold on the girls and offer up another boy.

Danny, I *have* to write about Danny: he was responsible for my awakening. He, too, lived along the boulevard, but in a big two-story house about a football field's length away from our grade school. We went steady between sixth and seventh grade, though we could've passed for siblings: matching blue eyes, dishwater blonde hair, and doubles on dimples. Danny was considered "cool," somewhat of a ladies man; all the girls wanted him, but I, Gail Soliwoda, nabbed him! We were of an age when boys and girls carried on a stage one version of dating: going to the house of a kid of the opposite sex solo, without a gawky string of others attached. One such date is branded into my memory.

Danny arrived at the house on a Saturday evening. His visit was all planned out in advance and approved by my mother. Earlier in the day, I scrounged up my allowance nickels and dimes and made my way to Teresa's to buy two cokes and a bag of chips to properly entertain my guest down in the basement where we planned on hanging out. As we reached the foot of the stairs, I paused to ask – awkwardly and way too soon – if he wanted one of the open Coke bottles I cradled in my arms along with the chips. Standing as close as he could be, he turned his eyes to me and said: "You know what I want." Yipes!!! A busload of frantic butterflies crashed head first into the gurgling pit of my stomach. Before

I could remember breathing, Danny leaned over and kissed me smack on the lips – a *real* kiss, not a peck. Not a peck at all! After coming up for air, we did it again, while the Coke bottles tipped in my arms and trapped us in a sticky puddle of a situation, or as I call it: the moment of my awakening. Danny's kisses loosened a fierce shudder of attraction in me – one that shook my body in a frighteningly deep and foreign way. The Coke lost its fizz and the chips lost their crunch; I hungered and thirsted for Danny alone. As my body blushed to a wild shade of passionate purple, my mind fell into a muck of Catholic questioning: was I experiencing sin? Was that what I was feeling? Was my blush dirty? Was I dirty? Evil?

Questions of religion and sexuality surfaced early and seemed destined to loom large in my life. They switched on the moment Danny ignited my body with the torch of his sixth grade lips. But my crush on Danny had been smoldering months before the actual day of my awakening; I still had a Father back when I first began to go woozy over him. Life in Erie, Pa. was still what you might call normal back then. A funeral at Blessed Sacrament Church killed normal.

....

Everything was blurred by tears: the church, the people, the Mass, Latin and English both incomprehensible. My father's funeral mass at Blessed Sacrament Church was so overall blurry that I recall nothing but that about it. Then, the long funeral procession of cars, headlights beaming in the full light of day, drove straight to Calvary Cemetery to bury my father. Guns were fired, Taps was played, and a triangularly folded American flag was placed in my mother's trembling hands.

I still have that very flag resting on a shelf in my adult bedroom. The flag was meant to stay forever folded, but once I felt compelled to open it up all the way, thinking Dad could stretch and get a breath of fresh air – you know, shake-off the musty feel of gone for a minute or two. Bizarre and nonsensical notions such as this have made a habit of punctuating my life.

Once the coffin was lowered into the ground and handfuls of dirt sprinkled thoughtfully - or spilled in despair -over the top of my dad's casket, the long line of cars processed to Greengarden Blvd. for food and drink. Our Italian neighbors had everything organized and ready to go on the home front. Not knowing what to do with myself once there, I resorted to what my dad had taught me, taking up my cocktail waitress ways and serving drinks with an angelic smile on my face. I impressed the crowd with my skills and myself with my hunky-dory-I'm-A-okay performance. But, when the funeral party ended and the last of the crowd exited the front door, our new identity struck instantaneously with a heavy and merciless thwack: we were a family of four with its head chopped off. *We looked like shit!*

This entire tragedy was big news in Erie, Pa. Articles with pictures of my dad were in the paper for days. Everyone referred to him as a hero, a real life hero! I came across a copy of an editorial printed in the Erie Daily Times newspaper on March 31, 1959. It reads:

"ONE OF OUR BEST

'Greater love hath no man than this, that he lay down his life for his friends.'

Bernard Joseph Soliwoda, the Erie fireman who died Easter Sunday morning after helping to rescue three-year-old Debbie _____who was cowering in terror under her bed in a smoke-filled room, measured up nobly to the standard of the Apostle John quoted above.

His bereaved wife, Irene and his children, Karen, Gail, and Timothy along with his mother and brothers and sisters, have this memory of his nobility to brighten the darkness of their grief and to help fill the emptiness of the days that lie ahead without his stalwart arm to support them.

They have the heartfelt sympathy of every man, woman and child in Erie and wherever the story of Fireman Soliwoda's heroism was read.

Bernard Joseph Soliwoda was an Erie boy, born and bred here. He went to Holy Trinity School and then to Erie Tech where he graduated in l938. He served four years in Pearl Harbor as a machinist with the United States Navy and returned here to work at the General Electric plant until he joined the Fire Department in 1951.

His interests were simple, centering chiefly about his family and church and his job. He enjoyed the respect of all who knew him, especially of his fellow firemen to whom his courage was well-known. The nickname they gave him testified to this attribute – Salty.

In short, Bernard Joseph Soliwoda was a credit to his city, to his profession, to his church, to his family, to his God."

The article goes on to announce a resolution by the mayor ordering the editorial to be placed in the Official Journal of the City of Erie. The editorial could have used an editor. "Ben Soliwoda was the salt of the earth." Clear and simple.

....

Prior to Dad's funeral, Blessed Sacrament Church had stood out in my mind's eye for its modest number of saintly statues, restraint in tacking on holy doodads, and all around absence of gilded domes and excess curlicues. It didn't smell of a moldy and damp past either. A sleek and modern look enfolded its interior and exterior, offering up the face of a lean and disciplined misfit among a brotherhood of overly indulgent church decors.

Every Sunday, major religious holiday, minor day of obligation, and 40-day stretch of Lent, church was a family affair. Lent amounted to a miserable run of time – the point exactly – lots of self-imposed sacrifice and fasting topped off with more meals than ever of smelly, boney fish. I don't know how either of my parents ranked in terms of being religious; there was no grand display of it in our household, no grace before meals on a daily basis - that was reserved for holidays. But I was encouraged at an early age – either by my parents or the nuns at school, I suppose – to kneel alongside my bed and say my nightly prayers. A family report card for religious effort might have netted us a collective C if graded by a generous soul. Faith itself, however, it is a tough thing to grade. Baptism into the Catholic Church anoints you with a boatload of inexplicable and sometimes conflicting truths to memorize and live by, most of them listed in the venerable catechism. It was repeatedly drilled into me growing up that *faith is both a mystery and a gift*, and I've never doubted it for a minute. It's a hell of a mystery and, most definitely, not something you can buy for yourself or anyone else. The biggest part of the mystery is: how long should you hang on if the gift never comes?

The Sisters of St. Joseph were charged with running Blessed Sacrament Grade School. For the most part I liked the nuns, though on occasion I'd run across a terrifying one, or a seemingly unhappy one, or worse yet, one who could see right through me. I didn't dare cross *that* kind of nun – my homework sailed in on time, all neat and full of effort. The nuns were robed in black full-length habits with white starched gimps resembling a formal bib or some other sort of chest protector, not unlike what adults tied around their necks while eating spaghetti and meatballs at an Italian restaurant. The smell of starch and ironing and black heavy fabric and perked coffee wafted off the nuns daily at the break of dawn. There was a period of time (a pretty long period, I must admit) during which I thought that the religious garb served to cover up the absence of certain body parts. For example, I didn't think that nuns had standard ears underneath the veiled headgear that encased their faces. And I didn't think that they went to the bathroom like the rest us – certainly not poop! No hair either. They were born without hair: God's ingenious way of assuring vocations. Yes siree, I had nuns all figured out.

It was during these young Catholic years that I slipped quite smoothly and naturally into the tradition of guilt. My mother had prepped me in her own silent way, but guilt at its purest came from Holy Mother Church, herself. There are lots of jokes out there about Catholic guilt, but once you've sampled the bitter taste of it you're disposed more to choking on it than laughing at it. The pressure of being good, knowing good, doing good, thinking good, praying good…left me queasy with doubts and distrusting of my own thoughts, inclinations, motives, and actions. I feared that a red-tailed devil was cruising Greengarden Blvd. with my school photo taped to the dash and hell's engagement ring sized and ready to slip on my pudgy finger – one sizzling hot boyfriend I could do without. Heaven was for saints and hell was for sinners: the clear and concise truth. I felt myself sliding towards the hot end of the poker. Where the hell was my gift of faith?

When it came to A+ sermonizing, most priests failed according to my needs and measure, but there were a few who popped up on occasion to deliver words aimed at moving the young and troubled of mind. The best among these were usually the visiting missionary priests who appeared once or twice a year to collect money for their work in faraway lands; they tended to preach with dramatic images and awe-inspiring words. When *they* spoke, my ears perked up big like a bunny's and I chewed on their words – like on a carrot – long and hard. Accounts of exotic adventures and intense challenges watered my budding romantic nature, sweeping my thoughts off to the shores of unknown lands, and transporting my body further than I ever dreamed possible from the pews of Blessed Sacrament Church. After such a Sunday sermon – feeling all pious and drunk on fervor – I floated airily beyond the heavy church doors into a bigger stretch of world: envision Saint Gail, halo and all! I recommitted myself to the path of righteousness…I would be a good girl… somehow, despite my inclination towards sin…despite Danny…I would be a good girl.

CHAPTER 5. LIFE A.D.

I remember only snippets, disjointed frames of our lives during the first weeks, then months After Dad. When I discovered that my mother was bent on packing up and giving away Dad's clothes and things, the reality of losing them, his things, was like losing him all over again. Why send away all that was left of him? They *belonged* to him, dead or not. Besides, to me they amounted to far more than "things." They defined the length and the breath of him, the full body of the man I loved. Feeling panicky at the thought of their departure, I stole a belt and tie – thinking for some reason that I needed to *steal* them. I would hold on to them just in case he returned. Shocking surprises could come in good flavors as well as bad, couldn't they?

I slept with the belt and tie tucked under my pillow. I cuddled with them. I sniffed and petted them. I talked to them. They *were* my father. Some days I wished the belt would loop itself back and let loose with one more whack, one more whooping so that I could shed tears for pain I could grasp. As his closets were cleared, a hidden trove of Easter candy came to light: yellow marshmallow chicks, foil covered marshmallow eggs, and jumbo, hollow chocolate bunnies with half jelly beans for eyes. Dad had stashed the candy, but he never made it back to hide it piecemeal for the hunt. The sight of it turned my stomach. It held not a lick of sweetness.

Night after night in darkness, my mother sat in one of the two matching cushioned armchairs in front of the TV listening to Perry Como croon love songs, his eyes tender and his voice plaintive and sincere. Her eyes appeared all together gone, blinded perhaps by the tropical sun of the past, and lost off the shores of Hawaii. I knew instinctively that she wanted to be alone, but I couldn't stand the sight of her sad routine – it threatened me. I needed to fix her. Uninvited, I took to plopping down right next to her in Dad's empty chair and chatting up a manic jibber in the hopes of teasing and tickling her back to life, back to me. As if I were no more than a pesky mosquito, she would shoo me away with the same nightly gesture of annoyance. Her aloneness filled me with doom. My dad was dead and my mom was lifeless - both of them gone to me. But I was determined not to amount to an added burden for her to bear, so I acted out what might make her happy. I acted like I was healed…I acted like I was intact…I acted okay with a solid performance. Unknown to me at the time, this early acting career of mine would lead to decades of struggling to untangle the emotional tatters I had stitched together and wrapped myself in.

One day I heard my mom talking to Grandma Smieciuich, her words coming through in hard sobs. She was *never-ever* going to care about anyone else again…*not even the kids… not anyone but herself.* I knew she was nearly out of her 36-year-old mind with grief, but that *wasn't* a good enough reason to explain why she shouldn't care about *me*? What did I do? Her reasoning seemed to have gone up in smoke right along with Salty. That damn two-story smoke-filled building choked up everyone but little Debbie.

Counseling might have brought us some relief, but in those days therapy was thought of as something reserved for wackos. We fell into a long and deep silence when it came to sharing and expressing feelings. We curled up separately and licked away at our gaping wounds in private. With no aid at my disposal, I resorted to molding a perverse interpretation of my father's honorable and heroic death: it befell us, and no one else, because something was intrinsically wrong with us, we were inferior, we were shamed, and we were marked with a bloody X straight across our Polish foreheads, an X that even a blind man could see. Shame trumped heroism. And I wore my version of it, my truth, paired like a second glove to the vibes radiated by my mother that I already wore on the other hand. Both of my hands were coated in yuck. It never dawned on me to blame

God for Dad's death, or to be angry at God for Dad's death. How could I blame God? A good Catholic girl would never blame God! This tragedy was clearly something we earned: a prize straight from the hell. It was the only logical explanation.

Sudden death brings more than heartless absence – it also brings the constant hint of danger. The irreversible ripping away of goodbyes and second chances can permanently cripple innocent left-behinds from the sheer shock of it. Ground once solid and firm can erupt in sporadic trembling, threatening to open up and swallow you in yet another random act of violence. The mirror you once recognized yourself in reveals a dusting of dread around your face, forcing your smile to look foreign and fragile. Your shadow marches in front of you instead of behind you, shading any and all forward progress forever. And as for normalcy, the kind you used to take for granted and think little of, it is relegated to album pages of blessedly ignorant family smiles of before.

....

So.......After Dad we didn't exactly float anymore, even with the name Saltwater strapped around us for support. We took to a kind of flailing, bobbing up and down type of stroke – gulping for air on the good days before being dragged under on the bad days. Without the assistance of our chief lifeguard we were abandoned to swirling currents going nowhere. The house on Greengarden Blvd. stood firm, but it was nothing more than a bone dry dock. My dad couldn't rescue us when we nearly drowned in loss: his last rescue had done him in. No more rescues for Salty and no more saved for us.

All of the kids in town worth mentioning hung out at the beach in the summertime. It was like a pick-up water bar for hormonally intoxicated youth. Every school-less sunny day turned into a drama-inflated beach party. Coppertone, baby oil, and salty sweat permeated the air, and radios blared teen tunes, dueling for dominance over the more natural sounds of crashing waves and screaming seagulls. Girls lay sprawled out on beach blankets pretending to sleep in the sun's rays while actually working furiously on their golden brown summer hides. Guys cruised the parked blankets, lustfully eyeing the early budding or fully blossomed boobs laid out before them like a smorgasbord. And in return, under the cover of permissive dark glasses, the girls curiously eyed the pooch size of each boy's wet and clingy swim trunks and the bulging, jiggling, snaking mystery inside that occasionally lifted its head skyward.

Most sunny days I blended right in, flirting up a sand storm and scouting for the next love of my life. But, on other days, I went on an underwater exploration for answers. I wanted to discover how long I could hold my breath. I wanted to reach the point at which my lungs threatened to explode, the precise moment before my head would burst into smithereens. I wanted to know what would happen next. The water was my smoke. I became obsessed with knowing what my father had experienced during his last moments without air. How much did it hurt?…how much did he suffer?…how long did it take? And, did he have time to think? Did he panic? Did he have time to think of me? I needed answers every bit as much as my dad had needed air. On rainy, non-beach days, I put a pillow over my face and continued my testing dry and indoors. Forever finking out, I never got truly close enough to the truth of his dying breath. I ranked closer to a yellow chicken than to a hero, but I kept on trying. Whenever I swam under water a big killer whale of a question automatically weighted me down.

....

You're probably wondering about the lawsuit. There wasn't one. Remember, firemen were family, and, besides, the times were not lawyer-ridden like today. The situation was a delicate one; blame would have been ugly. Well beyond any reasonable doubt, there appeared to be solid enough grounds to claim some form of gross negligence warranting a huge payout to us, the so-called "survivors." Certainly we would have won the case, despite losing everything that mattered. Where were all the sleazy ambulance chasers when we needed them pounding on our front door? A real kick-ass lawyer might have been able to talk my mother into filing a lawsuit to lighten, at the very least, the green portion of her crisis. But, for whatever reasons, she didn't. The financial security her mother-in-law had argued for so heatedly vanished in smoke. Seems that the built-in security applied only to *living* firemen at the time: death benefits were thinner than paper.

Oh, but we weren't without gifts. People gave us Mass cards, meaning a cash donation to a particular priest who in turn would dedicate a Mass specifically to the blessed repose of my father's soul. I don't recall the price tag for this service, but, quite obviously, these folks had not been informed – like I had been informed – of the straight-shot-to-heaven guarantee that came with suffocating to death on Easter Sunday. They should've given *us* the cash.

There was a TV (or was it a radio?) program called "View Point" anchored by a man named Dave Forsythe. Dave recounted for his Erie audience the fateful Easter event surrounding my father and made a plea for cash donations for the hero's widow and children, meaning us. I have in my possession a small aged and collapsing box stuffed with yellowed, musty smelling notes from some of the people who responded to Dave's pleas.

Dear Mr. Forsythe,
Enclosed please find one dollar. The gift is very small but we
are aged and retired, not a new, strange, story to you. How ever
on Easter Sunday! My husband and I had an anniversary of as many
years together as the young fireman lived. I wish it might be so
much more, one dollar is so little.

Another:

Dear Dave,
Enclosed is my note for Mrs. Soliwoda's fund. Probably many
people would like to contribute toward the fund but are unable
to send folding money, checks or even a money order.
How about putting coin boxes in banks and drugstores for such?
Corner groceries might be glad to have boxes also. I enjoy
your program keenly.

As you can imagine, gifts of $1 did little to improve our financial situation. A few generous souls sent $5, but that was the maximum amount noted in the box of cards. Collecting money on the airwaves was pretty embarrassing and humiliating - it turned us into beggars on top of everything else. We were looking more and more like all around Polish losers! At the very least, a full-blown lawsuit would've served set to vent our smoldering anger and pent up fury. But, we weren't like that. We were quiet. So quiet.

Through the mess of it all, time was the one thing uninterrupted in our lives: it didn't stop. One day, though still knee deep in despair, my mother was forced to raise her heavy head and think about survival. Thanks to Dad, we still had a roof over our heads, but we could hardly eat the roof. What was left of the family called for a re-shuffling and a re-assignment of roles. It would start with my mother, she would now perform the role of full-time breadwinner, minus the cigar and jokes. Karen and I would act the part of mini-parents, cooks, and housekeepers, minus the age and experience, and Tim would be the full-time child, the only one among us certifiably equipped for his task.

Since we weren't about to amass oodles of money from a lawsuit, *or* from begging, Mom signed up for night classes to polish up her dusty secretarial and clerical skills. Karen, Tim, and I were left alone on these nights, sometimes running wild and taking ruthless advantage of the sorry situation. Brother Tim bore the brunt of these evenings, as we, his parental sisters, bossed him around to within an inch of his skinny life. He hadn't retreated into the basement just yet – he was an open target.

Mom landed a secretarial job at the Erie Court House doing something or other with Veterans' Affairs, meaning she was absent from eight to five as well as a couple of evenings per week. She steadily climbed the ladder of secretarial success, eventually nabbing the post of top secretary to the top boss at a large company called American Sterilizer. Her top job didn't come with top money, but it did come with an increase in self-esteem, which she probably needed just as much. When I reflect back on her as a young widowed mother juggling like crazy to hold things together in whatever backass way possible, an aching sigh emits from my heart. She, too, was heroic, though I didn't know it or appreciate it at the time. After all, weren't parents **supposed** to do it all? And besides, I was a selfish sinner, a pitiful excuse for a worthy Catholic.

Before Mom set off to work each morning she scribbled a note to Karen and me instructing us on supper preparations – often meaning, which cans to open. We had the usual weekly serving of Spam, rotated in among corned beef hash, tuna fish, sardines, canned beans, fruit cocktail, and cans and more cans. We worked out of the freezer, too, particularly on Fridays, dishing up breaded fish sticks and tater tots on an island of ketchup. As for dessert, we became pros at Jell-O distribution, insuring that each petite fluted cup was filled to precisely the same level. On weekends, Mom took to the kitchen to stir up a big pot of something or other to last a few days. Being so close to Italians, she learned to whip up a mean batch of spaghetti sauce loaded with meatballs, sausage, and chicken chunks. She served it with a fresh loaf of crusty Italian bread straight from Teresa's Delicatessen. On these spaghetti weekends we nibbled on an earthly bite of heaven. I was mightily tempted to resort to my middle of the night refrigerator raids, but meat chunks were counted as carefully as grocery change and rationed out to last, so I was forced to curb my thieving ways. On occasion I thought of my restraint as virtue: a small stroke of victory over the red-hot hand of the devil.

For breakfast we were instructed to pour ourselves a routine bowl of cereal before heading off to school, but the kitchen cupboard teased with small boxes of Jiffy cake mixes (five for a dollar) stacked in a row. If we had a little extra time after Mom left the house, we skipped over the cereal and baked a cake. Twenty minutes of oven time and out popped a single layer of scrumptiously moist, warm chocolate cake to divvy up into two queenly portions for my sister and me and one minor princely portion for Tim - fair measure according to the queens.

It was around this time of household re-configuring that I made my first TV appearance. I'd entered an art contest and wound up capturing the first prize of a $25 gift certificate to Trask's Department Store. The contest required me to draw a portrait of my father, for it was a Father's Day competition. Electing to draw my father vertical and alive, rather than horizontal and dead like the picture camped in my mind, I sketched his upper torso in a suit coat and his head with a pipe dangling from his mouth. I forgot to mention earlier on the sweet smelling pipe that Dad smoked on occasion – all out perfume compared to his chewed up smelly cigars. Cigar perspective stumped me – I hadn't mastered foreshortening yet – that's why I went with the pipe. The pipe bowl was easier to fudge. This wasn't a sympathy win, by the way, the cards weren't stacked in my pitiful favor. No one knew that I was one of the Soliwoda kids belonging to the dead hero dad until *after* I won. That's when they decided to put me on TV. First, they came to the house to film me drawing at my easel, smiling idiotically like a real artist would never do. Then I went to the TV studio for an interview. I haven't a clue as to what I said, but I wore my groovy baby blue crew neck sweater and a gray pleated skirt. My dimples were more polished than my shoes. I'm making a point of mentioning it here because I don't want you to think that *nothing* good ever happened again on Greengarden Blvd.

Time became our friend. Thanks to the unstoppable nature of it, life slowly churned its way into a less bumpy version of existence. Time played fair with us. It never left us behind, and it never paused to gawk at us, either with pity or disgust. To time we ranked like everyone else. It kept doing precisely what it does: it ticked on, and so did we.

CHAPTER 6. A HIGH SCHOOL REVELATION

While wrapping up my existence at Blessed Sacrament School, Karen commenced a new one at Villa Maria Academy (VMA), a private Catholic high school for girls run by the same gimped Sisters of St. Joseph who ran the grade school. The high school's tuition was steep, but Karen solved that by being awarded a full scholarship – more of the papaya juice effect, no doubt. But, even if she hadn't received a scholarship, my mother would have found a way to get her there because it was clear to all that Karen's smarts warranted the price of sacrifice. The jury had to linger long and hard before determining what high school to plop me in when my turn came along. The verdict hit my ears like a full-blown miracle: I would attend VMA just like my sister, even without her smarts or scholarship. My mother must have flirted with Jesus, or robbed a bank to make the green appear. There was, however, one distinguishing tidbit to our like enrollments. Mine would place me in the commercial (business) track of the school, not the college bound track that Karen was sailing along. To me, the difference was as big as China. The commercial program entailed studying bookkeeping, shorthand, and typing instead of Algebra, foreign languages, and similar college prerequisites. I was assigned to the "trade school" division of VMA, a dead-end academically – an open highway secretarially. That's the way I saw it, anyhow, through a smudged up mirror reflecting the face of inferiority and small smarts. I bucked up and took what I could get. I resigned myself to the obvious: *"Okay, I'm enrolled in the Polish dummy program for losers. Dummyitis must be my diagnosis."* It was becoming clear to me.

I didn't ask for an explanation for this made-for-me decision – why be pummeled by the obvious. Happy to be attending VMA in any way shape or form, I determined to make the best of my fate. It seemed like a hundred years later before I heard, direct from my mother's very lips, the actual reason why she had tracked me commercially: money. She couldn't afford to send me to college. Her logic had nothing to do with *stupid*. In her practical way of thinking, she was offering me the best available: the road to job security. If *my* husband suddenly dropped dead, I would be able to collapse onto the financial sofa of typing, shorthand, and bookkeeping to sustain me. Her grief had converted her into a helluva nuts and bolts practical woman.

Despite the shadow of my tracking, watching hordes of fellow classmates stumble around in similar freshman puppy confusion made me feel close to normal and very much like them. And how I craved *normal*...being more like everyone else and less like my marked and tarnished self. The high school itself was located on West 8th St., a good enough distance from 33rd & Greengarden, a good enough distance from where our family shame was housed. Maybe, just maybe, the hallowed halls of VMA would lead to an escape. Fortified with hope I turned to action. It was time to work on a new me. I picked up a shovel and began to dig.

The troubled 11-year old in me watched from afar as my high school self dug a deep hole in my memory, in my brain. In that hole I dropped the bulk of my unresolved everythings and told them to hibernate there forever. I heaved shovelful after shovelful of dirt upon them and then stomped on them, snuffing out the hope of light, of healing. I was convinced that official burial would suffice to keep them gone. It had, after all, kept my father gone. I didn't stop to consider how burying can be so much like planting, how ugly growth can surface in a stunning display of later in life complications.

....

I threw myself into belonging. It's true that the commercial department had a tangible stigma attached to it (at least according to me), and likewise true that the most highly regarded positions, like Student Council representatives and class officers, tended to be awarded to college track girls, but…I set out to alter that lopsided picture and bridge the school divide. Being a pleaser, bridge building came naturally to me; I knew how to hear both sides out, empathize, and mediate. Having known all too well the bitter sting of being royally cheated out of a father, I housed a strong sense of fairness on all counts. There was no need for me to employ cheap gimmicks and tricks to bridge the school divide, I resorted to straightforward effort and sincerity. My pure and simple plan was to *like* everyone to death, and if some individuals defied likeability – as certain girls do – then, I would resort to *love*: good old-fashioned Christian "love one another." I had a mission. I felt appointed. The Road to Belonging rolled out before me as clearly as our newly paved driveway once had.

Other than that of pimply self-conscious creatures aspiring to womanhood, the student body shared another common feature: we all dressed in blue and white uniforms. Four or five hundred blue and whites marched to the guidance of a couple dozen black and white nuns and a handful of lay teachers, equaling nearly three solid levels of brick and black and white and blue. Our navy, knee-length, long-sleeved uniforms came with a medium sized zipper centered up one side and a shorter zip rising up from breast level to the pit at the base of our necks. The entire neckline of the uniform was circled with a detachable, white rounded collar, which required stiff starching – you could earn a demerit for uniform slovenliness or limp collars and cuffs, cuffs being the wrist version of the collar. The collar, with its heavy starch, reminded me of a baby gimp, a lesser version of being lassoed into religious life. Girls who had the money sent their collars and cuffs to the local Chinese laundries that had a solid reputation for quality starching. Without cash to spare, we starched our own. Karen's came out just so, not too stiff and not too limp, but mine tended towards crusty, with over-starched razor-like edges capable of gashing a circular VMA stigmata around my neck.

We wasted valuable time, as well, polishing and buffing butt-ugly navy blue oxfords to wear over white crew socks. The all-seasons long sleeved uniform rendered our arms toasty on hot days, but high school sweat pooled from an assortment of other things as well: panic, delight, embarrassment, anger, temperament, love and hate. Each of these tended to draw a noticeable white chalky stain under our uniformed armpits. Four years worth of the smell of sticky warm b. o. on that navy fabric is something not easily forgotten. But I warmly and gladly pulled the uniform over my head each and every school day morning, zipping myself right up into belonging.

High school had a great deal to do with fits – clothing was just one of them. No fit was more important, however, than that of a clique: one of those tight knit groups of like-minded girls who cling to each other for dear life, crazy-glued together even during bathroom breaks. There were cliques for smart girls and dumb girls, pretty girls and ugly girls, cool girls and nerdy girls, saintly girls and wild girls – even one for uncategorized misfits who cliqued together precisely under that category. Believe it or not, there existed a smattering of girls who couldn't manage to get their rear ends into the misfit barrel: they were the leftovers, the truly forsaken ones. Out to please and bridge, please and bridge, I dog-paddled from one established clique to another, backstroking on occasion towards the forsaken ones to splash them with a smile, lest they blow their brains out from loneliness or despair. Another heaping of guilt was the last thing I needed piled on top of my developing chest.

My strategy for all around belonging worked for the most part, albeit in varying degrees - tolerance and acceptance, I noted, were not the same thing. In a way, I shot myself in the foot by spreading myself so thin among the masses and not dedicating myself entirely to one select clique. I was slow to be included in many first round social selections because each clique presumed that I was more partial, or more belonging, to another. I was adrift at times, off shore from where and when the "real" fun was occurring. My particular manner of belonging could be categorized as vaguely universal: a cosmic bonding uniting me in sisterly fashion to every blue and white creature that walked the halls of VMA. A jaded person might have tried to sum up my intentions as "working the crowd," but I never encountered anyone who did – the masses had faith in me. Despite being trapped in a secretarial destiny that I didn't feel at all destined to, I was, nonetheless, elected to a respected position on the Student Council. A badge of authority was placed on my arm, even though I sat in front of a non-college bound typewriter. My strategy was working. My election signified one small mission accomplished – one tiny bridge across a conspicuous school divide.

....

My preoccupation with commercial vs. college and clique vs. clique one day vanished for good in the blinding light of my high school revelation. It struck at the start of my senior year. I was an active member of the school's Mission Club, whose sole purpose was to promote awareness of the needs of those living and suffering in underdeveloped countries (remember those missionary sermons?). Orchestrating Mission Day at the school was the club's main annual event, an all out effort to sensitize our classmates. Sr. Marietta, our super-animated, gung-ho leader, invited the Missionary Sisters of Our Lady of Africa – commonly referred to as White Sisters (due to their white habits, not their skin) – to occupy the starring role in the event. It just so happened that the band of missionary nuns had a training house for postulants and novices located in the foothills of the Allegheny Mountains in a small town called Franklin, Pa. not much more than a two-hour drive from our school. Residing there in partial seclusion, their work was to train and spiritually develop a tiny cluster of young American women eager and ready to join the ranks of a congregation dominated by European women and dedicated to working in Africa. Well, I tell you, the very moment the spirited troupe entered the school I lost my mind to them. My mouth fell open in awe. The energy radiating about them – from their flowing white robes, to their multi-accented voices, and cheery demeanor – registered exotic and captivating, near yet far. It was as if the entire continent of Africa had rolled through the doors of Villa Maria Academy and gobbled me up whole.

They began with a bit of history, recounting the almost one hundred year old story of how the archbishop of Algiers, Cardinal Lavigerie, had long ago made a plea in France for women to come serve the needs of the women living in North Africa. Eight young Frenchwomen responded to his call, collectively birthing the congregation. From eight in 1869 the number had multiplied to over 2000, representing 20 nationalities of women working in 14 countries of Africa. Some of the sisters standing before us had already rendered decades of service in Africa. They spoke vividly of life lived in such a foreign culture, life lived among masses of people saddled with daily hardships but alive with hope, descriptions of sickening horror and relentless beauty. Love trailed from their spoken voices and a far-away look glazed over their eyes, exposing a raw longing to be back in the arms of the continent they called home. These veteran missionaries were temporarily sidelined by their current duties: the not-so-romantic work of recruiting and training young girls to add to the ranks. That's why their feet were treading on the soil of VMA and not the soil of Africa.

First, their inspirational words folded around me like warm arms. Then, when they shifted to music, the sounds sent quivers up my spine and throbs in my heart. I was emotionally paralyzed. Grouped together on stage - veterans and novices accompanied by the steady beats of an African drum - they gave voice to a melodious flow in African languages and swaying rhythms. Their perfected high-pitched harmonies drummed up unthinkably wild passions in any number of us Villaites sitting mesmerized before them. They resonated within an ethereal jungle. It was crystal clear to me that only God himself could have sent such a tauntingly delicious mix of sounds to beat on our malleable hearts and confound our tender ears. With my senses going full out gaga, my eyes flickered back and forth across the wide canvas of faces before me, cementing themselves finally onto the circular saintly globe of Sr. Mary Peter. I studied her face, halo and all, contemplating it and appraising it as if it were a rare object of beauty poised before me. The clearness of it, the near roundness, the fresh pinkness spelled out a formula for purity. I zeroed in on her lips as they moved in foreign formations, swelling and puckering with musical determination. Then, pulling my eyes away to span over the whole of the group, I recognized the identical formula for purity multiplied many times over. My eyes stung, they burned...I blinked and blinked. Arms seemed to appear out of nowhere beckoning me, as an entire continent whispered my name. I blinked and blinked at my private revelation.

Simultaneously drained and full, I temporarily forgot how to function once they piled in their van, drove off, and abandoned me to my current existence. Was full-blown infatuation a sign of destiny? Did it have an honest and lasting chance? In a star-struck daze I wandered the halls of VMA. It's worth noting that the missionary clan had a profound effect on other girls, as well; for the next 48 hours a litany of professed intentions rang out to the tune of signing up and heading straight for the romantic wilds of Africa. But their fickle intentions faded fast – just like the drumbeats. Mine did not. Jolted to the core from the Mission Day experience, my inner life swirled in a state of dishevelment worse than the state of my side of the closet. *God almighty, Africa!* Sure, I wanted to escape...but *Africa?* I became obsessed with the idea of donning white robes, hiking narrow village paths in the far off corners of the Dark Continent, and befriending and aiding every man, woman, and child I encountered along the way. I felt a heavenly sweetness. I felt converted to the cause.

Several of my classmates perceived my spiritual light-headedness, but I doubt that any one of them believed for even a nano second that I would ever board a plane heading for Africa. For a simple Polish girl from Erie, Pa. to veer so far from the likely and acceptable chart of life's options was about as far away as you could get from belonging – what I had strived so hard for all along. The face of contradiction took shape before me: I wanted to belong *and* be different. I prayed like crazy – like 1959 Easter crazy – begging and bargaining, this time around for nothing more than clarity and guidance. My stunning, exotic revelation left me floundering over the question of whether or not I was brave enough for such a radical departure from the only life I knew.

....

Before Mission Day knocked me for a loop, I had managed to carve out a fine groove for myself in high school.

My freshman year was, quite naturally, dedicated to adjustments: classes, cliques, teachers, and so on, whereas, my sophomore year was steered by boy-driven drama. Cathedral Prep High School was the boys' official feeder school for VMA, meaning that most boy/girl matches were generated from within the two pools of Catholic hormones. During my sophomore year I found myself going steady with an Italian boy named Gary, a Prep senior. I say that "I found myself" because the relationship snuck up on me – almost without my knowledge. Due to the fact that Gary was a senior, our relationship raised a few eyebrows. The going steady business usually occurred within the same grade level, or, at most, one level up. Dating a senior two-levels up from me was almost like dating a certified man – and Gary possessed a jungle of dark body hair to reinforce the point. Wiry tufts coiled out of his shirt tops and a five o'clock shadow arrived around three. And he had a gigantic Adam's apple lodged inside his neck that bobbed wildly when we were together.

Gary was tall and relatively good looking – in a swarthy Italian way – despite two partially overlapping front teeth that caused kisses to be of the teeth rather than of the lips. Also, he was inclined to kiss in a full-bodied sort of way, a man's way. This, I believe, is where our age difference manifested itself the most. His kisses carried none of the syrupy sweetness that had poured from Danny's sixth grade smooches. The mere act of drawing close to me triggered panting in Gary: choppy, heavy, rapid breaths mimicking a horse taking a big whinnying huff from puffed out nostrils. Once our lips suctioned together around his cumbersome teeth, low and plaintive moans emitted from his throat, or his nostrils, I couldn't tell for sure – by then I was hotly distracted by the intense rhythm of the shoulder to toe gyrations summoning a teepee in his pants. *Yikes!!!* The bulk of it *freaked* me out! Like clockwork, the moment his gyrations grew in pitch and fervor, I wiggled my way free – politely, of course. And, as casually as if we had just ended a conversation on the weather, I thanked him for the date and declared it over, ignoring the look on his face indicating that he just might drop dead on the spot from cardiac arrest or some other merciless malfunction. He barely had the breath to whimper goodnight in an octave or so higher than his usual voice before I opened the screen door and closed it behind me.

When it came to comprehending my sexual self, it is no exaggeration to say that I understood *nothing* of it: I was certifiably stupid, no debate. But I suspected that back porch goings-on like the ones described above represented the shenanigans of older folks – folks beyond my years. My mother showed no inclination towards enlightening me, for *no one* talked about sex less than my mother. To this very day I can't recall her uttering the word "sex" more than a few times, each occasion strained with mortified reluctance. She got by substituting phrases like, "Oh, you know what I mean," or by casting a tight lipped look on top of a shrug of the shoulder – a blinking red signal to me of sin and shame. Info concerning sexuality and desire got securely filed under *taboo topics better left to ignorance*. There was an over-abundance of church talk floating about regarding the needs and nature of our souls, but an eerily disconcerting silence concerning the needs and nature of our bodies. The wall of quiet led me to conclude that sexual desire was hopelessly scented with guilt and exempt from the glorious fragrance of the rest of God's creation. Whenever my mind or body took to wondering about sex, I had no doubt that I was already in bed with the devil.

I wonder how shame could thrive so ferociously on nothing but a diet of baby green ignorance? My state of ignorance commanded that I drag a cartful of skewed and unhealthy assumptions into my adult life. I was unable to shake off associating sex with dirt and dirt with me. I could be a poster adult for why sex education should occur sooner than later.

Besides my attraction to boys, I had my share of girl crushes too – something not uncommon in an all girls' high school. Lots of girls were sweet on each other and friendships could rank as possessive and prone to jealous fits as boy/girl relationships. My crushes were mostly of the fickle fleeting sort, ones unknown to the crushee. They were birthed from many sources: a melody floating within a voice, a glimmer of distinct beauty in the tilt of a head, the powdery scent of softness on well-tended skin, or some other personal radiance observable to me alone. My inner bank of artistic sensibility was growing and swelling, setting off a barrage of impulsive responses to the physical world around me. When I discerned beauty – even in the most obscure and a-typical form – my eyes preyed upon it and my heart usually followed. I was blossoming into a sensate dreamer, ill suited for the factual and pragmatic certainty of secretarial land.

The high school years flung our bodies into a hormonal state of rage, flip-flopping between deep-set insecurities and ripening egos, while friendships and romances swelled and ebbed like the tide. And all the while schoolwork pressed hard and steady and without mercy. The combined pressure screamed for relief. Many of us found it across the New York state line, a 20-mile hop-skip-and-jump to where the drinking age was 18 and the good times rolled. In my junior year I had access to a late fifties, two-tone blue and white sedan to get me there.

Drinking practically turned into a major for some students. Being juniors, a good many of us possessed a maturity of look and manner that enabled us to belly up to the bar and lie through our teeth. The 30-minute drive got us to a couple of roadside dives crammed with other under-age Erieites equally thirsty for liquid magic. The term "designated driver" hadn't been coined yet, so the driver drank freely, just like everyone else. Seat belts weren't around either. Along with my mom's car, I don't know how I survived some of those drunken road trips. There were kids who didn't. Sadly, it was with some regularity that the local newspaper reported on teen fatalities resulting from bar hopping across the state line. However, despite printed evidence to the contrary, my friends and I believed ourselves to be invincible to road kill, so we carried on with our feats of reckless swerving abandon. There was something inherent in the nature of recklessness that appealed to me, both in drinking and driving; I was magnetically drawn towards any excuse to cut loose from my burdened self and fly wildly out of control like a spastic bird. Alcohol provided the means and the excuse. I could blame alcohol.

Peggy, my longtime buddy from grade school on, still takes pleasure in recounting the humiliating details of one NY road trip for which I wasn't the driver. Pickled flashes of it remain with me as well, so I can hardly deny it.

Malt beer was new on the market. It became the rage. With a higher alcohol content than regular beer, it guaranteed more bang per buck – though, probably not, since it was more expensive, but that's what I thought. Anyway, for sure it meant messing with the certainty of my previously established beer intake. My memory holds a fuzzy image of myself leaning against a brightly painted blue wall in a dark bar with music blasting and teen jibber-jabber shrieking when, suddenly, the room dislodges itself into a dizzying bout of tilting and spinning causing my stomach to rise to my throat and white stars to shoot out of my eyes... and...there I go... sliding down the wall in s l o o o o w m o o o t i o n . . . puddling onto the sticky ash covered floor.

Skipping the puking stage – which remains mercifully blacked-out (for me at least) – Peggy picks up the episode in my Greengarden Blvd. driveway.

Unlocking the front door, my companions, quite literally, heave me through the doorway and close the door behind me, hearing but not seeing me collapse onto the dining room floor. My so-called friends speed off like racing chickens, in the event that the ruckus rouses my mother. How I made it to my bedroom I haven't a clue, but when I opened my blood-shot eyes to the bruising morning light that's where I found myself sprawled out. If my mother held any knowledge of my teen drinking misadventures she never let on. She seemed to – or needed to – believe that I was responsible enough to stay clear of any "serious" trouble and "real" danger. I had, after all, worked insanely hard at portraying myself to be nothing more than a well-adjusted, happy young girl.

There were plenty of other occasions that didn't require us to drive all the way to New York to get toasted: crossing the state line was a "special drinking occasion" type of affair. Closer to home there were weekend parties hosted on booze pilfered from the liquor cabinets of unsuspecting parents. The sum total accumulation was generally enough to insure a party of sloppy drunks engaged in foolishness and heavy-duty making-out. We imbibed "sophisticated" drinks like SloGin fizzes and Grasshoppers, adult-like drinks, and, of course, sweet juices spiked with who knows what.

Alcohol made me chatty and funny. My humor was naturally of a quirky sort, but drinking gave it an added shot of pizzazz and a witty punch – so I thought. But, chatty and funny wasn't the best part of it: alcohol had the power to pickle and can all notions of inferiority, guilt, stupidity, shame…blah, blah, blah. After the first few drinks hit my gullet, life turned delightful and the world became one rosy planet - the moment was sublime!

Guzzling beyond the sublime, however, tended to knock me into morose self-reflection, followed by bouts of weepiness, followed by the need to find a bed before passing out. But, despite some nights gone sour, for the most part I steered clear of the darker side of over-indulging and imbibed in a sensible frolicking way along with a variety of pals. It was the social and expected thing to do. For the record, I should state that my weekend festivities *did not* in any way interfere with the higher purpose of Monday through Friday school business. As a responsible girl, I divided the two happenings like squabbling children, allowing each one a turn at being first and indulging both fair and square. I took pride in the balancing act of adding to and subtracting from the conflicting demands of a tight social and academic calendar. All in all, I considered myself to be performing an admirable job of fulfilling my pledge to make the best of my high school years.

Just when I thought I was shining bright, my sister grandly upstaged me in her senior year, unveiling a lofty pursuit that stole the show, one that made my junior year juggling act look like child's play.

CHAPTER 7. ADDITION AND SUBTRACTION

Addition and subtraction have become very familiar to me in a material and hands on way: it's how I create each and every sculpture. I find subtraction the more difficult of the two; I suspect that's why I've struggled so hard over the years to comprehend it, tame it, claim it, and have it speak for me three-dimensionally. I'm forever choosing the hard way to prove myself to myself.

Carving is 100 percent the pure work of subtraction. Staring at a block of stone, or a hunk of tree trunk, bark and all, triggers the process of believing – believing that if I am patient, if I look long and hard enough I will see through the thick of the material and directly onto the shapes stirring about in anticipation of release. My faith in carving has been more solid than my Catholic faith, for carving faith is tangible in woody smells, chips and splinters, flying fragments of stone, and clouds of dry dust. I have spent years in my studio alongside a silent hunk of stone or wood sitting in a dusty corner waiting for me to have the patience and insight to see into it, and me waiting for it to open itself to me. Patience and trust must build before the chisel strikes. Waiting has taught me that if I am attuned and open to possibility, the layers of material bulk will shed themselves seductively one at a time, until its inner being is released from hibernation and exposed to the light.

I've screwed up royally on many occasions, attempting to impose *my* will and design, working against the grain, battling to impose an identity, and relying on clever manipulation and technique to mask my chiseling deception. Such a forced and imposed engagement can be likened to an unhappy marriage in which each partner tries to craft solutions through determined inflexibility and pushy willfulness. The thing about these sorts of struggled pieces and lives is that they always look just like that: struggled. Carving out an authentic, convincing, and worthy resolution requires purity of motive.

....

Though I was apparently blind to it, Karen's senior year included, in its own way, the work of pure and patient discernment, and she did it without a chisel. After graduation, she announced her intention to trade in her VMA collars and cuffs for a starched gimp - yes, she had decided to join the Sisters of St. Joseph. Catholic high schools were known to provide fertile grounds for the annual harvesting of religious vocations; each senior class dutifully coughed up its fair share of girls. There were close to a dozen in my sister's class who headed towards the path of righteousness. I imagine that it will come as no surprise to you when I say that I have no recollection of the two of us ever discussing her decision in a sisterly like manner, no little bedroom powwows late at night. She held it close to her chest – the acceptable way of things in our keep-it-to-yourself household. The fall would find me with a room to myself. Karen's body would be pulled out of the family - subtracted, if you will. At least her removal came with notice.

As for brother Tim, he became virtually invisible once he fled from the den of females and settled into his basement pad. Absorbed full time with me-myself-and-I, I gave little thought to his reclusive absence – or was it my absence? Tim suffered a fair amount of injustice doled out from the hands of his big sisters. One time I talked him into turning over half of the hair cut money Mom shelled out for a visit to the barber. I convinced him that I could cut his hair just dandy. We could split and pocket the money. He fell for it. With great faith in my untested skills, I proceeded to butcher his fine blonde mop. Soon deflated by the sight of my own handiwork, I kept on cutting, as if he had a second mop of hair to destroy. Finishing up – giving up, I should say – with a phony sigh of satisfaction, I shielded him, almost kindly, from the worst of it by not offering a mirror view to the back of his head. Our mother was less considerate, "You look like a chewed up rug!" He got the cash back, and the next day the barber salvaged what he could. Mom tended to focus more of a protective eye over Tim since he was the child-designate.

As for my mother, she was still a relatively young and pleasingly attractive woman. In time she began to exhibit more than just mere survival: she showed signs of revival. She began to date. Clinging to Dad became my assigned duty; that's how I saw it because that's how I assigned it. It was my destiny, I was certain. That being the case, it was okay for her to move on, to step out. I could mind the territory of his memory while she had some well-deserved fun in her life. I had no intention of being an insensitive petty snit about it. Initially, my acceptance was all out sincere and selfless, but later ulterior motives crept in.

Mom made a sharp point of keeping us kids off limits to her suitors. Her dates qualified as discreet evenings out. However, after more than a few such dates, a certain tall, dark, handsome divorcee insisted on doing something special with us (the kids), so she bent her own rule and allowed him access to us, and us access to burgers and ice cream. I was a total sucker for this kind of maneuver. The price of the ice cream alone bought him my approval. And, also, he looked so…"Oh, you know what I mean!" And an after-shave spicy cologne smell wafted from him, a man smell my nose sorely missed. I welcomed it back, even on the bristled cheeks of a stranger. My senses began eating him up. Fortunately, my mother employed more than her bodily senses in measuring up her charming date. She took into account motives, as well. She asked around and discovered that this smooth talking, fine looking, cool dressing dude, also came with a reputation for being a widow/divorcee opportunist at large. He was circulating his way across town sniffing out the financial potential of the bereaved, abandoned, and vulnerable, and charming the school socks off shallow young twits like me. He must've suspected that Mom had come into some big bucks from an accident settlement, which, of course, was ridiculously far from the truth. Sometimes even our stash of Jiffy cake mixes ran low. Well…Mom showed him the door, if you please, and out he went: good looks, spicy cologne, and all.

Knock-knock! Another tall, sturdy, dark haired man rapping on the door, but a bachelor this time. Other than a quick introduction, Mom reverted back to her rule and kept this one at bay, where he was, in fact, grateful to be. When Bob Siry first walked through the front door, his glaringly shy, quiet, and self-conscious presence radiated with such awkwardness that I hurt for him. He seemed at a genuine loss for words when presented before two teenage girls and one shadow of a boy. His misery was so acute that we were rather forced to act softly towards him, exhibiting something close to pity. He was on the road to becoming an entrenched bachelor by the time he met my mom and fell head over heels for her, three kids and all.

She was 38 and he was 36 when they met. They dilly-dallied through dating, but eventually notched things up to something resembling courtship. That's when my mother began to gingerly blend him into our lives a teaspoonful at a time. As kids, we were materialistically impressed with the guy because he drove a silver Cadillac, the kind with pointy elongated tail fins. The car was meticulously polished, gleaming rich and elegant – so unlike us. And, in addition to the fine quality of the Cadillac, Bob, himself, possessed the fine virtues of a guy hard-wired-decent through and through. Yet, despite the obviously winning combination of a Caddy *and* a decent guy – due to my own little craving for recklessness – I rather fancied the thieving slime ball as being more of a good time joe. Luckily, my mother was the one being courted.

Another material benefit to this lumbering quiet man, custom-made for the Soliwoda code of silence, was the motorboat he docked at the marina. And this guy even possessed the patience to attempt to teach my mother and me how to water-ski on Lake Erie – an exercise in sheer embarrassment for yours truly. After repeated tries at remaining upright, I exited the water with ruby red rope burns whipped across both legs, testimony not only to my inability to stay upright, but also to my inability to fall properly. I had a way of becoming hopelessly flummoxed whenever people rattled off left/right, up/down, push/pull instructions for me to follow in rapid fire. My mind froze. Observation was always a better method of learning for me, but Bob hailed from a strict German background of 1 a.b.c...2 a.b.c...3... He was schooled in a regiment of logic and precision – a bit of a gritty rub against my stubborn skin. Employed by RCA as a TV repairman and training instructor, precision was likewise part of his job.

You wouldn't call Bob wealthy, as in Wealthy, but extended years of bachelorhood and rented rooms had enabled him to amass a considerable chunk of savings, affording him the frivolous luxury of Cadillacs and boats. Warming to us couldn't have been easy for an introverted bachelor facing the subtraction of freedom, the addition of long lasting obligations, and the cumulative terror of dwelling among alien teens. But, he was of the staunchly brave variety: he bit the bullet and proposed. In fact, he proposed on three occasions before my mother finally caved to his persistence and offered up her "Yes." He was a stoically determined fellow.

With her tiny word of acceptance, the blueprint of life on Greengarden Blvd. changed once again, but this time by addition.

....

Addition is a whole different ball game. When I sculpt by addition I build onto form, be it with clay, plaster, wax, wood, or any endless number of objects and materials at hand, even color. With an idea pricking my mind, I rummage around, searching for the first piece of matter necessary to move the idea forward, the very thing to displace space and accommodate a new presence. Often, it's no more than a piece of steel, something rigid to form the inner skeleton, something capable of supporting all that is to come. The role of that first piece of something or other is significant; it defines the core of the structure, it cannot be easily altered once established. Addition takes place from the inside out, the exact opposite of the outside in work of subtraction. Once the supporting skeleton is defined and set in place, the process of building commences in earnest. Mostly, I prefer to work with moist, giving clay to flesh out the bone-like armature into rotund volumes. Bulk is added in a controlled and deliberate manner, though it remains open to adjustment, open to forgiveness. With clay I can thoughtfully respond to the placement and performance of each squishy lump, assessing the impact one glob at a time. For me, the most pleasurable part of sculpting exists in this dialogue of process, this exploration into the myriad number of ways in which to decipher rightness. The slightest pressure exerted by the palm of my hand, the subtle indentation of my thumb, the distinct markings of a tool...any and all of it can alter the persona of the emerging creation, confusing a sly smile with a quizzical frown, a seductive glance with a hint of malice.

....

The addition resulting from marriage is far from subtle. My mother's landed like a brick among us. The atmosphere of the household changed dramatically, turning it topsy-turvy and sideways overnight. Passages of static air became displaced by the long strides and accompanying smell of a grown man in residence. There were new and pesky annoyances for my sister and me, like having to dress in more than bra and undies when darting from bedroom to bathroom, and vice versa, while tending to our teen regime.

For the last five years females had defined the main floor of our house. The reinsertion of man brought a twitchy air and a cramped feel to rooms and hallways that suddenly seemed too tight to accommodate. Bob's legs and arms appeared everywhere. They extended and hovered like those of a daddy long legs spider. True, we gained a boat and a Cadillac, but still…the invasion, the intrusion, took some getting used to. Poor Bob probably felt 100 percent more rattled and displaced than we did, but we were all about thinking about us. He possessed a bravery gene, no doubt – nothing like my dad's, but something worth applauding, nonetheless, considering the extra mouths tied to his "I do."

Tim was the main beneficiary of Bob's presence (not counting my mother, of course): finally, a man, a father figure, to validate his existence for the remainder of his formative years. I knew instinctively that my stepfather was a fine and sincere man, someone good for, and to, my mother and brother, but that knowledge wasn't enough for me to open myself to him. My heart was sealed off to anyone sounding of father – Dad's boots were off limits. Bob accepted me as I was, distance and all. He never tried to rank in my book as anything other than my mother's husband. He knew his place when it came to me.

I experienced a burning sense of embarrassment whenever I had to explain to someone that I had a "stepfather" and not an "original father" – feeling compelled to explain on the spot that my *real* father had died… *and* that my mother had waited *five* whole long and lonely years before remarrying, emphasizing the *five* to ensure that her alone time sounded respectfully long and mournful. Bewildered looks flashed back at me whenever I rattled on and on with this rambling, uncalled for explanation to any and everyone, strangers included. Inevitably, someone would make a gaff and refer to Bob as my father. I never failed to jump in and correct with "stepfather," refusing to allow even the most innocent slip of the tongue to hang in the air as truth. I felt ridiculous doing it, but I couldn't stop myself, I couldn't give Dad's title away, not for a second. What if he could still hear? It was bad enough that his wife was now hooked up with another man and they were sleeping in his very own bed. What if he could still see?

The year of the family addition and subtraction hubbub was 1964.
In May of that year I acquired a stepfather and in September I lost my
sister. Our family portrait was altered by math on both occasions. I was
a junior that year, bound to a slightly reckless social life, you may recall.
Maybe it was the soberness of Karen's decision affecting me, but my wild
life began to quiet down and settle in an air of seriousness. Self-reflective
winds whipped around me, tossing about universal questions in the air:
So, who am *I* and where am *I* going? Such existential questions befuddled
my classmates, as well, for we had reached the age of transition, the age
of wondering.

Many of us turned towards the women in black to aid us in our
grappling and help us identify our place in the world. I was drawn to
confiding in a petite, intensely quiet and humble nun, an English teacher
who smelled of tenderness, compassion, and coffee to pour my heart out
to. Her doleful eyes reflected wisdom and caring; they pierced my insides
and found so much more than my father buried there. In a mother-starved
way, I gravitated to her nurturing warmth, nearly collapsing at the foot
of her kindness and notice. Years of acting the part of A-Okay had left
me starved for attention and affirmation. I'd worked overtime to conceal
my wounds and ailments from my mother, convinced that she needed
my strength and protection, not my problems laid bare. With sad-eyed
admiration and trust I looked hopefully in the direction of my trusted
confidante. Maybe, just maybe, I could rid myself of all that was fowl and
smelly about me and drift, drift, drift airily towards blessed sweet.

With the approach of senior year, Anita – yet another Italian – became one
of my closest friends. When I visited her house, Bea, her short, plumply
pleasant Mom, gorged me on polenta smothered in homemade spaghetti
sauce. It was like feeding on pure Italian love. But, my fit outside of
Anita's house, and into her existing circle of friends, was less sumptuous.
Her friends were more of the super-intelligent type: not the type to pile
in a car and head for the state line to let loose and down malt beers on
a Saturday night. I squeezed in under Anita's wing. Our odd little clique
became known throughout the school as The Big 5, though I don't know
what was deemed Big about us. Our fellow students detected a convent
aura about the whole of us – maybe that's what made us look Big. Each
of us had glued ourselves to a favorite nun pal. My wilder ways were

increasingly tamed due to my association with The Big 5, but I kept a window cracked open to climb out and chew on a party bone every now and then. Ambidextrous, is how I saw myself.

VMA had its share of traditions and its most venerable was that of May Day: a ceremony dedicated to paying homage to the Blessed Virgin Mary. Bar none, the school's highest honor was that of being chosen May Queen. It was the role of the senior class to nominate girls within their ranks whom they believed to be most deserving of the honor, those who best exemplified the virtues of Mary. The top four nominees formed the official ballot, with the entire student body casting a final vote for the queen. I was one of the four. The nominees were called upon to circulate from classroom to classroom, rustling up votes through the delivery of a well-crafted and compelling speech. Having maintained a generic popularity among my classmates, I have to admit that I wasn't all that surprised to find my name on the ballot, despite the standard absence of commercial track student nominees. When it sunk in, however, that the whole to-do really was about the Virgin Mary and saintly virtue, the seepage attacked my under layers, for I burned with humility *and* desire at the same time. Such prideful stains of desire proved beyond a doubt that I did not deserve to be in the running - though I still wanted to be with all my heart.

The announcement came while I was sitting in the back row of my homeroom – my very own nun pal/confidante read my name out loud. I was voted May Queen for the class of 1965! Though I feigned being stunned, I shed real tears – tears of shame, mostly – for, not only had I hoped to win, I had half-expected to win. A simultaneous rush of worthlessness and elation ran through me. The honor showered me with the Mother lode of class acceptance and praise. It rained over my disgusting pride and me.

The heady excitement of the upcoming crowning effectively overshadowed my shame. I feasted on anticipation of the grand day. My mother bought me a long white dress to wear for the occasion, as required. And my attending court of honor (the remaining nominees, including one other member of The Big 5) dressed in long pastel colored dresses. Each of us wore a floral wreath on top our heads like a crown, though mine was more elaborate and distinct, like my honor. I wrote my own speech and delivered it on stage in front of the entire school body, thanking them directly for the great honor, but then turning my eyes and words towards the *true* Queen of the May: our heavenly Mother Mary, our role model for life. My earthly mother made my stepfather take off work in the middle of the day to play cameraman for the occasion, indicating that she must have been plenty proud of me. In his restrained and modest way, Bob seemed genuinely proud of me, as well. Quite naturally, many of the students and teachers took him for my father. Mother Mary herself must've zipped my lips because no clarification spilled from them that day.

The night preceding the crowning ceremony, I was invited to an authentic fraternity party. Welcoming some down to earth distraction, I went. Front and center was a giant punch bowl filled with an ice-cold, fruit flavored concoction that several guys started generously ladling out to me. Oblivious to the percentage of tasteless high-proof kick factored into frat punch bowls, I took to the sweet refreshing liquid like a parched desert traveler. Slurring, giggling, and stumbling my way across the dance floor, it became obvious that my coherent drinking limit had long gone bye-bye. Honestly, I never intended to fall into such a sorry state only twelve or so hours before my crowning, but there I was, major juiced. May Queen jokes buzzed about my ears, yuckity-yuck funny words at party time, but humorless blurs in the sobering light of dawn – the sunrise of my big day.

I woke with a hangover queasiness, and through a splitting head I foxhole prayed that word of my debauchery would not echo through the school halls before the coronation; particularly, not into the ears of the school principal, Sr. Brenda Marie, who generated paralyzing fear in each and every one of us.

When I arrived there was neither buzzing nor snickering in the hallowed halls – another apparent gift from Mother Mary. For the moment, I was safe. Now… all I had to do was lead a procession of girls in a pompous, looooong and slooooow march down the school's eeeeendless first floor hall…turn the corner and continue the march down the fuuuullll length of the school auditorium…while flanked by the entire student body turned toward me in song:

"Bring flowers of the fairest, bring flowers of the rarest, from garden and hillside and mountain and vale. Our dear hearts are swelling, our glad voices telling, the praise of the loveliest Queen of the Vale."

But, the riskiest part of the ceremony was yet to come; it arrived after delivering my thoughtful speech without a stammer. In front of everyone, I had to climb a stepladder and place a floral wreath directly onto the baby-blue veiled head of the life-size statue of the Virgin Mary. Sweat beads bubbled and mustached my upper lip as I ascended. With each step I feared that I might topple, or wobble, or worse yet, topple the Virgin herself. Concentrating every square inch of my pickled body, willing coordination into my shaky limbs, I moved with such focused deliberation that my effort could well have been taken for the epitome of pomp and circumstance, rather than the impeded performance of a hung-over May Queen. But, like some kind of modern day miracle, the ceremony went off without a hitch. The photos and slides that my stepfather shuttered that day reveal nothing more than a pious, reflective young woman dressed in white and crowned with a halo of flowers gazing up adoringly at God's Mother.

May Day was a prelude to graduation, along with a host of other activities that buzzed with finality, but none of it sufficed to distract me fully from the women in white. Several months had passed since their school visit – and my revelation – but they reappeared nightly in my dreams, cornering the playground of my mind. They came mixed among masses of black skinned bodies, screeching elephants and roaring tigers…wild drum beats and chirping whistles…they came with a Polish girl running through the bush alongside them. Whether my thoughts continued to drift there on the sheer wings of youthful impressionability or on the true breath of God's calling, I still couldn't say. In my dreams I didn't care, and in my waking missionary life began to feel like an embrace.

I can't prove in any logical way that this missionary business had anything to do with my father's death, but I always sensed a pulse there. Perhaps my words came out jumbled on that long ago night when I pleaded in desperation to God, when I offered him myself in exchange for my father's life. Perhaps God didn't understand the trade stipulation, the part that meant if my dad was dead for good, than so was my offer. Perhaps I was still on the hook for the promises I choked out that night. Or, was it the plain result of life turning serious at too young an age - the heart pumping too heavily with noble causes and lofty ideals? And, there's always the escape from Erie, Pa. theory to toss into the mix of reasoning.

So, here's where my ulterior motive for wanting my mother married enters the picture: before I could entertain departure of any sort, I needed fixed assurance that my mother would be cared for - my leaving could not be associated with abandonment. Without marriage Karen's departure from the family would have laid upon me an obligation to stay, for in my mind I remained Mom's caretaker – just like I remained Dad's memory keeper. Hooking Mom up with a proper husband equated to opening the door to freedom.

With the combined force of daytime thinking and nighttime dreaming, I mustered up the courage to write a letter to Sr. Mary Peter – the pink-cheeked angel my eyes had latched onto the day of my revelation. I poured out questions as well as my heart. I mailed the letter. Then I stalked the mailbox for days waiting for a reply. It was essential that my correspondence remain undercover, for I was not the least bit ready to see or hear or bear what my mother might think of my scheming dreams. She had been accepting enough – though far from thrilled – with my sister's decision. I didn't want to push her buttons or make her think that I was just out to top my sister.

Eureka! A letter in the box! But it was penned from another sister, the one in charge of vocations. It turned out that Sr. Mary Peter was a novice in training, therefore, not permitted to communicate with young aspirants, such as myself. However, my substitute pen pal welcomed my interest in the congregation and encouraged me to continue corresponding, writing out in detail my ongoing questions and thoughts. She, also, suggested that my family and I drive to Franklin, Pa. for a visit – a chance to size each other up, though she didn't use those words. Her letter dealt me a blow when she stated the firm fact that the age for admission was eighteen. My eyes bulged with a, *"What the…?"* I was set to graduate at seventeen. It would take six long months to reach the ripe and ready age of 18. When you're fired-up and hot-to-trot, six months looms like a long decade. And, obviously, a family visit was out of the question, so I had to settle for nothing more than rounds of clandestine letter writing. But, I took to praying more fervently, as well, hoping to hear God's rare, whispery voice through my ears, or my heart.

With the presentation of a diploma, my four years of life at VMA officially ended, immediately filing themselves away under "Ago." Collars and cuffs piled up limp, and clunky blue oxfords sat unpolished, zippered uniforms were donated as hand-me-downs. The Big 5 subtracted itself out of existence: four of five off to join the Sisters of St. Joseph – age not being an obstacle to their dream scheme. I was the fifth, the leftover. My college bound friends moved on to four more years of academic camaraderie, while my fellow commercial students and I stood our ground, equipped and ready to speed type our mark onto the world and document our new status in life. We scoured the same Help Wanted ads and scrambled our way across the east and west sides of town, interviewing to secure our secretarial futures in the real world of the working. I had been clobbered by a far rougher version of the real world six years earlier, so the mere material threat of unemployment seemed no threat at all. In graduating from high school I entered into the final round of waiting, waiting to subtract the past of me and create a new me one glorious glob at a time.

CHAPTER 8. BETWEEN HERE AND THERE

With four years of training for the joys of office life tucked under my belt, it was expected that I exercise my credentials and harvest their bland fruits. Actually, I had gotten a part-time taste of office work during my junior year, when I was employed three days a week after school by Holland Realtors to type real estate contracts for Jack Holland's wife, Laverne. Mrs. Holland was a stickler for detail, though I suppose a contract is nothing if not about details.

She was a stickler for her appearance as well: she sported a beehive hairdo of piled up curls, layered atop a copiously made-up face, and accented by stylish and ornate pointy eyeglass frames. She wore form fitting, sometimes cleavage revealing, above the knee outfits matched to perfection by noisily clopping high heels. I would hear her heels clop their way towards me and park themselves directly behind my chair, where the noise quieted to the smell of her middle-age scented body, as she leaned obnoxiously close over my shoulder to inspect my contractual typing skills.

At her clunking approach, my fingers dampened in anxiety and scurried blindly across the keyboard as if untrained, suddenly typing Greek, or was it Swahili? Cherry-flushed and smiling angelically, I turned my gaze up at her hoping that my double dimpled charm was enough to forgive my moment of secretarial collapse. Eventually, dear Mrs. Holland came to realize that I was quite a perfectionist myself, as long as she kept her bodily distance and waited for me to approach with a flawlessly executed document in hand. When I quit my part-time job, due to an overly fulltime senior year, she was visibly sad to lose me. Oddly, I couldn't quite lose her for the longest time: my heart raced and my fingers sweated whenever I heard the sound of clopping heels approach.

With the help of the Help Wanted ads, I scored a full-time secretarial job at Keystone Electric, an east side electrical construction company run by two Polish men. Dick and Sarge, the two Poles, interviewed me and then passed me on to Virginia, the also Polish office manager, who eyed me with a wary up and down look, noting and measuring my threatening youth and charm in a sly biased second. Perceiving threat in her squinty, medium cool blue eyes, I downshifted smoothly into awe, "I don't know how you've managed all this work by *yourself* Virginia! I can sure learn a lot from you." Oozing syrupy praise worked just dandy: I was hired.

As Virginia's baby flunky, I started off by being assigned the things she didn't want to do. She relished having someone to dump junk on and she flaunted her newfound authority as if she had actually earned it. One day Virginia called in sick – something she was freer to do now – so Sarge called me in to take dictation in her place. Well…I dazzled him with the trio of my shorthand speed, a perfectly typed transcription of his mumbled and jumbled facts, and my quick grasp of electrical jargon. A star was born! From that day on Sarge called upon me to take his dictation, not Virginia. She was miffed and her thin lips showed it – they hyphenated her ears. Our shared office space grew tight, as did the polyester skirts around her waist, but I stuck with flattery. I couldn't afford to jeopardize my paycheck because I suddenly found myself with financial commitments.

Having earned and tucked away no more than a few paychecks, I decided rather impulsively to buy a new car, and not just any car. A spiffy new sports model had just hit the market: the Fiat Spider. Bob accompanied me to the only car dealer that had one parked on the lot. It took only 30 minutes and his credit rating for me to become the proud owner of a snazzy, sporty white convertible. Not knowing how to drive its manual transmission didn't dissuade me a bit. That's how it is with me when lust squarely overpowers reason. I simply *had* to have it! My slick and frivolous purchase led to Bob and me spending a good chunk of time together, his super-size frame accordioned into my passenger seat as we danced a non-stop jerk and stall across vacant parking lots. But, thanks to his patience and my persistence, I soon cruised to the tune of confidence, my long dishwater blonde hair whipping in the breeze, heads turning as I whizzed by in such fine style.

But mind you, I didn't buy the car for *my* image; I bought it solely out of admiration for its shapely beauty. It called to me visually, sensually, and the call was irresistible now that I was backed by a weekly paycheck to flit away on such lavish eye candy. Yes…there appeared to be an obvious disconnect between my missionary aspirations and the material indulgence of a brand new sports car, but…I chose to embrace the neon contradiction, adding a tug-of-war suspense to the fork in the road looming ahead of me. Besides, if a lifelong vow of poverty awaited me, why not gobble up excessive goodies while I still could? And, with my mother now eyeing with trepidation the regular, foreign-looking correspondence arriving in the mail, the outlandish purchase was a comforting indulgence for her, as well. It served to sooth her with the balm of hope that a seductive and racy set of wheels could keep me happily parked in her driveway.

The only benefit I could divine from working over on the east side of town was that it offered up a two-minute drive to Grandma Poplaski's house, where I could eat a lunch prepared with old fashioned love. Her house was not excessively covered in doilies like my other grandmother's house. Stephanie's house was more lived in, more earthy, more dirty, more her. But she religiously dusted the crucifixes, statues of the Virgin Mary, St. Joseph, St. Anthony, and other miscellaneous saints that occupied her house; such in-house shrines were the norm for old-world Polish families. Overall, though, she cared as little for the state of her house as she did for the state of herself, yet she loved to cram her dining room shelves with fine crystal and quality china. Growing up I spent many weekend afternoons at her house dusting her cherished goods and re-shelving them for their secure life behind glass cabinet doors. The collection's main purpose was to sparkle and shine – just like my Fiat Spider. Grandma and I shared an eye for beauty.

Throughout much of her life she worked long hours on her feet, standing before a toy assembly line at Marx Toys. That was the price she paid for craving such fine objects of beauty, objects that glistened in her weathered house much like a trophy wife glistens on an old man's arm. I'm certain that underneath my grandmother's plebian manner lurked a diamond in the rough, an unpolished life-size woman destined to remain so. With something close to recklessness, she stocked the shelves of her china cabinet with more beauty than they might hold, and certainly more than she could afford, never weighing either.

That she didn't care more than a speck about the inside state of her house, didn't mean that she didn't care about the outside back yard, her beloved garden.

The flower garden was arranged like rows of crops, offering a twelve-inch walking space between each row for admiring and care taking. Roses were abundantly present, all types and colors blooming profusely like wildly fertile mothers. Thanks to Uncle Al's manual labor, Grandma maintained a semblance of garden control, though the happy growth sometimes ran wild and exploded into breathtaking floral chaos. Her garden was insanely spectacular at times, though my mother ignored every gorgeous bloom. She resented the garden because all of her mother's time and interest roamed outside, abandoning the disheveled inside to her, the eldest child, to tend to. While my mother coldly turned her back on the colorful spectacle, my grandmother couldn't walk by a single flower head without chirping: "Ooooh, isn't that beauuuutiful!" in Polish melody.

I held none of my mother's grudges towards my grandmother. Besides the house/garden thing, my mother nagged at her incessantly about her eating habits and the weight they carried, but Grandma deafly ate on with an almost primitive relish. She *loved* to eat! Her natural chubbiness grew into fattiness, and the fat of it held on long and tight before succumbing to the shrinkage of old age. Almost every outfit she owned bore testimony to her taste in food: the menu du jour displayed boldly in spotted signage right across the billboard of her sprawling belly. These spots drove my mother crazy. I concluded that the real culprit was Grandma's belly, a bull's-eye catchall that blocked spilled food from landing on the floor, instead of on her. Her generous table top of a lap openly greeted drips, globs, and splatters. They weren't her fault. Most of what my mother held against her mother, happened to be the very reasons I loved my grandma so unconditionally.

I drove to my Grandma lunches twice a week: a baked chicken leg, a serving of jiggling Jell-O chock full of fruit cocktail, and a scoop of cole slaw. Or: a baked pork chop, jiggling Jell-O chock full of miniature marshmallows, and a scoop of potato salad. Since Uncle Al still lived with Grandma, he, also, reaped the benefits of my lunch visits, Grandma prepared an extra leg or chop for him, as well. But I never ate lunch with him – or with her for that matter since she preferred the role of waitress – which was just as well because trying to make conversation with him induced indigestion. His presence in the house sounded mostly through the spin of his favorite records: *You are My Sunshine, Goodnight Irene...* unless Grandma had requested a kick-up-your-heels Polish polka for the lunch hour festivities. He was odd, so odd, so itchy to be around.

I'm referring to the house as "Grandma's house" because Grandpa had died of a heart attack in 1962 at age 66. He didn't topple over on the floor and die like my other Grandpa. He died on the operating table during surgery for bleeding ulcers – a surgery that was supposed to go well, but didn't. Mushroom goulash left the menu for good when Grandpa Alex left Erie, Pa. for good – the place he had settled in as a 14-year-old immigrant boy.

He departed solo from his homeland in Poland at that very young age, making his way to the United States of America. Leaving behind his family and all that was familiar to him, he ventured across the ocean and onto the shores of a land boasting of prosperity and promise. I've often tried to picture him arriving in Philadelphia in 1911 with nothing but a suitcase in each hand and Polish words on his tongue, but it's hard to capture such courage in an imagined picture. Somehow or other he got wind of work to be had in a place called Erie, Pa., so off he headed in the hopes of finding a place to establish his still growing feet. He found a job at the General Electric plant, where Grandpa Anthony worked, as well. Then he found Stefania Lipiniska, who herself had traveled from Lublin, Poland with her mother and brother in 1913. Passion snared them for keeps when Stefania became pregnant. They married and started a life together for better or worse. My mother, Irene, was their flower child, their passion fruit. She was the first seed they planted and harvested in Erie, Pa.

Grandpa corresponded with his family back in Poland, as well as sending them money. He hadn't run from them. He ran out in front of them, hoping that they would one day catch up with him in America. After he married, quite surprisingly, his family stopped responding to his letters, leaving him confused, hurt, and perhaps angry. Uncountable years later my mother discovered that Grandpa's family had not, in fact, stopped writing: his dear wife Stefania had intercepted their letters and hidden them for, what turned out to be, dusty decades, eventually forgetting they ever existed. My mother came upon the unopened shock of them after both of her parents had died. We could only surmise that Grandma's intent had been to stem her husband's habit of mailing off money to relatives, hoping hard and mean that silence on their end would end generosity on his. Her calculated cruelty disturbed me deeply. I tried to step back and into her practical leather shoes to better understand her deception, but I kept tripping over the footprint of Grandpa's pain. My mind just couldn't figure out a way to justify her behavior. Forgiveness was the only way around it, the only way to cleanse her, the only way to calm me. I forgave her for my love demanded it.

On days when I wasn't driving my cool and sporty Spider to East 4th Street at noontime, I carried a brown bag lunch and walked to the nearby Catholic Church. Around noon the church was mostly empty. Entering the dim, dank incensed vestibule – pausing to dip a finger into a tepid bowl of holy water and make the Sign of the Cross – I made my way to the privacy of a back pew to best conceal my intentions, for I wasn't there to pray: I was there to eat my sandwich and read. The book I toted along with my brown bag lunch was *The Agony and the Ecstasy*. Reading about Michelangelo while seated in a domed church was like adding espresso to the story. Eating a baloney sandwich and a Hostess cupcake in the house of God verged on the sacrilegious. Sorry, but it was the only place I could think of to simultaneously indulge body and soul, the only place where art and spirit could rendezvous like lovers. These inspirational time-outs sustained me through the grind of tedious office hours and they became the tonic of my survival when my waiting time became compromised by my first road trip to Franklin, Pa.

I planned on making my virgin drive to the Allegheny foothills with me myself and I, but, nonetheless, I felt obliged to inform my mother that Spider and I would be venturing off on a three hundred mile round-trip to visit my missionary pen pal. I lost sleep fretting over how to phrase the news and practiced delivering it in a jaunty tone that would understate its significance and dash any motherly concern. True to her close-to-the-chest manner, my mother expressed neither surprise nor dismay, swallowing whatever size lump formed in her throat, along with the need for any hard questioning. I welcomed her reserve like a genuine gift, for I was an absolute nervous wreck.

Cruising through the Allegheny mountains on a leaf radiant day – the convertible top down and my long hair haloing me in the wind – I arrived at the hillside drive of an impressive stone complex marked with a giant wooden cross rooted in a pine filled yard. Turning my earthly Spider onto the drive and parking it there, felt like I was dumping trash onto acreage of purity, sacrifice, and denial. As my engine died, a little white nun of wonder stepped out of a massive front door and greeted me warmly, commenting readily and enthusiastically on my gorgeous set of wheels. I had parked upon honest land. We chatted in the front visitors' parlor and then moved across a spacious entranceway to share a meal together in a private dining area. The rest of the house was designated as the novitiate proper; visitors were restricted for it was occupied with young sisters engaged in a semi-cloistered year of silence, prayer, and training. Scurrying white-robed figures could be glimmered flowing through the adjoining hallways, but the ethereal blurs kept their heads down and their eyes lowered as mandated by "custody of the eyes." Older, fully professed nuns, however, popped their heads in gaily to say hello, displaying friendly dispositions and effusive warmth. Each greeted me with a European two or three cheek smooch of welcome. Even their laughter radiated a holy calm. Calm was all around me.

The *most* vivid part of an all-around vivid day, however, was the occasion of afternoon prayer. Mounting the steps of the broad center staircase, I pulled open the weighty door to God's house and self-consciously inserted myself into the community of young and old in the act of prayer. As if stricken by a virus of disbelief, my eyes fluttered to adjust to the vision of a chapel such as I had never seen or imagined: space so sacred that my breath failed me, my eyes stung, and a dizzying sensation tingled throughout my limbs. And the silence…the utter silence of it resonated with the crystal clear voice of God. My ears were on fire.

The chapel, itself, was coated in the color of creamy white, and giant over-sized windows welcomed a pouring of sparkling daylight from two sides to. Twenty or so simply designed blond wood pews angled diagonally around a central altar, also simple, also blond. A large ebony cross was suspended over the back wall and a life-sized, but stylized, corpus hung from it posed in agony and signifying redemption. There was no other adornment present, other than the intoxicating smell of sunshine swabbing cotton wrapped bodies bent in prayer. I was overcome by a consuming desire to belong, not visit.

When late afternoon moved in to signal the time for my departure, I exited the holy confines and ever so reluctantly made my way back to

Spider. Sliding into my black leather seat I sat motionless…motionless in a sporty vehicle demolished of blue book value by the crushing impact of my heavenly day. Driving off, my rear view mirror hung with the image of a tiny white figure waving with gusto, until a curve in the road erased the shape of it. I headed home in a meaningless way, to a meaningless job, and a meaningless life in Erie, Pa.

Before departing from the glorious occasion of my visit, I was assigned homework: to write a short autobiography – a pre-requirement of the admission process. Thanks to my mother's tendency to hang onto report cards and such, I located a carbon copy of the autobiography I wrote back in 1965 stashed in a box of memorabilia in the basement. It came as no surprise to me to read that I chose to begin the account of my life with Easter's death. Then, I wrote:

> "I remember praying for strength for us all. It was then that I first realized the power of God and my need of Him. By the help of God, we were able to pick up the pieces and start life again."

Reading this blatantly strong declaration of my young faith surprises me and rattles my mind. It floods me with nostalgic pangs of longing for beliefs inherited and lost, for I am different now: ambivalent concerning organized religion and the faith demanded of it. Along with the nostalgia of it, it dredges up a bucket-full of cynical resentment towards the obligations of a religion that forced me at a very young age to believe wholeheartedly in so much that is unbelievable. However, before my Catholic devotion ultimately collapsed in torment, conflict, and doubt, it appears to have, at one time, provided me with comfort and consolation – though I can't quite remember how, other than reading about it. Nowadays, when I tilt my head upwards, it's to do no more than to set my eyes upon the vastness of the sky and wonder, be it with or without a divine creator: that is what I call prayer.

When I finally turned 18 in November, I was certain that I had cleared the last hurdle to admission into the White Sisters, my sisters, but something…something…maybe in my correspondence, or my visit, or my autobiography, led the Vocation Director (my pen pal) to recommend that I wait one more year before joining: 19, perhaps. I was CRUSHED! No…no…that doesn't begin to describe it: *I was obliterated, pummeled, destroyed!* The consensus on their end appeared to be that it would be better if I *ex-peeerienced* a bit more, *ma-tuuured* a bit more. They tried in vain to comfort me with, "God's time is not our time. If your calling is real, time will only strengthen it. Time will strengthen *you*." In other words, the test of time would serve to make or break my resolve, and that's exactly what they hoped it would do. They wanted time to do its work before they were called in to do theirs.

In re-reading my autobiography, I can much more clearly appreciate their reasoning and decision. My life's account rambles on at times with an overly generous smattering of artsy-feely stuff. It expresses more full-blown honesty and passion than it should have laid bare at such an early stage in our courtship. The autobiography just *felt* too much. It had the same problem I had.

The only – and I mean *only* – benefit that came with the setback, was the generous time frame it afforded my mother to better prepare herself for losing a second daughter to Mother Church. She surmised all along, of course, what I was up to long before I finally confessed my intentions. There was no doubt in my mind that she wanted me to join the convent and fly off to Africa about as much as she had wanted to be a widow. But my mother never *really* tried to all out dissuade me, or assail me with any hard-core objections, any guilt, any threats. Instead, she exhibited restrained acquiescence – like through a clenched jaw – choosing to tolerate my insistence on such a foreign road to happiness. The delay offered her the chance to hope for all she was worth that something, or someone, would materialize out of nowhere and alter my spiritual travel itinerary.

Many Catholic parents prayed, specifically, for religious vocations for their sons and daughters – the church even instructed parents to do so – but my mother wasn't among them. In having two daughters eager to leave home, forsake marital bliss, and join the convent, she guessed that she had gone wrong somewhere along the mothering line. To her, religious life equated to loss, further diminishment of our small family, the absence of grandchildren, the absence of Karen and Gail. My decision served up grief…silent grief.

I licked my time wounds by playing Nun: a new game, though similar in some ways to Church, our old game. In the locked privacy of my bedroom, I draped myself head to toe in white sheets, mimicking as closely as possible the clothing habit of the White Sisters. Then, staring into my full-length mirror, admiring the beatific vision of my own saintliness, I romanced upon my upcoming wedding to Christ. What I was doing wasn't any different than a woman trying on a wedding gown, primping and posturing for the most special day of her life, was it? For a soundtrack, I blasted Joan Baez records, inviting her soaring, plaintive voice to permeate the air and carry me deeper into my reveries. Ohhhh, I was *soooo in love* with Joan Baez! It's a good thing that Joan Baez wasn't any more physical for me than a record, for I might've been tempted to strip off my white sheets and run off across the highways and byways of America just to be near my singing-strumming idol. Sometimes, the most intense of my multi-sensory infatuations butted heads. I cleverly mediated any conflict between the White Sisters and Joan Baez by adapting my game to Singing Nun.

With such heavy time on my hands and heart, I started hanging out with my cousin LeRoy – the hilarious, artistic one. To my utter surprise, this seemingly innocent move led my plans perilously close to derailment, for LeRoy introduced me to his best friend Billy, a boy as Italian to the roots as I was Polish. I perceived Billy to be the spitting image of a true Bohemian artist. He was conspicuously different from the generic male population of my environment. Besides being gorgeous, tall and dark with a head of black wild curls, he was a painter, a true artist. Typically, he dressed in his signature long (almost to the floor) black coat, black boots, and black pants, with a colorful scarf flourished around his muscular neck. If you didn't know Billy, and you spied him sauntering your way dressed like a black shadow, you might instinctively lower your worried eyes and clutch your purse a tad tighter, or cross the street to avoid his threatening approach all together – such was the air about him. But a word with Billy was sufficient to vanquish all fear, for words exposed a sweet and tender soft-spoken man, framed with an offbeat, wry sense of humor and life. The only problematic challenge he posed was in trying to comprehend and/or appreciate his non-traditional "out there" take on life.

Well…we fell hard and fast into the pattern of soul mates stitched from top to bottom. We drank from the same well of intense feelings, and saw through the same passionate lens; even the quirkiness in our humor matched to a fit. Assuming my own version of his artsy dress code, I took to wearing corded, hip-hugging bell-bottoms (before most Erieites caught on), and perched a black beret on top of my head of dishwater blonde hair. In our hometown, dressed as we were and cruising around in a flashy Spider convertible, the two of us were a sight to behold. Grown-up locals gawked nakedly when we zoomed by – as if they had seen an honest-to-goodness UFO.

When Billy first entered our house for an official meet and greet with my mother, her wordless up-and-down appraisal of his less than "normal" appearance was loud enough, but her tight-lipped hello screamed panic. With desperation and practicality, and within a split-hair of a second, she tallied up pro and con columns for Billy vs. the convent, weighing and balancing a miserable choice between two thoroughly undesirable options for my life. When a nervous swallow roller-coasted down her throat, it all but announced that Billy had won out over Jesus – a quick and decisive ruling. An Italian-bohemian UFO was more acceptable to her than my departure.

Billy and I engaged in nature dates, and not just because he was broke. We went on extended beach walks and drove to the country for sketching expeditions, the type of dates we loved most. With a picnic of cheese, bread, and cheap wine, we searched out abandoned farm property offering romantic seclusion and landscape vistas. Coming upon a rustic and empty barn was like winning the lottery for us. We hoisted ourselves into a hay-less loft and spread our blanket across aged and rickety boards. There we lay close, sharing an appetizer of kisses and cuddles before thinking to open our picnic basket. After our actual eating feast, we took up pad and pencil and began to sketch from whatever choice views the barn openings provided. Billy was on break from studying art at the Cleveland Institute of Art, so I believed myself to be in the presence of certifiable talent. But he treated me like an equal, encouraging my talent and praising the work of my hands. I never thought of myself as an *actual* artist – except, perhaps, back in grade school while going steady with Larry Markowski and working on classroom bulletin boards together – and I, most definitely, never stopped to ponder a future in art. For an X-marked Polish girl trained in the likes of dictation, such a life seemed as preposterous as linking up with Joan Baez. Now, why a missionary life in Africa seemed more doable, I really can't say.

Billy was aware of my convent plans and aspirations. The first time we hung out together with LeRoy, I announced openly that I was on hold to become a missionary nun; all I was interested in was a distraction from time. Well…Billy distracted me all right. As we wiggled deeper into each other's souls, and cuddled longer in each other's arms, we chose to ignore the holy elephant sitting before us heavy with danger. Skipping about in fields of wildflowers and through days of bliss, we allowed our artistic odyssey and summer romance to extinguish thought all together.

When the time came for Billy to return to Cleveland and his art studies, we took comfort in knowing that a two-hour drive could rescue us from terminal separation and keep the thrill of togetherness alive. In fact, as soon as Billy settled into an apartment with his buddy Frank, he phoned, begging me to drive up for a weekend to see the place. Oddly enough, it just so happened that Frank's girlfriend, Sally, had been a commercial student along with me at VMA. I'd been friendly with her, of course, given my all encompassing "if I can't like you I will love you philosophy." Driving there together for a double-date weekend could be lots of fun, I said to myself. After all, it was only Cleveland, I said to myself.

I wanted to go, all right, but something in the very nature of the idea verged on sinful and inappropriate for the times (I thought anyway) – and I was wormily squeamish about broaching the topic with my mother, as well. I was certain that she would be scandalized at the thought of Billy and I sharing an apartment for an entire weekend. So, when my mother let out a chipper, "Oh, *that* sounds like fun!" I was flabbergasted and shot her a blank look of wonder. Of course, after thinking about it, her overboard enthusiasm wasn't perplexing at all. She clearly preferred risking the likes of a scandalous pregnancy to my going off to the jungles of Africa with the likes of Jesus. Her motherly blessing and enthusiasm actually served to calm my own queasy jitters. The trip was on.

Sally and I didn't bother to discuss sleeping arrangements - it was a "no-brainer" that she and I would share a bed, right? All four of us were Catholic. Surely, everyone would be on the same Catholic, no-brainer page when it came to bedding down for the night.

Their tiny apartment smelled of cold cuts, being that it perched on top of a run-down Deli in an equally run-down part of Cleveland. Basically, the place was one large room decorated with two tattered Goodwill armchairs and two beds separated by a yard of so of space and a worn sheet suspended from the ceiling, forming a billowing thin divide between the two beds. Sally and I deposited our suitcases onto one bed. A mini-kitchenette and bathroom were tacked onto the end of the room like an afterthought, nearly tumbling off and down the dim stairwell. Scattered artworks by both Frank and Billy dueled for prime wall space, exotic incense smells battled to conquer the salami odors wafting upwards through the floorboards, a host of candles shed a seductive light, and the

Beatles sang *Norwegian Wood*. One authentic artist's pad! I had never felt so grown-up before, so womanly. Cleveland felt grown-up, as well, all bustling and cosmopolitan compared to "Drearie Erie," or "Mistake on the Lake" – however you chose to see it and call it. We opened up bottles of cheap wine, Vintner's Choice or Pink Catawba or some other lowbrow fare – Blue Nun being the finest wine I knew. I couldn't wrap my hand around the glass fast enough for I needed to down a cure to my racing heart. A battle was brewing big time in my gut: Billy/art vs. Jesus/Africa. Both pairings seduced me with the possibility of glorious fulfillment.

Wine helps when you're toying with two lovers.

Wined and mellowed, the four of us strolled around town arm in arm, stopping to dine at a penny-saving greasy spoon specializing in cheap tap beer, and the likes of us. Tired out, we headed back and climbed the narrow dingy staircase up to the guys' pad. Unlatching my suitcase, I gathered my night things and headed to the bathroom to set my hair in jumbo size rollers guaranteed to keep me looking good for my second day in the city. *Was I clueless or what!!?* Upon exiting the bathroom, I found the trace of Sally's silhouette, along with Frank's, projected amorously on the candlelit sheet hanging between the two sides of the bedroom space. They patterned a human pretzel. I panicked! I was shocked! How could she? Then I saw Billy scantily dressed in a T-shirt and boxers staring at me. I don't know who was more shocked: Billy seeing me with a head full of rollers, or me seeing Billy lying in the bed that Sally and I were to share. The holy elephant had arrived. I could hardly fall to my knees and pray to God for help. Billy detected my terror, he swore that all he wanted was to *sleep* next to me, to be close to me, nothing more. Still, I was scared to death – remember I knew absolutely zilch about sex. With such complete and utter ignorance at my disposal, I envisioned the White Sisters morphing into ghosts before my eyes. I summoned my voice, my courage, and whispered to Billy that he would have to sleep elsewhere. Turning my eyes from him, he simultaneously rose and turned his body from me. Like a jilted lover, he rummaged about for a blanket, attempting to settle himself in for a night in the old armchairs, which he yanked together, placing them in front of the window to peer out on the desolate street below.

Noises percolated from Frank and Sarah's bed: rustlings and muffled groans, disturbing and threatening sounds that made my stomach queasy. On occasion, I had caused my own mattress springs to squeak and squeal like theirs now did, manufacturing such sinful sounds alone, but never with another. The candles in the room were extinguished, but the room glowed intermittently with light from fleeting traffic and washes of neon hues cast upwards from the street shops below. Gingerly, I wedged my rolled head into the pillow and prayed for the quick escape of sleep. But once the commotion of Frank and Sarah settled, the fidgeting frustration of Billy disturbed me even more as he flailed about in a vain search for comfort. I don't know how much time passed before I opened my sleepless eyes to Billy standing upright and staring out the window, rejection flickering from the pores of him. My fingers caved first. They moved to my head and began removing the rollers set in my hair – hopes for tomorrow's beauty flattened as I tossed each one aside. Beckoning to Billy, I whispered, "Okay." But, I had terms. My terms were that he would lie *on top* of the cover sheet and I would lie *beneath* the cover sheet – a cotton yin and yang. In my naive mind, the idea seemed like a safe and foolproof compromise, one that insured that both my beliefs and my body would be guarded from the dangers of man.

Billy behaved perfectly, but I did not. As we slept cuddled together through the night, I became unbearably aroused; the heat of his physical presence through the cotton seemed to penetrate me. Shutting down my mind and pretending to act through the deepest of slumber, I proceeded to wrap my legs around his leg (with the sheet still over him, of course - I couldn't totally violate my own rules) and hump my way to satisfaction in a one-way pursuit of desire. Humping his leg was the extent of my sin – a far cry from intercourse, I hoped, whatever all that entailed. In gentlemanly fashion, Billy restrained himself throughout, settling for pleasure from my indulgence alone. When I succumbed to the state of sleep, it was the equivalent of blacking out in shame.

In the morning light we acted like nothing had moved us but dreams, but I more than sheepishly recalled my lusty appetite as clear as day - certainly Billy recalled it, too, and God...*he* knew it forward and backward. My humping action is all that occurred throughout our weekend together, I escaped any fatal bullet, but I was dead certain that I had cheated on Jesus, even though he wasn't yet my spouse. My behavior was nothing short of disgusting. Sexual desire didn't sit on my lap as normal like it should have – like it did with most human beings. My bodily appetite scared me to death. I didn't know how to reconcile it with my Catholic and mother-based hang-ups. The pressure of such ignorance, such conflict, pushed me to run from that which my body threatened to lose control of – from Billy who could alter my future with only a second's worth of liquid love. My weekend in Cleveland spelled-out to me in capital letters the urgency of saying goodbye.

Billy was devastated, crushed, heart-broken by my goodbye, though the knowledge that I was leaving him for none other than Jesus, and not some other turkey of a guy, offered him a balm of comfort. He told me so. His misery informed him that he would never find another, and upon graduating he shipped off to Vietnam, as if to make it so. Being the cause of his pain was my greatest pain, for my own loss was soothed by my renewed purpose and sense that destiny was close at hand. I was spared the absolute void of our breakup, a void that he alone had to bear. I was re-routed from Cleveland, Ohio to Franklin, Pa. – both a two-hour drive from Erie, Pa., but in two entirely different directions. Sadly for my mother, my weekend in Cleveland did not bear the fruit of her last hopes.

With a couple of months still lingering before the date of my entrance, I turned to a safer distraction, one void of bodily temptation: a guitar. I taught myself to strum and pluck away in pure innocence. The guitar arrived as a going-away present from a bunch of my closest high school friends who had chipped in to buy it for me. Now my mirror revealed a far truer version of the Singing Nun game: a Polish Piper girl with a troop of half-naked village children trailing, clapping and swaying, clapping and swaying. But, unlike the tunes of Julie Andrews, I strummed and sang to those of Joan Baez: *Gabriel and Me, Sweet Sir Galahad, Wayfaring Stranger, Blessed Are, Last, Lonely and Wretched...* I, quite narrowly, broadened my repertoire with the addition of like-minded, folksy tunes by Peter, Paul and Mary and Judy Collins. It was the sixties, so along with timeless love, protest and social-minded-songs distinguished the bread and butter of the era. As my guitar skills improved, I took to composing my own lyrics and melodies. The words and simple chords to at least a half dozen of my songs are tucked away in an old three-ring music binder, which sits on a shelf in my current bedroom. It's a binder I can't let go of - it keeps moving with me. Most of my home-brewed compositions flow in the vein of the following:

I had some flowers and I watched them grow, how I watered them God only knows. I never thought the day would come along, when they would die and be gone.

Refrain: Child life keeps slippin' away, child you've got to find your own way. You've got to be a man, you've got to understand, you've got to look, search, ask, seek, before the time passes on, before the light is gone.

I had a friend he was so dear to me, we used to spend the day just letting' things be. I never thought the day would come along, when he would die and be gone.

Refrain.

I knew a fellow and his name was me, kind of stubborn, kind of ornery. I used to tell him that a day would come when he would die and be gone.

Refrain.

No comment.

Increasingly, I spent the remainder of my wait time in solitude, locked in nervous anticipation. As if already gone to my world, I distanced myself from friends and social habits. My beloved Spider was demoted in my eyes to nothing more than four wheels for getting me nowhere. My body lingered, still tied to the cord of its birthplace, but layers of me commenced to peel away and shed, detaching from the place that had born me and grown me, confused me and tormented me. I was in the final stage of removing myself from the *somewhere* and the *someone* of who I was.

An austere shopping list arrived in the mail from the White Sisters, showing everything I would need to purchase and bring with me on my day of entrance: men's style T-shirts, white cotton socks, white flannel nightgowns, polyester white blouses, a simple black bathrobe (this I had to order from a specialty catalog for nuns), one black button down sweater, and the ugliest old lady-ish black shoes available on the market. I shopped for these blandest of bland items with more enthusiasm than I had shopped for my sports car, thrilling over each find and handling it preciously, sacredly almost. A single compact trunk would easily serve to transport the entirety of my frugal, earthly possessions: my practical wardrobe of renunciation.

When the only-two-days-to-go-before-departure-alarm sounded, family emotions thickened into something dense and sliceable, like pound cake. Our well-established Soliwoda code of silence trembled as we verged on the teetering edge of an unthinkable family breakdown – one that I could not allow. I toughened myself, steeled myself, by recasting my mother, stepfather, and brother into no more than hired actors staged in a painfully awkward goodbye scene on television.

Grandma Stephanie took the family to a restaurant for one of her extravagant splurges: "Order *whichamacallit*...Lobster! Everybody, order lobster!" she encouraged. She *loved* lobster tails, allowing the drawn, golden, sweet butter to run freely down the front of her dress with trickling abandon, like a rivulet of sheer pleasure. To my mother's critical eyes, her sloppy stains registered as embarrassment, but they registered as pure delight to mine. *Whichamacallit* was Grandma's pet word, filling in for every single word in the English language that she did not know, or lazily bother to learn. No matter how she used it, I always knew what it meant.

I drove to the east side to deliver a goodbye to Grandma Smiecuich, who had slowly begun to distance herself after Dad's death, treating us as if we hung to the family by a weak thread, and nearly severing us altogether when my mother remarried, despite having done so herself with no apparent hesitation. Anyway, that's how my mother viewed the relationship, so, naturally, that's how I viewed the relationship.

Over the years, whenever my sibs and I performed a dutiful Sunday afternoon visit to her home, she customarily broke out the Mogen David wine, not a bit bothered by the nonsense of a legal drinking age. A box of Russell Stover chocolate covered cherries rested on a doily covered tabletop as permanently and reliably as a knick-knack. The cherries and the wine were offered to all guests, not just us - *forced* might be the correct word. Grandma never guarded the Mogen David bottle from us like she guarded the Seagram's 7 bottle from the grown men in her life. Sipping belly-warming wine and chomping into cherry-chocolate liquid made for a visit sweetened with far more giggles and pleasantness than an alcohol free visit could ever muster. With a goodbye peck – and maybe a five-dollar bill – we drove off from these visits high on sugar fumes, cheeks ablaze in Mogen David red.

My final goodbye visit was similar in that I drank the same sweet wine and plucked a chocolate syrupy cherry from the box, but it was different in that I spent the time trying to consciously absorb into my pores the home and mother of my father. I inhaled them as deeply as I could for myself and for him.

Exiting Grandma Poplaski's house for the last time, I nearly crumpled. She whimpered her goodbye with a strained high-pitch in her voice similar to what she had emitted when Grandpa Alex died. *Whichamacallits* stabbed at my heart so fiercely that I could not linger. All I could do was turn my back on her and drive away.

In bidding goodbye to my grandmothers I was bidding goodbye to my history, a linked Polish chain of born into and married into names: Tynecki, Wojkielwicz, Soliwoda, Smieciuich, Boczek, Poplaski, Lipinska, Cezkowski…There were skis tucked in there along the way.

And…the last stop.

Calvary Cemetery was forever crammed with folks going nowhere. I maneuvered my way through the narrow, winding roads circling and defining islands of tombstones and caskets of bones and dust, and parked no more than a few yards away from Salty's well-tended grave. Standing with my feet upon his patch of grass and my hand upon his cold stone provided me with a physical link to all that was left of him: a comfort of last resort. I needed to explain to my father that I would soon be carrying out my vigil of remembrance far away from Calvary Cemetery. I couldn't hover over him any longer, but I would keep on living for him no matter where I was. But certainly he already knew all that, for live pumping veins connected his 1959 death to my 1967 departure.

My travel trunk was loaded into the king-size trunk of the meticulously cleaned and waxed Cadillac. Then the four of us divided ourselves into the front and back seats to commence our last family drive together. I can't begin to imagine what Tim was thinking at the time, even though he had already been privy to one convent drop off, and I *couldn't* allow myself to imagine *what* my mother was thinking – no one wanted to ruin the drive by thinking or sharing. When we reached Franklin, Pa. and turned the Caddy into the driveway paving my way to freedom, a festive crowd and atmosphere greeted us around the bend. Two other girls, along with their families, had arrived before us, kicking off the party-like celebration. We were the last to arrive. There wasn't the slightest vibe of solemnity in the air for the occasion. But once everyone settled down – hellos helloed, names named, double cheek kisses kissed – our merry group adjourned to the chapel for a simple ceremony of initiation into the Congregation. While the sisters sang in heavenly harmony, the three of us newcomers exited to shed our earthly garb and don the simple garb of postulants. When we re-entered the chapel, we belonged. Our initiation was followed by a jovial reception with snacks and beverages. Our families contributed nothing but awkwardness and anxiety to the occasion.

Well, that's pretty much all I can remember of the day...the day I'd just about gone stark raving mad waiting for...the day that meant everything to me...the day that formally marked my escape! It was simply too much for me, too much to embrace, to grasp. All I could do was retreat into numbness - a safe place, another escape. My words, my movements, my thoughts came to me hazy, filtered through a mesh, until the moment arrived for my family to physically dwindle to three, then I shuddered. Such clumsy hugs and kisses...so, so clumsy...so, so strained. The three of them climbed into a hearse-like Cadillac and in neutral gray rolled down the drive and away from me.

BOOK TWO

CHAPTER 9. THE CONVENT

B ells sounded at 6:00 a.m. I woke in darkness on a firm and narrow bed of disbelief in a tiny dormitory cubicle outlined by a privacy curtain divide. I pinched my still beach-tanned skin to see if it recognized me. I drifted between the mountains of euphoria and the valleys of fear. I contemplated portraits of the new beginning and the new end of my life – it was now 6:01 a.m.

With haste I dressed, fitting myself into the garb of a postulant (the term used to define one starting out in religious life): black shoes/white socks, black skirt/white blouse, black sweater, neutral hairstyle. The black/white combination of the postulantcy would last one year before giving way to the pure white habit of the following stage: the novitiate, comprising two semi-cloistered years. The combined three years of training led to the profession of temporary vows, meaning the vows of poverty, chastity, and obedience being professed for one year. Thereafter, the vows would be renewed annually until readiness for final profession was sanctioned: a life-long commitment, a life-long marriage, to Christ and his work in Africa. This, in a pistachio size nutshell, was the long-range schedule of my new waking life.

At 6:15 a.m. the first activity of the short-range schedule of my life began with a half hour of private meditation in the chapel I so loved. The convent lingered in darkness, except for a dim glow flowing like holy lava from the slivered threshold of the heavy chapel doors. Electricity was one of hundreds of things we would learn to manage frugally. We three new postulants crept into the chapel, slithering into our assigned pew. We were quiet as tenured thieves, but the aberration of our black garb in a full house of white disrupted the ethereal harmony and slapped harshly like cymbals crashing onto morning silence. But, perhaps this radical intrusion stung my artistic blue eyes only.

Besides the design/harmony issue, the prayerful issue of meditation posed another problem for me all together, this one more impervious to my standard scrutiny. The purpose of the exercise was, of course, to focus, contemplate, ponder, and reflect on the life of Christ, searching for insights on how to live deeper, more spiritual lives. Meditation was designed as a cherished time of personal communication with God: like indulging in an intimate morning cup of coffee with your lover – sort of. Many sisters relied on the Bible as a meditation springboard, choosing a text and reflecting upon the lesson held within. Others needed no props whatsoever. They arrived alert and enraptured by the opportunity alone to spend quality time conversing with their Lord and Master. Discretely, I observed and pondered these meditation options, relaxing somewhat only when I saw the "Bob and Nod" approach occurring two pews in front of me: an older, sleepy sister's head nodding off onto her chest, then bobbing up violently, riled at the emission of her own guttural snort and her Bible, the word of God, hitting the floor. With the disturbance, a contagious outbreak of furtive giggles ignited simultaneously across all pews. A well timed "Bob and Nod" could reduce even the most devout soul into a blubbering, pink-faced ball of gulping snivels, until…control could be summoned from a deep reserve of discipline. My first early morning chapel visit taught me far more about the women seated around me than it did about meditation: they were human and they were a community. With that comforting knowledge, I relaxed ever so slightly into the rigid straight back of my pew.

At 6:45 a.m. we began Lauds, community morning prayer. Several groggy voices croaked and tuned up for the day, while others were pitch perfect from the start. Our postulant trio, Francine, Pat, and I, attempted as best we could to follow the unrehearsed script of the first day of our new life.

At 7 a.m. the bell on the front door jingled and one sister rose to prepare the altar for Mass.

At 7:15 a.m. a White Father (our Congregation's male counterpart, who also happened to have a training house in Franklin, Pa.) entered the chapel to celebrate Mass.

At 7:45 a.m., after having nourished our souls for a hearty ninety minutes or so, we exited the chapel and headed for the refectory to nourish our bodies for approximately thirty minutes. Souls apparently came with bigger appetites.

Breakfast was accompanied by silence, except for the clattering of dishes and wares, the hissing of steaming water kettles, and the gulping pouring sounds of hot milk and coffee being funneled into cups and bowls. We lined up to a buffet table spread with European type breakfast offerings of cold sliced meats and cheeses, homemade bread and jams, and yogurt and fruit. Having breakfasted so long on Jiffy cake mixes, I was at a loss as to what to take, how to take it, and how to eat it. Some sisters drank their hot milky coffee out of bowls!

By 8:15 a.m. I was queasy in the stomach, physically exhausted, and teetering emotionally: a brand new 5'6" wreck! And to top it off, in my morning rush, I'd forgotten to roll on deodorant, so swampy puddles of nervousness pooled under my arms and soaked the pits of my brand new black sweater, inviting anyone nearby a potent whiff of the young, the vulnerable, the anxious.

After breakfast, there was a personal break for bathroom visits and the like before the start of a two-and-a-half-hour period of assigned charges, more commonly known as chores. This particular morning, however, the three of us were directed to meet with our new Mistress of Postulants, Sr. Felicia, for a mini orientation covering the upcoming 12 months of our life together. The four of us together would exist as a tiny sub-congregation within the whole. The three of us dressed like baby penguins would waddle behind our elders until we learned our way. Twenty-four hours earlier we amounted to complete and total strangers, yet now, we three would share close to every waking minute together. Such forced bonding would appear unnatural and unwelcome in most circumstances – prisoners experience it – but *everything* we were about was unnatural, opting for poverty, obedience, and celibacy, in particular. We were no longer about nature. We were about spirit, and the power and push of that spirit made the seemingly unappealing every bit appealing, even desirable.

At 11:45 a.m. we gathered back in the chapel for communal prayer.

At 12 p.m. we revisited the buffet table, but this time it was loaded with hot and hearty dishes, some recognizable, some not. I was half-starved from the toll anxiety had taken on my appetite days prior to my departure, so I eyed the home cooked offerings with a fair amount of relish, making a beeline for what appeared to be a mound of mashed familiarity. It went without saying that whatever we put on our plates we ate: wastefulness would be scandalous. I heaved a hearty forkful of mashed potatoes into my mouth: *Gulp!* My eyes bulged and my throat constricted – both cried out to my brain: *"What the hell is this?"* I couldn't inquire out loud even if I dared to because lunch, too, was a conversation-less time. A sister was regularly assigned to read during our noon meal, so while we chewed and swallowed we directed our attention to the likes of Thomas Merton's *Seven Storey Mountain*. I directed my attention on the grueling challenge of consuming – what I later discovered to be – a gluttonous serving of mashed turnips. I didn't even know what a turnip was, but I quickly learned one sure thing about it: it was no potato! I was reservedly less gluttonous after that, particularly of multi-national offerings disguised in ever so clever and reconstituted ways, and unidentifiable soups that pooled in indescribable colors.

After lunch we behaved like authentic Europeans and headed to our cubicles for "une sieste" before an afternoon of instruction. I collapsed onto my bed, shoes and all, and stared up at nothing. I had overdosed on much more than turnips. Six hours of convent life, two whole years of waiting, and 19 years of living converged to devour me. The alliance was close to swallowing the last bite of me when I rallied, rummaging frantically through the baggage of my youth to find what I was looking for: a switch marked "automatic pilot." I flicked the switch – I had flicked it once before, when I was 11. *Zap!* I drifted off for my European siesta.

When a bell chimed, sounding the end of naptime, I rose with an induced air of calm and made my way to class. Throughout the year our curriculum of study would focus mainly on: the History of the Congregation, African Culture, Spirituality, and French. Information and instruction was doled out by an assortment of sisters, but our primary teacher was Felicia, herself. Imagine my surprise when I discovered that Felicia sprang from unadulterated Polish roots, just like me. Yet, there she stood, a living example of an intelligent woman who appeared to harbor no trace of shame whatsoever over her heritage. The fact of it caused me to cast a questioning glance over my shoulder to my mother back in Erie, Pa.

Around 3:15 p.m. we broke for afternoon tea before continuing on with classes till around 5:30.

Back to the chapel for Vespers, the second of three of the eight hours of The Divine Office, which we observed daily.

At 6 p.m. we shared a light, usually cold, evening meal a bit like breakfast, as our main hot meal was always served at noon. More silence.

Afterwards, everyone congregated for a period defined as "recreation," though as postulants we "played" separately from the others. Finally able to exercise our tongues, it was during this evening time of board games, singing, sewing, and conversation – along with the bi-weekly busy hands work of sorting and folding community laundry – that we became acquainted with one another.

Laundry nights announced themselves by a mountain range of near identical white everythings waiting to be folded, sorted, and delegated to the appropriate personal cubby. Our community totaled around twenty-five and every single item that each of us owned was tagged with our hand-stitched initials in a designated corner. Despite the similarity of the items composing the mountainous pile, sorting through the laundry of others revealed plenty. For example: you could easily tell which sisters had most recently returned from serving in the mission field because even their underpants appeared homemade, patterned in a boxy, one size fits all shape. You could also identify the sisters who held their vow of poverty to the extreme, week after week folding threadbare remnants of dissolving undergarments capable of offering little but the time it took to slip them on. I wanted to stitch R.I.P. on the worst of these sorry excuses and put them to eternal rest.

Detecting the trace of private, human bodily stains was the most disconcerting part of laundry folding time. In such a chaste environment the handling of intimately worn garments seemed to verge on immodest. And what about sinful thoughts? Couldn't such activity offer an occasion for sin? Growing up, there were nuns and priests who had spoken in such terms, like the nun who said never to wear patent leather shoes because you might see a reflection up your skirt.

Observing these mortal stains on the garments of my goddesses took some getting used to. The fantasies that I had long associated with them butted up against a household of flesh and blood secreting women – not porcelain figures suitable for a mantle or sainthood. I was on the fast track to discovering whether or not my fabricated version of an otherworldly existence could survive alongside the reality of stained laundry in hand.

At 8:30 p.m. we congregated in the chapel for Compline, the final prayer session of the day.

By 9 p.m. we were tucked in our curtained cubicles, simultaneously dressing into the bedtime garb of white night gowns and dark bathrobes, and making our way to the communal washroom/bathroom – WC as the toilet portion was called. We filled our enamel washbasins and returned to our cubicles for a sponge bath, of sorts. Full showers would be individually assigned once every three days on a rotating schedule.

My first night visit to the communal washroom rattled me in a way not unlike the laundry stains. Of course, we weren't supposed to be observing each other in any way whatsoever – remember "custody of the eyes?" My peripheral vision, however, lacked such discipline and extended left to right the entire length of the bathroom. At night the veil of a full-fledged sister (postulants didn't wear veils) was removed and replaced by a night-kerchief tucked and tied behind the ears. I spied real ears. Then I spied clumps of carelessly mowed hair sticking out. Real hair. Upon identifying the owner of the hair and ears, I determined that both constituted unsightly baggage compared to the veiled simplicity and beauty of her daytime being. A perverse and illicit tingle of excitement flooded my body at these nocturnal sightings. You would have thought that I was off huddled in a dark corner with an X-rated movie rolling before my eyes. Ears…hair…necks…all hanging out, rendering these saintly women all but naked to eyes like mine. I felt embarrassed for them, and for me, and I cursed the ridiculously wide range of my God-given peripheral vision.

Walking back to my cubicle, water sloshed from my basin all along the way. Eventually, I learned that placing a towel over the basin prevented this sloshing waste of water and the hazardous floor conditions it caused. There was a lot to learn in living simply - the simplest things could be so complicated.

I set upon lathering up my odiferous armpits, realizing a second too late, that face first would have been more sensible. Oh well, the finer points of the routine would surely settle in with time. Staring down at the murky gray, scummed over water in my basin, I prayed that it held the first layer of scrubbed off impurity and fear; I hoped that my second day would start off purer than the first, and the third purer than the second.

Lights were out by 9:30 p.m. Rigid, I laid in the dark, hands folded across my chest as in death or in breathing surrender. Within short minutes a cacophony of unfeminine snores commenced, the sounds of consciences settled enough to drift off into a noisy lullaby. Mine was far from settled. Yet, Jesus must've loved me still, for despite the throngs vying for his attention, he tiptoed into my troubled mind and with the mercy of a savior flicked out my internal lights. I slept.

The end of day one.

....

Fear not. I won't be dragging you through each and every day of my convent life, hour-by-hour, thought-by-thought; I just wanted to give you the twenty-four hour flavor of the many days to come. Each one hummed to a mantra of similarity and stacked up like baby steps to heaven. As postulants, we were the equivalent of a rough sketch in progress, an exploratory scribble of possibility, while the more tried and true others resembled a more refined version of a work in progress; there was always more work to be done, no one was ever completed. The dawning of similar days did not give rise to a horizon of boredom. Attuned repetition exposes nuances and nuances expose variation. This is how I lived among my sisters: in days of varied repetition.

The assignment of morning charges arrived weekly posted on a rotating list, all fair and square. Our religious army of womanhood held command of everything about us: gardening, landscaping, vehicle maintenance, carpentry and plumbing projects, as well as the usual domestic chores of cooking and cleaning. Many charges were pleasant, easy, and desirable, such as dusting and mopping the chapel, or organizing the priest's vestments, or helping the cook with peeling potatoes, shucking corn, trimming green beans... Laundry duty was less than pleasant, though being assigned to the "tolerable" laundry division was far better than being assigned to the "intolerable" division – meaning that of the women on the rag. Economic prudence allowed little concession to disposable goods, so we stuck to the old-fashioned way of handling menstrual needs, even though a goodly number of us, rather mysteriously I thought, came to menstruate at approximately the same time of the month. Imagine, if you can, fifteen or more bloated women battling emotional meltdowns in synchronized periods of heightened sensitivity and borderline madness. If not for the bars of silence and custody of the eyes constricting us, we might have gone hormonally nuts and broken into holy catfights. The more squeamish among us prayed that our name would not appear under the column marked: "Le Petit Linge" (little linen, or rag). However, in such a fair and equal society, it was guaranteed to show up there sooner or later. When it did, the assignee had to first collect the odiferous buckets stationed in all the WCs the night before laundry day, depositing them in the basement for Sr. Exilda, the resident saint in charge of directing the nasty business.

Exilda, in my opinion, was the most charming, endearing, and humorous character among us. Her accent sounded a mishmash of east coast English, Canadian French, and African musical tonalities; her face dispensed a hodgepodge of mime-like expressions able to talk entirely without words. During class time she instructed us on African history, personalizing the vastness of the continent with vivid tales from her multiple decades of life and work in Zambia. She spoke of the country as if she were speaking of a beloved child – a child who encompassed her whole heart, a child who continually tugged at the entirety of her. We sat spellbound, as she slipped back into time and into her story: sometimes an unbearably tragic one, sometimes a hysterically funny one. This glorious woman, this teacher of ours, was regularly saddled with, what the rest of us considered to be, the most deplorable of chores. I'm certain that she volunteered for it.

Exilda gathered the buckets left to her and emptied their contents into a giant pair of wash sinks for a cold-water rinse and an overnight soak. In the morning, well before her help arrived, she'd already drained and re-rinsed the twin seas of red. Then, in silence the two of them transferred the soaked cotton rags into two commercial sized wash machines. While waiting for the wash cycles to spin out, tubs filled with bleach water and enormous pots of boiling water were readied for the following step. Buzzing to a finish, the cottons were removed from the machines and deposited into bleach tubs for soaking, then into the boiling water pots for sanitization, then into a cold-water rinse, then through a wringer, and then into the dryer.

Our arms swung in chain gang unison: down, up, over…down, up, over…."Lordie, Sweet Lordie, I'm down, I'm up, I'm over…soak me up, wring me out, dry me up…I'm down, I'm up, I'm over." Muscles tightened with the shifting loads, while the chorus continued, and the morning lengthened. There was no time to miss a beat for timing and flow were everything - as noted by the items at hand. As the dryers emptied they emitted a scent of salvation. The damp, musty laundry room filled, as did our arms, with the warm breath of cleanliness and the comfy smell of purified cotton. The transformation of blood red into white was complete – our very hands and arms serving as God's instruments.

Note to Exilda:

Please forgive me wonderful woman, if I have erred in recalling the stages and cycles of laundry day, even though I know that you are long removed from such earthly charges and concerns. But, only this telling can express vividly enough how being with you, under even the most unpleasant of circumstances, was simply heavenly.

Like into a glove, I managed to wiggle a fit with nearly any and all of my assigned charges. There was a rare but certain beauty in the oneness of everyone performing mundane chores in synchronized silence, toiling to create a physical place of harmony, much like our orchestrated prayer times created a spiritual place of harmony. The days were ridiculously rewarding in their similarity.

Then Pogo came along.

I was never much of a dog person, so being assigned to Pogo, our formidable male German Shepherd, was more than a tad rattling. My caretaking duties involved feeding him, walking him, releasing him to do his business, and assuring that he was locked up securely whenever the White Fathers visited – or any man, for that matter. Pogo hated men; the supposed reason being that a man had mistreated him while at a tender puppy age. This dog of my assignment managed to push two buttons in me: motherliness and fury.

Venturing out for our walk one day through the wooded trails behind the convent, Pogo took to the dog work of sniffing, chasing, and digging with raw abandon. I watched amusedly as he romped freely through the wild of it – experiencing a slight touch of envy. When I lost sight of him, my commanding "**Pogo!**" failed to hail him back, as it usually did. Scouting him out in dog-like fashion, my ears detected a whimpering in the distance.

I tracked the sounds through brush and bramble and discovered Pogo cowering under a clump of shrubs trembling and shaken, his head, face, and neck pierced with countless porcupine spines, and his eyes pleading, "Mommy, help!" I couldn't coax him up onto all fours, so I ran to fetch a wheelbarrow, and with adrenaline-laced effort hauled him back to the convent. One of the sister drivers rushed us to the vet's office. Pogo was immediately sedated for the grueling ordeal of spine removal. Fortunately, his eyes were spared from the pointed attack, but not much else from his husky neck up. His wobbly body listed heavily upon me as I ushered him home and down the basement stairs to his living quarters, comprised of a rug and a bowl of water in a warm corner. His swelling head reflected an appearance that only a mother could love. I was his mother. His need pushed that button first.

The sister who regularly functioned as chief cook for our brood was off duty on Sundays. Everyone took a Sunday turn at filling in for her. Having no previous cooking experience, when my turn came up I resorted to an all American staple, but added a designer touch to it. Taking a hot dog in hand, I sliced it lengthwise deep down the middle, laid in a strip of cheddar cheese, and tidily wrapped a thin slice of bacon around it in a fat and lean candy cane twist secured with a tooth pick at each end. I prepared two dozen or so of these fancy hot dogs with meticulous care, adjusting bacon angles, trimming cheese ends, inserting tooth picks just so…not too deep, not too shallow. Two loaded baking trays depicted pork and cheese masterpieces aligned like soldiers presenting in dress uniform. Setting the trays aside on the kitchen counter top, I headed off to chapel to join the community in prayer – though as cook for the day, I would have to sneak out early to pop my designer dogs into the oven.

Darting back into the kitchen, my legs froze in a mid-step halt, as my mind-boggled eyes scoured the empty counter top, and my back foot dangled awkwardly in space as if waiting for a sure place to land. I peered in the oven; perhaps some helpful Henrietta beat me to it and put them in to bake. Empty. I opened the jumbo refrigerator door; perhaps some helpful Henrietta felt that I shouldn't have left pork out unrefrigerated. No designer dogs. I panicked. My meal up and vanished!

In that very moment of desperation I noticed the swinging door leading from the kitchen to the basement ajar - something caught, wedged under the threshold. With a metallic sounding grate, I freed a baking tray, scattering about nothing but toothpicks. **Pogo!!!** Charging down the stairs I hurdled over the second tray angled against the bottom step and surrounded by more toothpicks, a couple hot dog pieces, a mess of cheese strips, and zero bacon. Around the corner Pogo's body lay slumped on his blanket - he looked hungover. His head and eyes barely lifted towards me before collapsing under the pork-laden weight of his gluttony, maybe even guilt. Nun or not, I hoped that 24 slices of raw bacon would do him in forever and free me from his relentless dog-like behavior once and for all.

But, I had no time for revenge. I needed a miracle reminiscent of the multiplication of loaves and fishes, minus the starting loaves and fishes. While standing stricken in the kitchen, an elderly sister entered to help with any last minute preparations needing attention. With wet eyes, sweat beads across my forehead, and a quiver in my voice, I blurted out details of the hot dog heist, for which I was ultimately responsible. You see, the swinging door leading to the basement was supposed to be latched at all times – part of my Pogo responsibilities. My carelessness invited Pogo to dinner.

I watched in awe as my experienced helper performed her own brand of miracle: instantly filling an empty table with bread, yogurt, sliced meats, cheeses, tomato slices…while heating up a pot of leftover soup in a hurry. All I wound up contributing to Sunday's dinner were the cups of Jell-O I had prepared to balance out the heavy fatty dogs. As the community marched from the chapel into the refectory no one seemed remotely aware of the catastrophe, or the miracle, or my shoulders drooping and my head hanging.

I never attempted to repeat my culinary artwork, though it had nothing to do with Pogo and bad memories. I was into originals. As for Pogo, I forgave him for pushing my fury button. How could I reside among saints and not forgive?

Regarding my family nestled in the familiarity of Erie, Pa., I dutifully wrote to them on a weekly basis and my mom dutifully wrote back. I was not homesick. I felt home, despite all the foreignness, I felt home.

Mom's handwriting was executed in an evenly slanted, straight-lined cursive script, but the script, as well as the content, had a tightly wound feel to it: a correspondence drafted from the tip of the finger, employing words that did not pierce the skin. Besides letter writing, during our postulancy we were permitted visitors on a designated Sunday afternoon once every three months. I was the only one among the three of us to have family living nearby, so I was the only one to have family visit the first time around: my mom, stepfather, brother, and Grandma Poplaski. Laying eyes on them was painful, close to embarrassing, for they looked awkward and exuded hesitation and discomfort. They knocked on the convent door like beggars, hungry for a glimpse of a girl they might yet recognize as their own.

My grandmother had never been physically demonstrative with my mother, thus my mother had never been physically demonstrative with me. I followed suit. Also, we had never before been apart for more than a few days, so none of us knew how to greet each other after such absence. This was new territory. I approached to touch them as if something might break on contact – maybe me. My mother and I leaned in awkwardly, cheeks barely touching, light fingertips on each other's shoulders, feet positioned as far away from each other as possible to insure no unnecessary bodily contact. We stood in a tee-pee embrace, crossed and bound at the top for a speck of a second before coming undone.

Tim wore an expression of dull misery – he was fifteen and visiting a convent, what else could he wear? I still regretted the "Shut up!" I had tossed in his face eight years earlier when he greeted me at the door with, "Hey, Ya! Guess who died?" Now, with a long overdue act of sisterly consideration, I escorted him to meet Pogo, watching carefully to determine whether Pogo hated all forms of males or just the fully-grown type. Tail wagging, Pogo immediately took to licking and slobbering over Tim's teenage skin. I offered my brother the best thing I had to offer that day: a dog distraction from the clumsiness at hand.

The hellos and goodbyes of our three-month visits remained strained and pressurized, but the time in-between eased with the welcoming warmth and distraction of the entire community, jovial chatter, and shared stories. My mother kept both ears tuned to notes of dissatisfaction from me, nuances of regret, but the music she hoped to hear didn't sound. Regret was not a tune I danced to. I was devoutly determined to march to the drumbeat of my mission. My happiness must have been a stinging comfort to her.

....

Pat, Francine, and I formed a gawky sort of trinity; I contributed a goodly share of bumbling missteps in the configuration. Pat walked with a hiccup in her step due to one leg being a tad shorter than the other; she moved about with a jolly lopsided bounce, even on the dreariest of days. She was older than Francine and me, already college educated and Peace Corps trained in Africa. I felt stupid around her (more stupid than usual). She spoke with an air of sophistication emanating from suitcases in her brain crammed full of academic and traveled knowledge. After voicing an intelligent comment or question, she had an irritating way of gazing directly at me with a quizzical expression, searching my round face for a glimmer of comprehension. For seemingly eternal moments she kept her eyes steadied upon me, though she knew I wouldn't comment, she knew I didn't know. I felt it. My insecurity labeled her look *malicious and hurtful* – deliberate taunting aimed unfairly at a secretarially trained Polish girl from Erie, Pa.

However, Pat wasn't teasing me. Her actual cruelty was in overestimating the extent of my worldly knowledge. I faulted her for the miscalculation – someone with such formidable intelligence should have known better. And I had another brittle bone to pick with her, as well. Despite Sr. Felicia's position of authority over us as Mistress of Postulants, Pat conversed easily and, seemingly, on equal footing with her. Their companionable way of relating flushed me in green, stupid jealous green.

Francine grew up in Chicago, but despite a big city upbringing, she bore a wholesome country girl air about her, which was reflected through her robust size and hearty laugh. She aimed to accomplish good in the world by becoming a nurse as well as a nun. When something tickled Francine's broad funny bone she would grip her stomach with both arms, fold over, turn ridiculously red, and – after a long and breathless buildup – erupt into squeals of teary convulsive laughter. Yet, despite these uninhibited outbursts, her thinking mind functioned in black and white, like her clothing. With my own mind swimming in pools of gray possibilities, I often crashed into the brick wall of her clarity with a deadening thud. Nevertheless, we managed to get along – though no one ever mistook us for two peas in a pod – and it was a good thing we did because we wound up spending more than our Franklin years together.

Even in the confines of a convent, it didn't take long before my romantic side rendered me smitten: this time with Felicia. Clever, intelligent, deeply perceptive… she was all of that and more - though not particularly attractive in a looks kind of way. My eyes, however, defined her as beautiful due to her stunning character and nature. I maneuvered my physical being as close to her as possible whenever I could, resembling the likes of a needy, clingy child. A type of maternal malnourishment afflicted me. I craved coddling and praise from a grown woman. Making room on my highest pedestal, sliding over Joan Baez and my high school confidante, I elevated Felicia alongside them. Given her placement, a ferocious and childish jealousy knocked me about whenever I saw her and Pat sharing a private and informed laugh.

Felicia identified my crush before I could digest it myself. She was keenly intuitive and I was probably ridiculously obvious. One day the unthinkable happened. She sat me down on a sunny afternoon and asked me point blank: "Do you have a crush on me?" *I died on the spot...oh, how I died on the spot!* Perspiration and red-faced shame poured over me, I wanted to run from her, from the question hanging in the air between us. Eliciting nothing but silence from me, she continued in the vein of: "Such feelings are understandable when you're young...you don't need to feel embarrassed...they're normal..."

At the sound of "normal" I almost breathed, but the shock of her comments continued to knock the wind out of me, like her opening question had. How could such feelings be normal? Weren't they shameful? Like in "Catholic" shameful? Her willingness to speak to me openly, honestly, and acceptingly was perhaps the most precious gift I'd received to date in my life. Discovering that people talked about such things was sheer revelation. I was stunned! She made it sound as if the ugly in me was natural, completely natural. God almighty, what a well-kept secret! My crush folded into pure gratitude.

Though my emotional progress crawled, my artistic progress jogged full speed ahead; a maturing creative talent unleashed itself. I was assigned to the no-work-at-all work of designing Christmas cards, Easter cards, sympathy cards, note cards...all in stylized African designs for our own use, as well as for sale. I advanced to creating enormous felt banners to hang from the white chapel walls, marking changes in the liturgical season or major religious holidays. The community called me an artist, just like Billy had. Professionally speaking I was a complete imposter since I had no training, but for practical purposes I was authentic and suitable. Living as a nun and working like an artist, unbelievably, my fantasies converged.

....

Progression through religious life is marked by specific ceremonies, the end one being the profession of final vows. Two sisters within our household reached that stage during my first year, compelling the lot of us to prepare as if for a heavenly wedding. On the appointed day, the music seemed to lift the rooftop of our sacred white chapel and admit the blue sky of God's breath. Each sister proceeded to recite her vows, then dropped to her knees and prostrated herself before God, the altar, and us. Prostration - the offering of still breathing bodies, white garbed corpses of the living laid out in willing surrender before the love of their lives, their God. I had never seen such a thing, such a holy sight. When they rose upright they glowed like angels.

The ceremony that would arrive to mark my own religious progress was the taking of the habit, and a new name. I was scheduled to become someone else, Sister Somebody Else. I had fantasized over name choices, just like over every other aspect of convent life. My sister, Karen, had chosen the name Sr. Alexis for her new self – a nod to Grandpa Alex Poplaski. Something like Sr. Mary Bernard or Bernadette would offer the same to my dad, but I didn't care to flaunt my private devotion. Instead, I wrapped my tongue around names rippled with flair and/or fervor: Magdalena, Fiona, Angelica, Amadeus.... But my name choices - the best and the worst of them - were suddenly washed away by an unprecedented tidal wave of change rising within the Catholic Church.

Between the years of 1962 to 1965, when I in high school partying and daydreaming, the church was engaging in the Roman Catholic Ecumenical Council known as Vatican II, convened by Pope John XXIII, and carried on by Pope Paul VI. In a sentence, at least semi-accurate, the purpose of the Council was to revitalize the church, restore unity among Christians, and promote dialogue with the contemporary world at large. The church hierarchy drafted numerous pastorals to provide instruction and guidance to the faithful in all realms of Christian life. Vatican II catapulted the church into becoming more relevant and in touch with the times.

It took a few years for the hefty bulk of their directives to be interpreted and digested within religious communities, Catholic parishes, and the vast lay community. The White Sisters – being a forward thinking and adaptive tribe of women – jumped on the bandwagon of change more quickly than the masses of tentative others. In Frascati, Italy, where our motherhouse was situated, representatives from our provinces worldwide gathered to determine how best to respond to the Vatican II's call for change within our own congregation. A multitude of adaptations were voted into our way of life – two of them landing like a sledgehammer onto my well-rehearsed script of anticipation.

The white flowing habit that I had fallen in love with was modified to within an inch of its former life. It was contemporized into a white, long sleeved, belted shirtwaist type of affair ending mid-calf and layered over with a white scapular (a broad piece of the same fabric draped front and back over the dress.) A gray version of the same dress was introduced for the purposes of travel and public appearances – gray insuring a more neutral fit among the laity. As for the veil, it became a radically shortened cloth wrapped about our heads in headband fashion, exposing our necks, our ears, and the top fringe of our hair. The whole world would now be privy to what I so furtively spied during communal washroom visits. And all that robed acting in front of the mirror for nothing. I would get little more than a glorified school uniform.

As if tailoring my flowing whites wasn't bad enough, name changing was nixed, as well. From now on all newcomers would stick with their birth name, and the entrenched others would be given the option of reverting back to theirs, or not. In short, I would be Sr. Gail; in long, I would be Sr. Gail Soliwoda. Unbelievable! Even in escape, I remained sentenced to the exposure of my body and name. The demands of change introduced me to the harsh rub of obedience and the costly sacrifice of poverty; I had to forego the romantic accessories I had long lusted after. But there was little time to wallow in pity or regret: I had to sew. If I wanted to be ready to march down the aisle for my own ceremony, I had to cut and stitch my own shirtwaist habit. Sewing machines geared up and hummed like crazy.

Having completed our first full year, Pat, Francine, and I swapped out our black skirts and white blouses and blended in with the flock in Vatican II garb. Dressed accordingly, we began a two-year stint of novitiate training. The first year, known as the canonical year, would be served out in a semi-cloistered state of silence; family visits would drop to one only for the entire year. This intensified, disciplined period of spiritual development was like a 12-month test of our resolve.

For nothing other than good ole' efficiency's sake, the decision was made to merge our dual training houses in Canada and the U.S. into one, the one being in Franklin, Pa. French speaking Canadians were due to invade our dormitories with foreign tongues. Their imminent arrival filled me with a rush of excitement and anxiety because in my localized mind Canadians were as exotic as Aborigines. Side-by-side with them, I would feel so "Ooh, la la!" sophisticated on a daily basis. Though I'd been engaged in a good faith effort to study French, on my tongue it sounded as if I should call my grade school speech therapist asap. I was deathly afraid of making a fool of myself in front of the exotics. It never crossed my mind that, given all the silence we were about to endure, communication could occur with no more than the accent mark of a smile. In fact, the night the Canadians arrived – two vans crammed full of them – it became obvious that we would communicate just fine with a hearty recipe of kindness, knowing glances, decimated French, and halting English. After all, each and every one of us had signed on to the same life. Pat, Francine, and I willingly shed a layer of our American skin to accommodate a more diverse grafting of needs and thoughts. We adapted to the changing times – just like Vatican II required of us.

....

The first year of novitiate passed like an austere routine performed before flaming golden leaves, falling white snows, blooming pink tulips, and warm blue skies. The time was reflective and calm…yet, in an inexplicable way, it disturbed me. My mind declined to honestly admit or acknowledge any sign of distress, so my touchy gut bore the brunt of its presence. With little warning, I was prone to doubling over with stomach clenching spasms forcing me to retreat to my bed for horizontal bouts of agony. Tests for ulcers and other gastro-intestinal suspects turned up negative; the unofficial diagnosis was psychosomatic distress. I was left to heal myself with the generic script of dealing with it. Obviously, one or more of my topsy-turvy boats over loaded with emotional baggage had become unmoored and drifted into the tide of my intestinal canal, disrupting the digestion pattern of my new life. Determined and stubborn as I was, I refused to link my physical bouts of turbulence to any aspect of the religious calling. My ever-vigilant superiors, however, connected the dots and took "special notice" of the signals being transmitted from my body. Despite my craving for motherly attention, I was not hungry for *this* type of attention. I did everything I could to make myself invisible.

Identical seasons of the year – the leaves, the snows, the flowers, the sun – cycled through the second year of our novitiate, depositing us on the doorstep of professing our first round of temporary vows. Our mood was as titteringly euphoric as graduates facing commencement. My Canadian pals were scheduled to return to Canada for the ceremony, enabling their families and friends to more easily attend the celebration. We three Americans would remain in Franklin, Pa., on our side of the border, for the same sort of reason. Sr. Claire, who had served as our Mistress of Novices over the two years, called me to her office one fine day just a few weeks before the official end of the novitiate term. Two steps into the sunny room and I began shivering to a forecast of stormy news. She delivered it swiftly, like a knife to the chopping block or a twist of a duck's neck: "Sr. Gail, we believe that it would be in your best interests to postpone the taking of vows."

My head rolled off the block…my breathless pale face lay there: one side stoic/obedient, the other annihilated/ humiliated. Pat and Francine were given the green light, but I was stalled at yellow. Despite her reassurance that the delay would be for six-months *only*, and *purely* in my best interests, it spelled nothing but failure in my vocabulary and dredged up the poisonous toxins of stupid and shameful. After three years of non-stop giving it my all, doing everything asked of me, attempting to please, convince, and fit, I was barred from approaching God's holy altar. While sickening panic and confusion rumbled through me, Sr. Claire rattled on about the beneficial possibilities of new surroundings and experiences… they would help me grow, mature, provide practical insights into the reality of religious life outside of a secluded convent. *Mature* was the only word I really heard – the key word – she couldn't fool me.

And so it was. In February of 1969 I sat back and watched as my two companions marched up the aisle to pronounce their vows in a heavenly ceremony surrounded by family and community. There wasn't a spot in the lineup for a Maid of Honor – no consolation prize for me. Belief and bulldog determination guided me through the murky waters of rejection; whether I liked it or not, I needed to believe wholeheartedly that God's will was directing the high and low tides of my life. I had, after all, spent three years being drilled in "Your will be done," not mine. I swallowed my beheaded pride and unceremoniously surrendered my will.

Despite such a leveling, I was soon swept up in the excitement of heading to our community in Washington D.C to serve out my sentence. The vibe in an "active" missionary community – albeit functioning in the U.S. – was far different from the insular community life in a house of training. Wearing a veil while tucked in the foothills of the Allegheny Mountains and wearing a veil out and about in the cosmopolitan chaos of Washington were distinctly different experiences. The sisters stationed in D.C. were engaged in a variety of activities: college studies, mission appeals, work among the African expatriates, and, scouting for vocations.

They sifted through and blended among regular people on a daily basis. The congregation's mission on the home front was a critically important one, and though everyone longed to serve in Africa, we were called upon to take a fair turn at performing the behind the scenes support work needed to further the cause. The home mission was: spread awareness, raise money, and train young women.

Once in Washington, I occupied space among an eclectic mix of multi-national women. My dimpled youth triggered surges of mothering hormones to flow in some, though I now tried to discourage such outpourings - I was there to mature, after all. My stomach pains traveled with me, but over time the knotting eased to the flexing muscle of my rock hard determination. A large brick house on the traffic-filled block of 53rd and 16th St., N.W. replaced the secluded fortress of Franklin, Pa. I found myself living life as an unsilenced nun among the people. It was time to try my wings, or as it so happened, a bus.

I was assigned a part-time day job working at the Center for Applied Research in the Apostolate (CARA) in its African library. To get to work I hopped a bus at a stop directly across the street from our house and rode my way to P Street. In my gray traveling garb I jostled among the public transportation crowd feeling grossly conspicuous. For a creature forever longing to belong, that bus ride was pure misery. Curious glances and stares forced blushes from me. I resorted to custody of the eyes for my own salvation. Being tossed back into the real world dressed as a nun was rattling, actually terrifying – I reappeared in a new mode of misfit.

On my bus ride, out of the corner of my eye, I observed young lovers, mothers with children, elderly twosomes, professional types, vagrants, and rebellious looking teens traveling homogenously in the same direction. Though riding right in the midst of them, my appearance signaled a direct express to God. When I boarded the bus, I felt like I was delivering an early morning slap in the face to their sleepy consciences. Occasionally, a man would rise to offer me his seat on the crowed bus, sometimes a very old man. Mortifying as it was, I felt that I had no choice but to accept for I was certain that his gesture of respect was directed towards the church and not towards me personally. I had to humble myself and accept. There was no place for hatred in my life, but there was no denying that I absolutely *hated* these bus rides with a passion. Who was I among these everyday people? After living through three years of radical change, the nagging question remained absolutely the same.

Two Canadian White Fathers were involved with managing and updating the CARA library, while I worked at keeping the stacks organized and assisting those who visited with their research needs. I managed to adapt to the librarian demands, but working sandwiched between two adult males addressed as "Father" made me feel like a pickle in between peanut butter and jelly. I breathed more easily in my part-time evening job, teaching secretarial skills to African American women at Sacred Heart Parish. Though I'd never taught a day in my life, I felt qualified.

Our Washington house served as the arrival/departure headquarters for sisters entering and leaving the country. Because of it I met a fascinating array of women coming and going, forming fast friendships with some, like Beverly – though in Beverly's case we'd connected long before we ever met. It was back when I was drawing a paycheck at Keystone Electric. I'd read in a White Sister newsletter that a certain young sister was in need of a coat before heading off to Zambia, so, feeling as if I was directly participating in her mission, I sent the money off for Beverly's coat. Now, years later, upon her return from Zambia for health reasons – jaundice and pesky complications – we met face to face. Bevo, as I came to call her, and I shared an artistic kindred spirit - we clicked for life at hello. Living within our diverse Washington community it became readily apparent to me that there was no one-size-fits-all mold in the congregation: similar clothes – for the moment, at least – but uniquely crafted bodies, minds, and souls. If Beverly fit, so could I. She was confirmation and comfort to me.

While swimming through my six-month pool of D.C. time, I honed my singing nun skills, strumming away on my guitar, accompanying the hymns of our daily liturgy. "Sincerely Mediocre" was the name of my tune, but their was no guitar competition within the rest of the group, so I ranked as a star. I woke one morning to the stunning realization that my life was constructing an amazing resume: artist, librarian, teacher, and singing nun. And I was only getting started.

My superiors held true to their word, in August of 1969 I was permitted to approach the altar and profess my temporary vows in Washington, D.C. My family drove up for the occasion and stayed with us for a few days. The sisters were flexible and gracious about vacating their rooms to accommodate family guests. As to the longed for ceremony, the memory of it is buried under an opaque haze similar to the one shrouding the day I entered the convent: another emotional blackout. I had a knack for disappearing from myself at the most important times.

Taking leave of Washington, I returned to the meandering foothills of the Allegheny Mountains, where the next phase of my journey was being deliberated. Pat had left to join a small group of sisters studying in St. Louis, Mo.– she was directed to complete a M.A. in Religious Education before flying off to a post in Africa. But Francine was still in Franklin, where she'd been sitting tight awaiting my return, for it seems that the two of us were thought of as a pair in terms of the future. Both of us needed further schooling before being deemed mission ready, and that meant college...yep...*college!* For the Congregation, my zero college prep background posed an added burden to that of college finances: as well as scouting for a free four-year ride for the pair of us, they had to find a place willing to accommodate my academic shortcomings. One such place generously stepped forward to accept the challenge and offer the gift: Villa Maria College in Erie, Pa. – the big sister college perched right next door to Villa Maria Academy, my very own high school.

I was returning to Erie, Pa.

Unbelievable!

After all that...I was returning to Erie, Pa.

CHAPTER 10. COLLEGE

Though both in our early twenties, Francine and I found ourselves sharing a college dorm room identical to the other rooms occupied by typical 18-year-old freshmen girls. Ours was plopped dead center on the second floor of the south wing, with the wing's communal bathroom and shower block situated almost directly across the hall from us. It was quite awkward at first, being herded together with these girls as if we were all one and the same. Despite my having landed right back where I was born into life, I felt stranger than ever. Gritting myself for nothing but sourpuss looks and teenful snickers from the dorm inhabitants when they discovered nuns residing among them, I was rather flabbergasted to find them friendly and accepting of us. They actually seemed to relish the novelty of having two young missionary nuns for neighbors.

Though no more than a few years separated us from the lot of them, our dorm mates treated us as if we were ripe old souls, sure-footed, and all knowing – nothing like holier-than-thou party police out to spy and snitch on them. Their admiration was flattering, and a bit addictive; I found myself adapting to their vision, offering comfort and counsel to many as they poured out their hearts over A to Z. Our room became nearly as frequented as the bathroom: girls popping in to say hi and chew the fat, and/or girls propped against the doorjamb, need plastered across their faces, if not outright streaming tears. On many nights a cluster of bodies beckoned me to don my guitar, strum a chord or two, and ignite a spontaneous hootenanny. All in all, we settled into a fine ole' time socially. Francine wasn't as into the scene as I was, but she tolerated it, and me.

I marvel that our superiors trusted us enough to cast us out without a White Sister net about to haul us in if personal storms kicked up windy and wild – obviously, our current mission was to sink or swim. The Sisters of St. Joseph ran the college, taught at the college, and occupied the top floor of our dorm building. They also volunteered to keep an eye peeled in our direction and extended invitations to elevator up to join them for special occasions. Most of the nuns came across as warm and welcoming to us, but some came off as inflexibly rooted to the right of community privacy, viewing our presence as a charitable nuisance. In their eyes we differed little from the students they were obligated to deal with all day long, and they were possessive of their time off.

Francine and I maintained a low profile during these privileged top floor gatherings, staying relatively mum, clinging to the corner of the room, and smiling away like wallflowers plastered in gratitude. I was, also, uneasy up there because Karen – I mean, Sr. Alexis – belonged to the same Congregation, though she lived and taught on the east side of town. I would have preferred mysterious origins, being among people who knew nothing of me. After helping myself to a plateful of fancy food, and guzzling a couple of topped off glasses of respectable wine, I'd mosey towards the elevator and descend back to my dormitory level. Staring out the window from my room, I scanned a patch quilt of parking lot spaces threaded to an exit drive. It was good to have an exit in sight, though, until my current mission was accomplished, I wasn't going anywhere.

Though not entirely certain of its precise meaning, the word "sociology" sounded of service, so I chose it as my major – I didn't deem myself remotely capable of succeeding in any other field being offered. I dove into my semester class schedule with determination and daring: a generic menu of first year necessities, augmented by Social Psychology, and an independent research project on Existentialism (which I would also discover a meaning for).

The research project led to page after page of effort at analyzing atheistic and Christian existential philosophies; page after page of attempting to grasp the human condition as interpreted by men named Kierkegaard, Sartre, and Heidegger; page after page of exploring existence and nothingness, freedom and choice, the individual and systems; page after page of pondering the absurdity of existence and the existence of the absurd. And to flesh out my research, I created a portfolio of handsomely designed illustrations, hoping to pad my grade.

Existentialism tested the thinking powers of my Polish Erie girl mind like nothing before. I wound up with a monster headache, a crisis of faith, and a grade of A. Such a wealth of reasonable questions, posed in such a wealth of reasonable ways shook the cornerstones of my blind faith with a rattling strike of logic. My mind unraveled, opening wide to the temptation of questioning and the turmoil of doubt. My encounter with existential philosophy was akin to rubbing sandpaper across my soul, leaving it in a raw and tender state. After only one semester of academic and spiritual debate, I became alert to the dangers hidden within higher education and reasoning.

To relieve my philosophical brain blisters, two upper classmates – Joan, quiet and shy and Teri, vivacious and chatty – applied the soothing balm of R&R to calm and relax me. One of them had a car, Joan I think, so we headed off campus on occasion to loll around Lake Erie, sip wine, and engage in conversation that rolled back and forth like waves between silly and serious. My religious habit failed to conceal the piece of me that had partied hard on the very same beach sands not that long ago. Yet, despite venturing back to the secular shoreline, I felt circled by a halo of security more impenetrable than the cloth covering me: a universal chorus of White Sisters cheering me on.

A few students about campus eyed me with a look of pie in the sky admiration – just like I had Sr. Mary Peter the day the White Sisters visited my high school. Sylvia, a junior at the college gazed at *me* in that awe-struck kind of way – her rose-colored glasses denied me any and all shortcomings. Most surprisingly, I found myself sitting on the opposite side of the admiration glass. Though my association with Sylvia was brief, after a full 25 years or more of losing track of each other, a friend tracked her down with the help of an old address book, asking her to share a memory or two of me for a surprise fiftieth birthday album being prepared for the occasion. Here is some of what Sylvia wrote:

"Sr. Gail entered my life at the beginning of the winter semester of my junior year at Villa Maria College. Gail was like a magnet that drew my attention and friendship immediately. Later on as I reflected over my own life and Gail's effect on it, I almost began to question whether she had truly existed, or if she was an angel sent from above to guide me through those two years.......If this all sounds a bit too emotional or if you laughed when I questioned Gail's existence as real or heavenly, forgive me for this is honestly the effect she had on me."

It's mind-boggling to consider that Sylvia could've siphoned so much out of me at a time when I persisted on seeing myself as muddied by earthly and spiritual inferiority. My own experience, as well as hers, leads me to wonder quite regularly whether or not people appear as bonafide blessings delivered to us in time of need, or if it is *we* who dress them up accordingly to respond to our needs? Which one?

Just when I'd settled into an established social and an academic groove, Sr. Marie José D'or – the Belgian Superior General of our Congregation, who regularly resided in Italy – arrived in Erie, Pa. (of all places) to pay a visit to Francine and me (of all people). She was making the rounds, visiting all of the White Sister communities in North America. The two of us hardly qualified as a "community," but she included us anyway, making us feel special and terrified. Marie José D'or was a medical doctor, an intellectually and physically formidable woman with an audible French distinctly different from the Canadian version I believed to be so resplendent. Her French words sounded how butterflies looked: fluttering delicate wings sustaining fragile bodies aloft, then...landing softly with gentle grace. Remarkably, her accented English sounded melodiously similar. I grew woozy listening to her and fearful of any clunking sounds that might tumble off my lips disguised as words. She reminded me of God.

Despite the generosity of Villa Maria College and the Sisters of St. Joseph, Marie José did not believe it to be in our best interest to be deprived of the daily support of community life. In St. Louis, Mo. there existed what was referred to as a House of Studies: a small gathering of our own sisters residing as a community while undertaking course work in preparation for their mission abroad. Marie José suggested that we relocate and insert ourselves among them upon the completion of our second semester at Villa Maria College. After voicing that surprising and ruffling opinion, she turned her attention to my brainy decision to pursue sociology, pointing out that the U.S. version of it was unlikely to be relevant or useful in Africa.

To my utter amazement, she was more interested in discussing my artistic potential, so I dragged out my portfolio of existential renderings and displayed them in front of her. They seemed to impress her…sooo…I decided that they impressed me too. "We need to find a college in St. Louis where you can study art," she said as clearly as a cloudless day. It was all I could do not to break out in convulsive giggles, but I bit down on composure while she explained the need for art programs in African secondary schools still bound to the British standard of education. The notion seemed absurd to me (not in an existential sense) as I had always envisioned Africa as a Motherland of primitive and cultural genius. But the art she was referring to constituted an imposed interpretation, not an innate one. Besides, who was I to argue with the Superior General addressing me face to face in beautifully accented wisdom?

At Villa Maria College I was situated roughly four miles from my Greengarden Blvd. home, but I might as well have been in Egypt. As missionaries, White Sisters expected to live great distances away from their families. I was expected to partake in the expectation by pretending that mine, too, existed a great distance away. I saw them on three brief occasions that year – not enough to abuse my privileged circumstances, but enough to give my mother far more of a daughterly indulgence than most White Sister mothers had. She didn't dare balk at the scarcity of my visits for she knew that she was blessed by my proximity and the certitude of my safety.

When the academic year ended, however, I departed Erie, Pa. for good…a second time for good. My mother's indulgence was spent.

....

The exterior of our St. Louis house on St. Andrew's Drive looked as unobtrusively normal as could be - nothing convent-ish about it except nuns going in and out. Francine and I moved into a large attic bedroom space already occupied by Pat, who had settled in a year earlier. There we were once again, the three musketeers. And to top off our reunion, there was Felicia, who just happened to be stationed in St. Louis pursuing her own studies. Our familiar little tribe was enhanced by a few others engaged in various fields of study, and two distinctly elderly sisters devoted to running the household and involving themselves in the doings of the Catholic parish nearby, for whatever soil we settled upon, it was deemed part and parcel of our mission to serve as active members of the local community. Adding to our ranks was a steady stream of transient sisters passing through for a summer course or two and causing our bricks to bulge.

A neighborhood ordinance must have existed prohibiting adult numbers like ours to reside under the roof of one modestly sized house, but our blend of intrigue and charm appeared to exempt us from such notice or complaint. Our neighbors likely thought of themselves as insured against evil, nestled so close to a houseful of God's women. Within my new community I felt insulated against the threat of existential doubt - community life served as a downy comforter.

My sophomore year commenced in the art department of Fontbonne College, a previously all girls' Catholic institution that had recently dipped its toes into co-ed waters. Handfuls of males drifted about campus in what could be interpreted as a hellish or a heavenly situation – several landed in the art studios. I was accepted into the department based on talent and/or potential (so I was told), but I was, nonetheless, terrified of my place within it, terrified of failure, terrified of my teachers, terrified of the males so near. Around men – mostly older men, such as teachers – I was burdened by a self-conscious unease that could best be described as longing. I would have to contend with the unease day after day, accepting male guidance and criticism as if I had lived with such givens quite naturally all my life. And there were other uneasy confrontations that I had to accustom myself to.

Almost knocking over my own easel, I squirmed on my stool and averted my eyes the first time Big Mary mounted the model stand in figure drawing class and dropped her robe. My face was as blushed over in pink splotches as her body was in fleshy folds of gold-tinged cocoa brown. Fully naked, she paused to take in the space around her with nonchalant eyes, and then commenced with a litany of movements: stretching this way and that, raising and lowering arms, twisting her torso right then left, straddling a stool….until…*"Hold it!!! That's it!"* bellowed from the commanding voice of Mr. Torrini, our short but bigger than life drawing professor who was also the head of the art department.

Big Mary froze into the pose we would sketch from. She was named, pure and simple, for her size: pendulous breasts draped her abdomen and belly rolls layered over the triangular patch of her kinky black pubic area, which from then on I considered more public than pubic. Her head was regal and her full lips swelled with an expression of naked superiority. Big Mary was a fixture around the art departments in town; hundreds of students had been given the opportunity to explore her body with charcoal in hand. As Mary settled into my vision as a live organic shape, I came to forget about the startling nakedness of her, focusing instead on my interpretation of her: linking black lines of limbs and folds, gesture and attitude, expression and style into something my professor might view as promise.

Criticism was a brutal staple in the department and skin toughening a requirement for survival. After all, the life of an artist wouldn't come easy, so it made no sense to pad the truth of it - an art department was no place for crybabies. I felt obligated to prove myself above and beyond my classmates because of the, "What are *you* doing here?" kind of looks I got on occasion. I muscled up a feisty will to not only survive, but to conquer. Exploring the act of creating something from nothing was as compelling, challenging, and troublesome to me as exploring the mystery of faith; I set out to scale two towering but vastly different mountains simultaneously. Dealing with criticism remained a hard swallow for me, but confronting nakedness began to go down more smoothly – my habited, clothed self no longer blushed while sipping tea with a model robed in nothing but skin. In the unorthodox confines of an art studio we looked bizarrely normal together. But, I have to say that, if Sr. Marie José herself hadn't whisked me here with the wand of her approval, I would've never with a straight face been able to call what I was engaged in training for the mission.

There came a point in my studio work when my garb hung on me like a problematic burden. I needed a more sensible outfit to handle the messy demands of sculpture, the area I had chosen to major in. The field entailed semesters of down and dirty physical labor. Luckily, the winds of change stirred up by Vatican II continued to blow, eroding our modified garb into the optional realm of skirts, blouses, and veils off or on. I opted for the update, but carried it even further by slipping into pants for plaster mold making days, when I knew I'd be splattered head to toe in caked on hardness. The Pope had encouraged us to be one with the people – by slipping into pants I was following his orders to a tee.

By the end of my sophomore year, I experienced a whiff of personal comfort – not up to par with the formidable comfort displayed in the moves of Big and naked Mary – but comfort, nonetheless, in my own skin. It had toughened nicely, making it clear to my professors that "the nun" just might work out after all and prove herself deserving of their time and effort. I edged my way into a select circle of the most promising.

It was just like another clique, actually, this one distinguished by an air of artistic superiority and a splash of arrogance. I clung to the outer rim of the inner circle because where I dwelled such traits were frowned upon. A strikingly tall male student, the apprentice and protégé of the particularly short and Italian-mannered Mr. Torrini, captured the first prize for arrogance within the group. His long and muscular frame prowled through the sculpture studio – populated by a gaggle of female wannabe artists – on masterful paws like a lion king circling the den. His macho air was backed by the weight of pure talent, but still, I longed to see him take a second-rate tumble right in front of the rest of us and suffer an honest-to-goodness taste of humility - it would be good for him, I figured. Possessing a fairly intuitive sense of others, however, I did consider the possibility that he could be 50-percent bluff: that deep down he was authentically shy and insecure like the rest of us – though I couldn't intuit precisely why he would be.

He and I went out of our way to avoid each other, he being arrogant (or shy) and me being me. Routinely he took to gobbling up more than his fair share of studio space for his super-size projects, forcing me to retreat to a tiny nook where I could concentrate without the glare of his critical eye turned to evaluate the thump of my mallet to chisel. I'd convinced one of my professors to teach me the basics of wood carving, though carving wasn't being taught at the undergraduate level. As a young girl I'd experimented with carving balsa wood in my basement, attacking the soft wood with nothing but linoleum cutting tools, screwdrivers, and gusto. Having earned my beginner's stripes through finger-fulls and knuckle-fulls of cuts and scrapes suffered to render little carved heads of Jesus, I now felt entitled to proper instruction and appropriate tools.

Something in me felt moved to carve, destined to carve. Without yet knowing that college and art were chiseled into my future, when my mother casually mentioned in a letter that the cherry tree across the boulevard – the one Peeping Douglas and I had climbed – had just been cut down, I wrote back asking her to save a hunk of it in the garage for me. Years later, when she and Bob drove seven hundred miles to visit me in St. Louis, that hunk of cherry wood weighted down their trunk with possibility. That piece of my cherry tree history came to reveal from within a seated girl tugging on her pigtails. She was a compact and efficient fit – she'd been waiting to prove it.

My daily studio presence provided endless fodder for mischievous and tarty asides from male teachers and students alike. Some were whispered out of the sides of their mouths while teasing with leering eyes; others were broadcast through a bullhorn of adolescent-like bluster: "Hey guys, here comes the nun! Know what "nun" means? It means NONE!!!" At the sexual innuendo they penis chuckled like a band of twelve year olds, but I'd become somewhat accustomed to their male blabber. I had my response down pat: raising a mature and arched eyebrow to the lot of them, I responded with direct and chilly eye contact and walked right on by. A figuratively oriented art department was bound to elicit verbal strokes of sexual design – they seemed as normal as pencil applied to paper, even when pointed at me. The combination of my silent scolding and physical unavailability kept a perpetual flame lit under them.

As one might expect in a Catholic college, art students were viewed as the chief purveyors of rowdiness both on and off campus. Pushing limits was, after all, pretty much the same as creative exploration. How many colors could you mix before creating muddy? How many drinks could you mix before throwing up? Our department orchestrated memorable studio parties: food extravaganzas heavy on Italian samplings, jug wine, and chummy loose-lipped art speak. When it came to off-campus parties, I was tagged priceless as "Sr. Gail, the designated driver." No mandate existed prohibiting nuns from drinking, but many of my fellow students thought that I couldn't, or wouldn't, so I didn't – not much anyway. At some parties teachers and students alike turned ridiculously sloppy, encouraging nun jokes to flow freely in my honor.

Mother Superior called the nuns together and said, "I must tell you something Sisters. We have a case of gonorrhea in the convent." "Thank God," muttered an elderly nun from the back of the room. "I'm so tired of Chardonnay."

Oh my…so much yuckity drunken laughter bellowed. I left those parties with a carload of inebriated jokesters, chauffeuring all over town to roll out one party animal at a time, each insisting on a slobbery goodnight kiss and a mushy repetition of thanks. I was just like a carpool Mom after the prom.

When summer rounded the bend and classes took a breather, my attention was diverted back to the sisterhood, a higher plane of existence. I was assigned to the summer collection circuit, mostly because of my youth and my driver's license. It was grueling to drive across the country to visit the list of Catholic parishes assigned to us by the Society of the Propagation of Faith, and far worse to preach and beg for their money to support our mission. Missionary orders were annually offered a teensy slice of rich American pie, but you had to travel far and talk fast to get it. No one in the community was ever gung-ho to be assigned this type of travel assignment, except for Sr. Cephas – she loved begging on the road.

Cephas was a wee Canadian sister in her mid-seventies registering less than five feet in height and potently seasoned from multiple decades of service in Africa. She spouted mission stories as naturally as birds warble. With maps and a calendar of destinations in hand, the two of us packed up a red VW Beetle and hit the road for the better part of the summer. I was the sole driver, her job was to keep me awake with her warbling and to keep us aimed in the right direction. We were surely at the top of the list for the cutest and oddest little twosome traveling the U.S. highways that summer. We banked on that, in fact, to help loosen up tight wallets.

En route, we boarded with any religious community able to offer us a bed for the night (a universal generosity routinely extended throughout the sisterhood). If there was no convent to be found near our destination, we plopped ourselves on the doorstep of the parish rectory, a stuffy, creepy sort of option. On occasion, we had the misfortune of being received by an entrenched and pampered diocesan priest who eyed us like pests on his property; a type of fellow fiercely territorial over the money, minds, and affections of his parishioners; an unwelcoming sort, even in the face of our charm. Fortunately, such stiff-necked clerics were the exception along the way.

Women ascending the pulpit and passing out collection baskets were new experiences for most of the laity, so Cephas and I often startled the crowd when we rose from our seats to assume the tasks. I reflected back on the times at Blessed Sacrament Church when the presence of a visiting missionary priest had pierced the minds and hearts of Sunday churchgoers, perhaps none more than my own. Now, with no mission experience to speak of, I was charged with working the same magic. Cephas and I took advantage of our time on the road together to tune up and practice blending into each other's verbal groove. While tag team preaching we were able to catch on deftly to each other's retreating beat.

Standing together before a mike too high for her and too low for me, we looked and sounded like a spiritual vaudeville act exhibiting the gift of tongues. When faced with larger parishes and multiple services, we divided ourselves up between the anti-social 7 a.m. bunch, the 8:30 a.m. eager to go to breakfast bunch, the 10 a.m. entire family is finally dressed bunch, and the 11:30 a.m. we can't procrastinate any longer bunch. And some parishes held Saturday evening masses, as well, providing us with an audience of those hot to trot on a Saturday night – those with no intention of waking Sunday until the morning had been slept away.

When Cephas ascended the pulpit solo she relied upon compelling tales of village life and irrepressibly peppy enthusiasm. As for me, I relied upon the inspirational vision of my youthful dedication to Christ, and my ability to infuse charismatic sincerity into every word I uttered. Staged on the pulpit, all trepidation fell way to a physical urge to deliver the performance of a lifetime – strangely, the same type of urge materialized every time I put my hand to clay, or plaster, or wood…

Boy, did we rake it in!

Some churches - the conservative dinosaur type - wouldn't allow us, being women, to pass the collection baskets, but when permitted we moved about from pew to pew, offering each and every donor an appreciative smile, while pausing for the unprepared – or the unwilling – to locate wallet or purse and cough up an escape from our eyes. Some looked close to stricken, like they'd been robbed on the spot. At the end of the service, we stationed ourselves at the back of the church, reiterating our thanks and chatting with those wanting a bit more of us. These Sunday fundraisers called for us to be at the top of our game – we had only a tiny window of opportunity to make the sell, clinch the deal, and hit the road.

With thousands of miles and dollars racked up behind me, September led me back to the studio, where I itched madly to be. Along with advanced studio courses, I still had a few more academic requirements left to satisfy. Great Religions of the World sounded like a course that could deliver three credits without a problem, but as I delved into the breadth of it my mind began to butt, once again, against the full nature of my Catholic faith. When I read about Hinduism, I felt called to it; when I read about Buddhism, I felt called to it…I couldn't decipher whether I was being enlightened or strangled. I delved into each religion presented with such determined interest that A's appeared routinely at the top right hand corner of every paper I wrote. But, what I really needed was an A in faith, my own Catholic faith.

Often unaware and unable to decipher the difference, my morning time of spiritual meditation morphed into sculptural contemplation. Both offered solace and doubt, both held possibilities and questions too great for my mind to set straight. Fragments of both slipped from the sides of my thoughts, and when I bent to retrieve them, others spilled out from the top, and when I finally managed to bundle the confused mess, the bottom gave out. God, there was so much involved in shaping a believable existence, material and spiritual.

I took to accumulating a list of false idols, mostly early twentieth century sculptors who dared to veer from a formidable past to give new expression to the figurative, to apply more radical shape and color to what their restless minds conceived. They didn't exactly reject the past; rather, they sorted through it, deliberating over what elements deserved to be carried into their own expression of the present. Glue could not have bound me more to the heart of their purpose.

I gravitated to the work of Arturo Martini. Familiar shivers shot up my spine when I read about his life of physical and mental turmoil: a life of erotic desire and Christian devotion...a life of torturous and bitter self-criticism...a life of being wed to the human figure but never content with it, always wanting more from it. Within his dilemmas I fell prey to a festering unease that came to settle upon me as my own.

The work of sculptor Marino Marini simply brought me to my knees: I worshipped it. He was my Einstein. He was my Art God. The perfection radiating from his forms was as elusive to me as it was real. The horse and riders, the dancers, the portraits...all restrained yet bursting with fullness, with life. His symbolic figures materialized in explosive purity from the dream edges of his inner reality and mythic vision. The harder I tried to dissect the rightness of their parts, the less I grasped the whole of them. It finally seeped into my consciousness that the honesty they delivered was beyond any formula for understanding. That was his brilliance. His work spoke its own language. His forms could not be transcribed. The bewildering dilemmas linked to faith and art absorbed me with a spongy fullness that led me to cry out for the sole purpose of soaking up more.

Time was being absorbed as well.

My college years were suddenly being tallied, totaling a prolonged time of testing on multiple fronts, but a cherished time that I hadn't expected to wrap my arms around and call my own. Each semester afforded me euphoric highs and despairing lows, but my destiny kept me anchored.

With a degree in hand, I was ready to graduate on to another continent.

My exact assignment within the vast continent was due to arrive via the motherhouse in Frascati; I waited for it like an irrepressible two-year old. Then…one day, as sure as the sun dotted the horizon on a clear dawn, it appeared in writing: *Malawi!* Maaa-la-wi. Ma-laaa-wi. Mala-wiiii. I pronounced the name of the elongated southeastern African country over and over again with melodious twists, until each variation inhabited my mouth as comfortably as my own tongue. My job would be that of establishing an art department in a secondary school in Likuni - Sr. Marie José D'or had precisely predicted such needs. The "department" would consist of me – a faculty of one.

Upon entering the convent, I never imagined that I would have to wait six and a half years before flying off to my mission – I mean, *God's* mission for me.

CHAPTER 11. AFRICA

My journey commenced with delays. Not the plane kind – the paper kind. I applied immediately for a work visa for Malawi, but I had to have it physically in hand before taking flight. The White Sisters and White Fathers had worked in Malawi for decades so there shouldn't have been a problem, but there was. Missionary newcomers, first-timers, were being scrutinized more deliberately, and much more slowly. My criminal check was A-Okay since stealing candy money from my mom didn't count, nor did all the Catholic guilt I harbored for non-criminal offenses. No one seemed to know exactly what the "official" problem amounted to. Rather than wring my hands and fret stateside, it was suggested that I fly to Frascati, Italy and sample transitioning into a European culture while twiddling my restless thumbs. Surely, the visa would arrive soon…surely, very soon.

Boarding the plane, I lifted my feet off the U.S. ground as if they were a pair of five-toed wings. I boarded with no sadness, no regret, no reluctance, no fear; I carried no sense of departure, only a sense of destination. If the plane chickened out and refused to fly, I would span the ocean myself, carried on saltwater waves when my strokes exhausted themselves. I would not be detained. Doubt was a relic of the past – at least for this voyage.

Upon landing in Rome, a tall six-foot-plus Dutch sister bent low to greet me with European kisses and a brand new accent for my ears to toy with. She loaded me into an infant-sized car and took to the Italian roadways like a wrong-sided banshee heading for the repose of the vineyard-laden hills of Frascati. We turned up the drive to what appeared to be a vast and formidable stucco and tiled estate. Several sisters appeared to greet me with fawning enthusiasm under the arched portico. I felt like a prized puppy, a novel American breed rare among this pack of full-blooded Europeans.

Within the Congregation, American sisters amounted to few and far between, and young ones thoroughly rare. As to the language situation, barking may have gotten me further than my French did. The Congregation was officially bi-lingual, French and English, but here French flowed as freely as the Frascati wine found sitting on the tabletops at meal times twice a day, as casual as water. I was ushered towards a small private room in one of several adjoining wings, feeling more disoriented in that mazed womb of a motherhouse than I had ever felt traveling the church collection highways of big and broad America. Instinctually, I resorted to the tried and true programming of my early convent days: I held my head up, dimpled my cheeks, and followed the crowd.

Now that I was in Frascati, no one was quite sure what to do with me. After two days I was handed some lire, walking directions to the local train station, a map of Rome, an Italian pocket dictionary, and the opportunity to explore the Eternal City all by my lonesome. St. Peter's, the Colosseum, the Pantheon, museums and cathedrals, museums and cathedrals, museums and cathedrals…all so impressively numbing in abundance and magnitude. By dusk my attention settled on the tangible number of times my rear end had been pinched while sandwiched in buses among groping, short, bald-headed men determined to feel a piece of my "nun means none" body. Other women dispensed gestures of nonchalant aggression, elbowing and whacking these determined feelers, but I didn't dare. After a few lone day trips of soaking in the crowded, honking splendor of Rome, I took to wandering the quaint narrow alley streets of Frascati lined with market vendors, observing with amusement the emphatic voices and gesticulating arms negotiating for hunks and handfuls of fresh this and that.

A week passed.

Two weeks passed.

No papers. No visa.

I began to lose weight – all that fresh Mediterranean food. The mother hens appeared worried about the shrinking American chick for I began discovering extra allotments of chocolate and biscotti propped by my door. Others resorted to the more blatant initiative of filling my mealtime plate, though self-serve was the norm. Collectively, they feared that my lost pounds reflected loss of happiness, loss of spirit, generated by the prolonged anxiety of my waiting, which wasn't true. The food was just different. Lighter. There was no loss of spirit in me. In fact, I felt like I had just earned a PhD in sophistication. And *that* went beyond, even, *my* wildest fantasies.

Weeks four…five…six and seven I lived the life of an Italian artisan. Silver and golden jubilee ceremonies were approaching for six of the sisters residing in the motherhouse. I was commissioned (the appropriate word in my mind) to design and create original sculptures for each of them. Portraying various poses of supplication and praise I modeled prophet-like, stylized figures directly out of plaster. They reflected a subject and style that was bound to please, nothing questioning or evocative, and certainly no nakedness. Plaster hardened under my nails, paint splattered on my smock – I was a picture of authenticity.

Week eight arrived with a bright idea: rather than continue lingering in Europe, why not linger somewhere in Africa? And there I was, riding a night train to Belgium where I could "quickly and easily" secure a visitor's visa to enter Burundi (north of Malawi, but at least on the same continent) and wait out my paper vigil on African soil. As I boarded the packed train, burdened with two suitcases of worldly possessions plus a guitar, a swarthy, elderly Italian man tore the baggage from my hands and half-dragged me into the six-seat compartment already occupied by him and four additional men. Ushering me into a snug middle seat between him and his buddy, I served as a pillow for the two of them all the way to Brussels. Their hands roamed in their "sleep" so I stayed awake - on guard against Italians.

Our house in Brussels swelled with a community of a dozen or more unfamiliar faces and not a trace of English. It was there that my November birthday rolled around, but I kept it to myself. Several days later, I discovered that my mother had tried to track me down by phoning Frascati, but language barriers prohibited her from tracking me further. Left to observe the day alone, I took a stroll heading for a pastry shop that I had salivated by a few days earlier. A proper birthday treat was in order: sugar would sing to me, if no one else. I stood back and watched for a long time as hurried women shoved their way in and out, rattling off their list of desires at frightening speeds, and in words I couldn't begin to decipher. Eying a creamy, promising beauty, I stared at every speck of it for long seconds, while a woman behind the counter stared at me. Then – as if hit by a bullet – she shot a question at me with a wounding tone of impatience. My tongue stuck to the roof of my mouth. All I could do was point to the beauty behind the glass, while raising another finger to convey "one." Though I knew simple numbers in French, the choice between the "un or une" of the occasion froze my lips. Gingerly transporting my birthday present back to the privacy of my room, I closed the door, and with an air of sinful indulgence bit into what I hoped would make the day traditionally special. But it was fluffy air…too fluffy…filled with cottony meringue… almost nothing…almost no birthday at all!

After three weeks of a "quick wait" in Brussels, my paws gripped an entry permit into Burundi. Burundi was selected because Sr. Gyslaine, a youngish Canadian, ran an art department at a secondary school in rural Mugera, part of the larger province of Gitega. Alongside her I could witness first hand what my own job might look like, and – *Alleluia!* – Gyslaine spoke English, though she taught in French and Kirundi. A plane connection landed me in Nairobi. I carried twenty dollars worth of travel money tucked in my gray pocket – sufficient for the five hour scheduled layover before my departing flight for Bujumbura. I discovered the hard way that the word "schedule" meant little in this part of the world, and "soon" meant that *nobody* knew when. My connecting flight was canceled with no more than a shrug of the shoulder; *perhaps*, there would be one later, or *surely*, the next day, and *maybe*, I could get on one of those, *if* they came. "*No problem!*" flashed a wide sparkling smile across the ticket counter.

An unsettling military presence pervaded the Nairobi airport: straight-faced and heavily armed soldiers spaced themselves apart like structural beams. Between them sat rows of rigid back chairs and a basic concession or two. I stayed fixed on my spot, seated in front of the ticket counter, in case a plane from heaven's own airline dropped from the sky, all willing and able to soar to Burundi unscheduled. When the personnel shift changed at the ticket counter, I re-presented myself, re-explaining my situation: "Soon," the fresh face responded. Then…another change: "Soon." After nearly thirty hours of "Soon," and just when I feared a second sleepless night under military guard, the word "Bujumbura" rang over the PA system. I leapt to my feet feeling as fresh as a daisy!

Flying over the verdant, ribbon terraced hills of Burundi was like spying on paradise, but upon landing at the airport the vision was crushed by a sea of faces that had known far too much horror and far too little paradise. Tribal wars had ravaged land, bodies, and minds, burning scars of caution into the somber and darkened eyes of the masses. It was the end of 1973; 1972 had been a year of abominable ethnic violence between the Hutu and Tutsi. History's estimates now number killings well over 100,000 in as little as a three-month period of time. Both tribes had bloodied their hands for years, but 1972 took on the grim face of Hutu genocide. Bleak reality had never penetrated my dreams - it now unnerved me.

Looking past stark stares, I caught a glimpse of a welcoming face, a face free of caution, coming my way: a fellow sister. We headed for the hills without delay. Tarred roads quickly disintegrated into potholed, rutted looking cow paths offering what little they could to any four-wheeled vehicle daring to roll over them. We weren't traveling far in terms of miles – kilometers I should say – but it took over three hours to navigate the wily terrain; even without the customary flat tire along the way.

Mugera was couched in between hills, some appearing to sag with the clustered weight of plentiful banana trees, and others munched bare by scraggly cattle eking out a life in slow motion. The mission complex embodied the heart of Mugera: a convent, a primary and secondary school, an infirmary, a small orphanage, a work center for learning trades, a seminary, and a church. Village huts were scattered about, tucked into the folds of hills and hidden behind banana trees – nearly invisible when rotating full circle to drink in the panorama. **WHAM!** It finally hit me: *I was in Africa! God Almighty…. I was in Africa!* Shuffling my feet, dust scatter-jumped around me settling conspicuously on my sandal tops and between my toes, the colored earth licking me in welcome. How I loved the red dust – I could roll in the dust – I could eat the dust.

Gyslaine became my translator, instructor, and pal, introducing me to her students and escorting me along village paths to meet and greet her many acquaintances. Together we talked shop, sharing art ideas through minds climbing the same vine, relishing the gift of easy compatibility in a far away land. I trailed behind her like a distracted toddler gawking open-mouthed to the left and to the right, every pore of me working overtime to absorb the exotic newness of it all. Her friendship supported me like a crutch. It steadied my nerves and heart when the images of a country depleted of both joy and blood made me tremble. Each and every day my eyes opened wider to the strained pairing of beauty and sadness existent in the land of Burundi.

Christmas arrived about a week after I did in the hills of Mugera. An all out liturgical and musical extravaganza was planned around a midnight mass certain to be over-crowded with those from remote villages journeying on foot for several hours to join in the praise making. Early in the day tiny moving specks appeared in the far distance like ants seeping from the hills in single file, growing incrementally in size as the day progressed and the peopled lines neared. At the stroke of midnight, when the church burst full and spilling with the crowd, the singing ignited with such volume and intensity that the potent harmony of it all but raised the roof.

After the service had sung and praised itself out, the assembly poured out into a darkened night pierced by spotty and flickering fires – dancing erupted and local beer was enthusiastically imbibed. Gyslaine and I were milling about enjoying the happy flavor of it all when I heard a "thunk" – maybe it was a "thud" – then closer to us, another "thunk-thud," then closer yet, another. The eyes of those around us sparked with knowing. Gyslaine quickly caught on. She yanked on my arm and told me to start walking, quickly but calmly. More stones showered our path before our bodies disappeared down the hill, sufficiently away from the pitching arm of someone dusting up hatred on such a "Silent Night, holy night, all is calm……".

By now, it came as no surprise to me to learn that all "soon" talk of a Malawian work permit had silenced. Looking for an alternative occupation on the spot, Gyslaine led me to an area where I could get my hands on large hunks of seasoned wood, and then to a small shed where I could set up shop. I unpacked my precious carving tools – which had won out over other precious goods vying for space in one of my two suitcases – and devoted my time to subtracting away at the grain of unfamiliar wood, releasing figures that emerged as African as the native wood itself. A steady stream of curious on-lookers flowed by; everyone interested in my methods, my progress, me. It was kind of like teaching without teaching. When I wasn't out in the shed sculpting, I tried to be useful in anyway I could. One night I assisted with the birth of a calf - a problematic birth. I didn't have to stick my hand "you know where," (as my mother would say), but I did have to hold the lantern precisely there with a steady hand while another sister did just that. As the gooey, skinny-legged wonder emerged, I felt a surge of relief – almost lactating myself on the very spot. When the mother cow died a week later from complications, I was grief-stricken for the skinny-legged orphan, the abandoned one.

After three months in Mugera, fresh paperwork was officially filed for me to stay put; it appeared as if Malawi would have to be penciled out of my destiny, for the wheels were rolling fast to make my stay official. It took the threat of my new assignment to make the old one materialize. That's how stuff happens, of course! Word came a week later that everything was finally lined up for my departure to Malawi. I didn't want to go. Along with my heart, a routine had rooted, and I was tired of being shuffled along. All of me wanted to stay put and build a life in the banana-laden hills, but…obedience stared me down with commandingly unsentimental eyes. So, I pulled up my tender roots, wept in Gyslaine's arms, and trekked on like an honest-to-goodness missionary.

....

Another airport landing….another airport greeting.

From Blantyre, located in southern Malawi, yet another White Sister face met and escorted me out onto a paved road heading towards the country's center, the newly appointed capital city of Lilongwe. I arrived in the former Nyasaland nearly a decade after the penning of independence from Britain in 1964, and after the consequent formation of a one party Republic in 1966, and after Dr. H. Kamuzu Banda was declared: His Excellency the Life President of the Republic of Malawi Ngwazi Dr. H. Kamuzu Banda – a long title for a long time. The Ngwazi (the shortened version) returned to his homeland of Malawi after having studied in the U.S., practiced medicine in England, and served prison time in Rhodesia. He returned to lead his country to freedom and prosperity. Believing that its future was in the land, he encouraged his people to devote their energy to cultivating its power and potential, rather than fleeing to its cities. The land held the promise of wealth from tobacco, tea, sugar, and groundnuts for export and reliable maize to fill their localized bellies. The likes of tribal terror in Burundi had not erupted among these rural people mostly content to bask in a spirit of nationalism on a stretch of peaceful land. Language-wise, the Achewa of the central region constituted the country's largest ethnic group, making Chichewa the national language while utilizing English as the official language of government and commerce. I could speak again in whole sentences.

The road we traveled was bordered with parallel dusty walking trails and scrawny, empty handed men walking several steps ahead of heftier women balancing full baskets on their heads and babies slung on their hips, or tied to their backs, or both. It was the walk of the land. But, as I continued to peer out the window at the seeming inequality of their walking division of labor, I became alert to the rather startling flash of smiles aimed in my direction. Malawi felt distinctly different.

The Lilongwe community occupied a large fired-brick house serving as the Provincial House (home base) for all of our sisters scattered throughout mission posts within the country. I wasn't assigned to that house, but we stopped for introductions and, so it turned out, another reunion with Sr. Felicia whose journey from St. Louis to Malawi had been without delays – she was not a newcomer. She had spent several happy years in Malawi before being assigned to training the likes of me in Franklin, Pa. For me, her renewed presence was like having sunny assurance at my disposal, even though I was heading further west to the mission complex of Likuni – the type of in-the-bush setting I had envisioned and hoped for.

Heading out from Lilongwe, the road narrowed considerably and then deteriorated into dusty ruts before depositing me in front of a row of brick and basic staff houses situated alongside the Likuni Secondary School for Girls, a boarding school. Our house was a tad more spacious than the others because it served to accommodate the Headmistress of the school. Even though the school had turned from mission run to government run with teachers considered civil servants, Sr. Fernande, one of our own, still filled the role of Headmistress.

With me included, our Likuni community totaled five. Each of us was accommodated with a tiny private room, not counting the flesh colored geckos that considered every wall their own. My four companions all hailed from Canada, so French, English, and Chichewa mixed and mingled like alphabet soup. Each language offered up a fair share of prized words that defied translation – the most precise and best of all words to serve the occasion – so we bounced around.

Our cook was a young man named Levison; we would have looked like selfish, pale fools if we had attempted to do our own domestic work. Foreigners, "azungu," were expected to employ as many locals as possible and besides, our school duties left little time for daily household concerns. Levison appeared regularly at pre-dawn to light a fire under the outdoor metal drum serving as a hot water heater, and then prepare breakfast.

Afterwards, he swept and cleaned the house and yard and cooked our midday meal before returning to his family in a neighboring village. When the thin grayish-brown slices of cow tongue first appeared on my noontime plate, I was like the cow itself: speechless! Such supposed delicacies seemed anything but. I filled up on mpunga – good ole'rice – until I could adjust my thought and palate.

It didn't take long for me to come to the realization, once and for all and for good this time, that I was *finally* in the place, the very place, I was destined for. I viewed the extending flat and open countryside around me as a welcome mat rolled out by the hands of a most polite and winsome people. It was as if my everyday feet had landed on the ground of my finest dream. Even the chilling whoops of hyenas heckling in the night could not shake the sureness of my footing.

But I couldn't get cozy just yet. After a month of Likuni life, I was sent to the old city section of Lilongwe, with its one main street of Asian shops and a Chinese restaurant, to enroll in a live-in, three-month intensive Chichewa course. I would do my art instruction in English, but the life lived around me occurred in Chichewa. I needed and wanted to connect to the richness of it, even if my efforts were translated as misunderstood. A total of four enrolled in the course: a young German fellow, a British male doctor, a Canadian Marist Brother, and me. Our instructor was a Canadian White Father, an established veteran who knew the culture and language of the country like he knew his face in the mirror. I was locked in with guys only for three whole months.

After establishing a somewhat of a toehold on the language during the first month, a rule was enforced banning all conversation in any language other than Chichewa, no matter how important or incoherent. It was one of those tough-love whacks across the head (tongue in this case). Even the nightly and rowdy recreational card games shuffled before the generator turned off had to be dealt in Chichewa, resulting in unnaturally quiet wins and losses before it turned naturally dark. Learning vocabulary was one thing, but learning the music of the language was quite another: the inflections, the high and low rhythms, the accompanying gestures and facial expressions. The whole of it represented a bundled package of life – so much more than mere words. What enamored me most about the language was the abundance of rhyming agreement that floated words into melody:

*Chi*rombo *cha*chikulu *chi*ripo. A big wild animal is here.
*Ti*rombo, *ta*tikulu, *ti*ripo. A tiny wild animal is here.
*Zi*rombo *za*zikulu *zi*ripo. Big wild animals are here.

Then, there was the sageful wisdom and poetry held within their proverbs:

Pang'ono-pang'ono ndi mtolo. Little by little is a bundle.
Mlendo ndi mame. Visitor is like dew.

Any foreigner who could rattle off the appropriate proverb at the appropriate time was respected like an elder. "Visitor is like dew," means simply that a visitor appears for a short time and then disappears – evaporating like dew. Some proverbs I could barely comprehend in English for they were so finely stitched into the pattern of a different life and landscape. After three months of exercising slow and steady progress as in, "Little by little is a bundle," the course ended. I headed back to Likuni to stumble over my accomplishment and instruct in the comfort of unmelodious English.

We were far from a bunch of crucifix waving, proselytizing missionaries bent on condemning and converting. Our purpose was one of simple presence, living and working among and for the good of the people. In some ways we set about working ourselves out of our very own jobs, for it was our goal to Africanize the institutions we had founded and maintained throughout the years. This modernized interpretation of missionary life both comforted and suited me, for despite my sense of belonging in Likuni, fevers of faith continued to strike me as fiercely as malaria struck others. I would have preferred malaria: a disease testifying to my presence in Africa, not threatening it.

Testifying to the sincerity of our intentions, our Congregation had founded an independent religious order of Malawian women to afford native girls an alternative to joining our foreign ranks, best assuring that they stayed put among and served their own people. I had met one of these sisters, Sr. Perpetua, back in St. Louis – she had arrived in the States to study. We offered her a place to live among us, helping to soften the hard edge adjustment to country and culture, or so we hoped. I was assigned to explaining to her the basics of life in America: how to use a phone, how to cross the street safely, count out money, make a purchase, eat our food...and how and why people used under arm deodorant – given the offensive odor she detected in them and her natural preference for going without. Now, I stood as she once had, noting why phones and deodorant were superfluous, observing how street crossings were as rare as money and the occasion to spend it, and pondering how to eat her rice with my fingers. A perfect Chichewa proverb no doubt exists for this serendipitous flip of the coin, but you won't find it on the tip of my tongue.

By the time September classes commenced at the Likuni Secondary School for Girls, I had prepared not only my classroom, but also four dozen mimeographed, hand-bound copies of a 55 page book of art instruction for beginners. The book contained broadly generalized chapters on topics such as color, perspective, printmaking, fabric dyeing, and standard design principles. Except for the numerous pages and illustrations that I took the liberty of plagiarizing from art store "How To" manuals, which I had horded for just such a purpose, I wrote the book myself. I figured that plagiarism under religious circumstances would be exempt from consequences – just like religious groups were exempt from paying taxes. The books were a huge hit with the girls from day one, for they loved having something tangible and weighty in hand, a possession. I, myself, relied upon the weight of them for solid direction and plotted planning.

The school boarded about 250 girls between the ages of 15 and 22. Many had gotten a late start on their secondary schooling due to fierce competition and any number of other tough circumstances, but having secured their coveted spot, they now ranked among the highly privileged. The country was far short on schools and teachers, for education often boiled down to money, particularly in developing countries. Behind the classroom buildings existed a row of dorm buildings. The dorms were interiorly lined with row after row of thin-mattressed cots and small cubbies to accommodate each student's sparse tally of possessions. Perpendicular to the dorm blocks was a rectangular dining hall where the girls, and periodically the teachers, ate family style seated on stools tightly tucked around long tables. I always seemed to land there, seated between giggling students, on fish day. Each prepared fish was divided into three supposedly fair servings: head section, middle section, and tail section. For some reason the head section was most coveted, so as I stared at the set of concave eyeballs set before me I tried to see "gift." The girls always insured that a head be served upon my plate. I'm not entirely sure if it was out of respect or devilishness.

The students wore uniforms to class, burgundy colored cotton skirts and white blouses with a burgundy trim around the neck, though most of my photos show them posed in the native chitenje – an approximately four foot-by-six foot rectangle of brightly patterned cloth traditionally wrapped around the lower body and tucked in above the waist (above the breasts on some women). Despite boisterous colors and wild patterning, no variety of chitenje stood out more radically than the propaganda version which garbed the country: cloth printed in the red, green, and black colors of the Malawian flag, bordered by catchy government slogans and symbols, and portraying illustrious images of the face of His Excellency Ngwazi Dr. H. Kamuzu Banda.

As for myself, I dressed in plain skirts and blouses and went without a veil. My wardrobe was entirely colorless and without distinction in my eyes. It was a law of the land that all skirts and dresses extend below the knee. Exposing the naked back of the knee (considered risqué), or daring to wear pants (bad American influence), could land a woman swiftly in jail. Women displaying their ignorance by arriving at the airport in pants were refused entry into the country until properly attired – as were longhaired males, until submitting to a haircut on the spot. Pants, naked knees, longhaired males, all were frowned upon. All were foul western influences worthy of censor.

Broadly speaking, Malawi did not possess a grand heritage in the visual arts, the compelling primitive sort westerners commonly associated with Africa. Consequently, my students were lapping up newness. During my first days of teaching, positioned in front of the class, the girls stared at me with piercing intent – as if my face and body comprised the sole lesson of the day. But as I moved from words of explanation to projects in hand, their attention shifted with equally probing intensity to the creative task before them. It was mind-boggling to witness my English instructions effortlessly translated into the shapes and colors of their own lives – all of it radiantly distinct from the mimeographed words and uninspired examples within my concocted text. The vast majority of students displayed inherent skills from the get-go, but there were a few whose hands moved as clumsily as I sometimes did standing at the head of the class.

Nearly all of the students had grown up in villages where women crafted and fired clay pots for functional purposes. The idea of manipulating clay for the sake of design form alone, however, was a curious indulgence for most. My curriculum introduced them to expression for expression's sake in a variety of ways: the novelty of non-functional art. I remember the howl of collective glee when I produced a box of scissors – brand new ones that actually cut. Each pair had to be shared by two or more, but the scissors cut with such divine ease that their patience was well rewarded. When it came time to dip brushes into tempera paint we rationed it out a dollop at a time like liquid gold. We maximized the minimum.

Every time I wrote home I begged shamelessly for supplies: "Mom, could you send three large-size bottles of Elmer's glue, four rolls of masking tape, two dozen paint brushes…" Erie, Pa., though so far away in every way, was my most accessible source for art supplies. There were some materials, however, that were offered up for free, compliments of the land, like clay and soapstone, but the time and effort required to harvest them was costly in its own way.

A two-hour walk from the school sat a village reputed to have fine pottery crafted from the smoothest of clay dug from the bottom of a treasured golden creek bed. A student shared this bit of precious info with me, necessitating a class safari. Off we went, each girl striding straight and easy while balancing an empty bucket on top her head. Our village visit was pre-announced via the local grapevine. Upon arrival a host of women greeted us formally, one at a time, as is the synchronized custom: a half curtsy, with the left hand clasping the right wrist and the right hand extend for a single brief and airy shake, while the head nods in a bow. The formality was performed in total silence until each and every woman in the welcoming party had touched hand to each and every one in the visiting party.

Then, the words of greeting (the how are you? of the English language) sounded in the rhythmic beat of a full Chichewa welcome. After the gestures and words, we were invited to advance into the compound where pottery making was in progress. A rickety chair was set in place for me, as the girls folded naturally to the ground to observe with new interest the veteran techniques for producing and refining perfectly shaped vessels. After a silent and perfect demonstration, we paraded single file behind a single file of women, making our way along a narrow and descending path towards the source of their velvety, ochre colored clay. We dug quite easily with our hands into the generous mushy creek bed, filling buckets, propping them on heads, and marching our way back to the mission, weary and satisfied and singing. Returning, we faced the task of immediately digging a pit deep enough in the ground to moistly store the bounty of clay harvested to satisfy a semester's worth of needs.

Moving beyond function, we fashioned free-flowing shapes and strung them together as mobiles and wall hangings. Drawing upon my students' knowledge of leaves and roots, we concocted stain-like glazes to add to our brew pot of experimentation and discovery. But the firing process itself – with its tendency towards exploding air bubbles in the clay – tested our enthusiasm by sporadically serving up charred fragments and burning disappointment to those who an anticipated holding their very own work of art.

After weeks of clay play – kneading it, forming it, firing it – we turned our eyes towards a much firmer substance, a much greater challenge some might argue. North to the hills we journeyed to quarry manageable chunks of soapstone for our round of carving. With an oozing amount of personal passion, I poured out my knowledge of subtraction, the process of identifying and releasing life from within one plane at a time. Soapstone is firm like stone, but mercifully soft for stone. It easily releases to the scratch and scrape of metal files – particularly brand new ones fast-tracked from Erie, Pa. The students proceeded to fill their nostrils with clouds of self-made dust, while their hands amassed the scrapes and blisters of repetitive filing and polishing…filing and polishing… Carving involves sweat and patience; reward is slow to arrive, if it arrives at all. My passion was less than convincing. The girls were ready to move on with my book of tricks. The lack of immediate gratification inherent in the tedious process of carving caused the group to let out a whopping cheer when we moved on to the chapter on tie-dyeing and batik. We toyed first with more root and leaf dyes, but achieved barely a tint of success. "Mom…could you send an assortment of Rit cold water dyes ASAP?" The Rit worked like magic! Banners of effort hung out to dry everywhere, waving and whipping about like flags of wild success.

At the end of each semester it became tradition for the students to mount their very own art exhibit. Shooing away the resident geckos, we transformed every square inch of wall space, along with every speck of table space and shelf space, into a ripe and abundant harvest of artistic achievement. But, more inspiring than the display itself, was the communal pride the students donned for the occasion: it was the loveliest garment I had ever seen.

....

Besides shipping things my mother wrote about things, though a featherweight blue aerogram could get swept up in the skies and take four weeks (or longer) to drift its way down on target. Mom was turning into a pro at the fine art of international mail; at the post office her face was becoming as familiar as a stamp. She held on to a good number of my letters over the years. Mine to her, besides requests for this and thats, were filled with vivid descriptions of daily life and pen and paper assurance that I was, indeed, healthy and happy – the only news she really cared about.

In one letter I recall offering her advice on how to deal with brother Tim as he inched his way into the manhood lair of females and sex, for she had hinted of frustration. It was I, Sister Gail, who legibly wrote out the god-forbidden word "s e x" in my response – my mom still managed to avoid it as if she couldn't spell it, or couldn't spare the ink. Her way of handling Tim was to punish him with silence for his natural inclinations. It was that damned Soliwoda silence still echoing in my own ears that made me risk bucking the trend in blue ink. In rereading the letters she amassed from me it's embarrassing to note just how **much** stuff I asked her for, and it wasn't all art supplies: a Timex watch for Mr. Ziba the history teacher, a 34A bra for me and a 36C for Annette, a half slip and panty hose for Fernande... Each White Sister serving in the missions was allotted a modest monthly allowance for personal use, meaning for anything from stamps to underwear. Mine was $5 per month, or however many Kwacha that transcribed into. Mom's generosity was like an off shore bank account.

I came across other letters, few and far between, that scrolled inward, touching abstractly upon other forms of need and sacrifice in my life – things that my mother couldn't buy and put a stamp on, things that were part and parcel of my chosen life style. Usually, by letter's end I doused them in some trite and watery platitude such as: "Everyone is called upon to make sacrifices." I was alluding to the pick and pull of physical love threads that at times unspooled from deep within my body and knotted themselves in a mess of choking desire. All I could do was to breathe my way through the tangle of them.

Life wasn't fully absorbed by work and prayer alone: we socialized, on occasion, with the Marist Brothers who taught at the neighboring boys' school. The brothers relished a good party and they had no problem splurging to concoct one. A sizable selection of cocktails and fine wine testified to budgets far fatter than our own. Also, they passed out cigarettes – Dunhill's, no less – so I puffed away, as did a couple of other liberal-minded members of the sisterhood. It wasn't that I cared for cigarettes or needed to smoke, it was just that when the generator clicked off at 9 p.m., conversation and a smoke partnered well with darkness and cocktails. The foursome was about as close to the wild side as I could get without having to fret over sin. I had voluntarily wed myself to follow a path of deprivation, but the country itself offered a sufficiency of it; running from a taste of frivolous pleasure now and then seemed beyond the call to duty. Gratitude is what I felt, for the fine taste of God's material blessings.

And, back to the cigarettes, I had neither the time nor money to get hooked on them, and not a clue as to the mechanics of inhaling. Truthfully, what drew me to the cigarettes being passed about was the burgundy and gold trimmed Dunhill box itself - so square and thin, so distinctly and properly British. It was a French White Father buddy of mine, Pierre, who took to providing and visually spoiling me with these fabulously packaged smokes.

With a chiseled face set over a rugby muscled neck, Pierre was strikingly handsome. He enjoyed the company of our homey Canadian-American community, as he himself resided in Lilongwe among solely Malawian clergy. I might have been fantasizing again, but he seemed especially fond of *my* company, though he acted with a common casualness towards me, yet something.....? He and that neck of his actually played on a rugby team and one day he invited me to town for a tournament match. There he was, sweaty and charging like a bull, his full body pulsing, a drenched team shirt plastered across his thoroughly hardened chest. I noted these things, these male parts of him, but I didn't *feel* them, not in any way whatsoever. Then, my eyes fell upon Malcolm, the British doctor with whom I had studied Chichewa for three solid months. He jogged off the field to the sideline and over to his beautiful wife and two young children, and it was the sight of that perfect family touching upon each other that nearly sank me. It wasn't the man alone, it was the man with his wife, with his children; it was the whole team of them in possession of each other. Under his satiny shorts I glimpsed the defined bulge of everything I didn't and wouldn't ever know; I saw her squeeze into him – into it – with a push of familiarity and ownership that left me starving.

I can still picture every detail of the scene that emptied me so fully.

You might, quite naturally, be inclined to tie my longing to the price of chastity, the vow of celibacy, but chastity was not the vow taking its toll on me that day. It was poverty that leveled me on the spot. I had never felt so poor. When I witnessed that heart-stopping moment, on that particular day, in that particular way, I barely possessed the strength to stand.

....

The daily routine of the school year was interrupted annually by a government-mandated event known as Youth Week. Teachers were called upon to organize student activities geared towards bettering the land; essentially, it amounted to a week of a multitude of hands offering up free labor. For example, some groups focused on agriculture, toiling in the fields, while others concentrated on transportation, helping to clear and repair paths and roadways. The initiative was meant to fan national pride and assure that those privileged with the gift of education remain sensitive to, and connected to, the needs of the land. Stretching my mind to link a qualifying project to art, the word "beautification" popped into my head. "That's it, we'll beautify a village. Brilliant!" We made contact with the chief of the village closest to the school to ask permission for a white woman and a group of students to spend Youth Week painting designs on the fronts of their village dwellings: *beautifying* them. He couldn't have entirely comprehended our request, but, nonetheless, he laid out his village to us like a blank canvas.

We prepared for our mission by sketching out a variety of border designs for door and window openings; we didn't attempt more than simple patterns because we were aiming for quantity as well as quality. Next, we mixed up several buckets of variously tinted, lime based powder paint (like pastel whitewash), the only choice available to us to deal with the scope of our project. To apply the paint we gathered an assortment of bristled brushes, rags, sponge pieces, and frayed twigs.

Except for mine, all heads were topped with a bucket of paint as we marched towards the village in the early morning dawn, causing a rare stir of curiosity to rise along with it. After traversing a couple of miles of narrow, rutted, and dusty road, we neared the heart of the village. There we halted, waiting to be formally welcomed before marching any further. Greetings doled out, I commenced with what must have been a riotous Chichewa rendition of our mission. At the sight of nothing but bewildered and befuddled faces, one of the students came to my rescue by re-interpreting my spoken mess and spelling out our beautification project. Project aside, the huddle of villagers standing before me appeared hypnotized by my dishwater blonde hair and blue eyes. Toothpicks couldn't have held their eyes open any wider.

The chief had three (maybe four?) wives, so I soon became aware of the pecking order of problems facing me. *Each* wife wanted *me* to paint their quarters, along with those of their extended and extended families. The students were demoted to the rest of the village. My plan had been to wander among the girls, fairly dishing out suggestions and assistance, but I found myself trapped by multiple wifely demands and taming jealous eruptions. My personal week of civic responsibility wound up being spent on equalizing the preferences of a group of wives who had no desire to be equal.

Though having packed lunches, we were presented daily with batch after batch of chimanga: fresh and hard fire-roasted corn on the cob that we could not politely refuse. Marveling, I watched as the girls chewed through six to eight ears of hard corn apiece – my kernel infested insides bloated miserably after two. Which led to the problem of relieving myself when the fill of corn worked its way rather urgently to the exit hole of my gaseous body. Well, there was the village latrine, of course: a fenced off maggot infested pit that tested my desperation with repeated cruelty. Mother Nature had never provided so poorly, in my opinion.

As the sun lowered in the sky, we marched home for the night wearily excited over each day's progress. As was the custom, a group of villagers accompanied us nightly, nearly half of the way home, singing and clapping pleasurable beats of appreciation. Dawn appeared to surface too early for the next several days. Each of us rose stiffly to greet our obligation and execute our artistic labor. Walk…paint…heat…corn…pit…smiles… walk…songs…dust…*Zikomo*, thank you, echoed in chorus. By the end of Youth Week the village was practically a tourist attraction for locals. A village area of 60 plus hut like dwellings were, more or less, successfully adorned with paint, and I weighed in five pounds lighter from corn. We had bettered the country; we had beautified a small sliver of it - through, at least, one rainy season, maybe two.

....

As a community, we were fortunate to have use of what we termed "a vacation/retreat house" located on the shores of Lake Malawi – that long wet body occupying an eastern length of the finger thin country. The lake encompassed 20 percent plus of Malawi's size and, supposedly, bred more species of fresh water fish than all of North America and Europe combined. It represented a long stretch of Malawi that we didn't have to concern ourselves with teaching or healing or counseling, a place where our time and effort shone upon ourselves. We enjoyed enough privacy at the lake to feel at ease donning a swimsuit and picnicking on the shore, even though we were never truly alone.

Little heads tended to pop up like native plants: children planted at a respectful distance for the sport of gawking at pale-legged women frolicking between sun and water. Women totting babes on their backs and laundry tubs on their heads paid little heed to us as they neared the water's edge to scrub and clean in the jumbo-sized washing basin. Jackson, the property caretaker, was charged with keeping the house tidy and guest ready, as well as cooking for any occupants. We brought our food along with us, but he provided the freshly caught fish. Though not a fish fan, Jackson's preparation, of what was commonly referred to as Chambo, had me forking in gluttonous mouthfuls and returning for more. He served doctored fish, headless boneless fish in a crispy and spicy coating. I found myself passing over the sweet fill of dessert in favor of the rare fill of fish.

Having access to a "vacation" house didn't exactly spoil us, for we rarely had the spare time to make it there. The greatest luxury of the place was its offering of liberation from the eyes of our students and fellow teachers, relief from our responsibilities and their expectations. It was a blessed sabbatical from the stereotype of nunhood. I suppose you could call it "letting our hair down," though none of us had quite enough to do so. Instead, we blatantly flaunted the backs of our knees before the approving sun.

Back in Likuni, I was no more than a gawker myself when nature offered up her own entertaining and fascinating exhibitions free of charge. The atmosphere was downright carnival-like when the yearly flight of Inswa, cicada-like insects, set to swarming: zillions it seemed, surfacing from the ground simultaneously, sprouting wings, and flying about madly for a 24-hour heyday before dropping back to the ground, dead. Their emergence triggered a feasting binge on the annual delicacy.

At the onset of darkness, adults and children alike rushed to gather around any outdoor light bulb they could find, and while swarms of

Inswa buzzed liberated in the glow of it, they proceeded to pick them from the air like flying candy and pop them into their delighted mouths. At dawn everyone scurried about to sweep up the remaining downed corpses for frying. Even within our brick walls, Levison managed to fill a pail's worth to carry back to his family for dinner. Fresh, plucked from the sky hors d'oeuvres were a bit much for me, but I did – before a crowd of curious students intent on sizing up my spunk – crunch down on a sampling of the fried variety: a munching gesture of diplomacy assured to gain me support.

Visually feasting on the human dances of Malawi provided a more acceptable and satisfying fill than the night dance of the Inswa. Though I've forgotten all the names, I ranked the dances of the land as the richest and most vital art form within the country – at least in my eyes. The majority of them were gender specific, choreographed for groups moving to beating drums, sounding whistles, and song. On weekend nights large concentric circles of girls formed around a bonfire on the school field and aligned their bodies in a harmony of gyrating movement – one that appeared simple and understandable in nature, but wasn't. On occasion, when I mustered the nerve to step in among the circle of sure-footed and hip-swinging girls, it was with the comforting certainty that nothing my clumsy body would do could disrupt the rightness of their rhythm. Their dancing spoke a language learned in the womb, and then as babes tied to the undulating backs, hips, and rears of their mothers.

For special occasions, the students from the boys' school came to join in the dancing festivities, injecting thunderbolts of hormonal energy into the night with their gender radiant power. The male dances were both gorgeous and militant, comprised of aggressive gestures coupled with tender sways, the two rubbing together like sticks threatening to ignite. When the boys and the girls danced together it was if the earth had married itself.

After receiving over a year's worth of letters post-marked from Malawi, my mother's abiding hope that I would bolt from Africa and dash back into the loving arms of Erie, Pa. began to fade. If she expected to see me anytime soon, she would have to find another way. I was well into my second year when plans for a family visit were laid like a fresh egg of possibility. Grandma Stephanie was fired-up, ready and eager to cough up the cash to fly my way. She had, after all, ventured on numerous senior bus trips to visit shrines and casinos in the U.S. and Canada. How hard could it be to travel a wee bit further to set eyes on her beloved granddaughter? Letters packed with options, questions, and specifics flew back and forth across the skies with a fiery sense of urgency.

"What about a side trip to Victoria Falls?" I wrote. Two hundred dollars per would buy us airfare, two days and a night at a first class hotel, and all our meals – grossly expensive in my mind, but they were sold on it. The three of them, my mother, my sister, and my grandmother, were booked to spend two weeks in August in my part of Africa, a time of year when neither rain nor temperature would threaten, and when Karen and I would both be absolved from teaching. The Sisters of St. Joseph had come around to effecting what the White Sisters had done, letting go of religious names and antiquated looking habits, so my sister would arrive on the continent as plain ole' papaya juice Karen. Besides a side trip to Victoria Falls, I was advised by those "in the know" to calendar in a trip to the Luangwa Game Reserve located in neighboring Zambia. An animal safari was routinely considered a tourist must do, particularly by tourists and travel agents.

As the family travel plans solidified on paper, an unannounced sentiment proceeded to invade and ruffle me. The bravado I'd long associated with leaving my past behind seemed to soften at its core. The thought of home and family heading my way jolted my heart with a direct bolt of longing.

On her side, Grandma Stephanie was stricken with two formidable problems of her own: 1. Her legs 2. Her passport. Being in her early seventies, she was fixed to legs that acted out against a lousy combination of age, lifestyle, and weight – mobility was priced to pain. As to her passport, she was denied one in a timely manner simply because she'd been born in Poland. The grim pair of obstacles left her absolutely down and grounded while my mother and sister took to the skies, flying towards me. Canceling out Grandma Stephanie from the reunion was rough on the heart, but as the arduous nature of the trip unfolded it turned into something more akin to a blessing in disguise.

I braced myself for setting eyes on my mother and sister for the first time in over two years, mostly because I didn't want to do the unthinkable and cry like a pathetic baby. In…and out…in…and out…lots and lots of deep breathing while I waited at the one and only arrival gate at Lilongwe airport. Then…through a fumed haze…they materialized crossing the tarmac. The three of us wore an identical stunned mask of surprise.

Fortunately, our family nature and training kicked in automatically, allowing each of us to swallow the emotional lump in our throat. In a minute or two or five or ten, we were acting just like we had living together at 3304 Greengarden Blvd. - Erie, Pa. had landed in Malawi. What was totally different, however, was that I was *tangibly* introducing them to my magic kingdom, and to my magical extended family of sisters, friends, teachers, and students. I was *sharing* my private world. Suddenly, I wanted to force feed them with the vividness of the dreamscape that had lured me away from them years ago. I wanted them to savor it, to digest it.

My mother's suitcase was stuffed with goodies, including Manhattan Mix (the traditional family cocktail) and SHAKE 'N BAKE (a new product on the market apparently worth transporting all the way to Africa). News quickly spread to the painted village that Amai Gailo (my Chichewa name) had received "mlendo" (visitors). Within a day of my family's arrival we found our Likuni doorstep heaped with baskets of bounty: groundnuts, eggs, bananas, and, yes, corn. In addition to our treasure trove of food, we were gifted with an authentically rare and priceless offering, something that most veteran missionaries had never been favored to receive: an invitation to attend a village Nyao ceremony.

The Nyao represented a secret society in the central region of the country. Their ceremonies, costumes, and dances revolved around elaborate, dramatic rituals linked to the childhood and adulthood rites of initiation. The Nyao and the early brigade of missionaries had butted heads in their time, each viewing the other as a threat to the well being of their traditions and beliefs. The face off remained until the missionaries inched their way towards enlightenment, learning to respect, if not honor, local customs and native beliefs. Foreigners could witness staged spectacles of Nyao dances performed at massive political rallies. The government framed the performances as a portrait of camaraderie between past traditions and modern progress. But, rare, rare, rare it was for a white skinned missionary woman to be invited to an honest-to-goodness village initiation in the deep, deep, deep spooky black stage of night. The privilege was an undeniable expression of the chief's lingering gratitude and appreciation for his beautified village.

The identities of society members were kept secret. Performers masked themselves with fright provoking costumes made from all sorts of things, such as feathers, hides, grasses, leaves, and paints concocted into terrorizing animal-like imagery. Stories circulated of murder befalling those who dared to divulge the identity of a society member – although the current punishment for such an offense appeared to have softened into a stiff payment of cash/goods to the village chief. Still, few dared to test the watery boundaries of retribution, for it was a well-known fact that Nyao members acting in the throes of dance-induced frenzy were exempt from the laws of the land. The Nyao pumped hot traditional blood into the veins and arteries of the local population, whether they liked it or not.

I didn't know enough to be scared, though others let off a whiff of it on my behalf – out of range from my mother and sister, thankfully. On the designated night, we drove the car and parked it at a respectable distance from the village, walking the rest of the way accompanied by villagers who appeared out of nowhere to escort us into the heart of the night. The village had become "oh, so familiar" to me in daylight, but what I saw now, and what I heard now, caused goose bumps to rise in the chilling heat of the night. In a somewhat expected manner, we were formally welcomed and then escorted to three rickety chairs, but everything else appeared different: the smiles crazier, the whites of eyes wider, the sweat heavier, the entire physical atmosphere tinged explosive.

My heart felt as if it was beating on drums, or was it the drums beating on my heart? The intoxicating tension in the air roused the ole' high school drinker and reckless driver persona right out of me. I tipped the bottle of prevailing threat and chugged a big swig of its honey-coated dare. It egged me on further: I envisioned a make-believe Hollywood movie with three white women from Erie, Pa. being stirred about in a colossal, finely crafted, clay cooking pot. One of the three was proudly spouting off the precise source of the ochre clay used to fashion the vessel of her boiling demise.

Casting a glance in my mother's direction, and noting that she appeared terrified beyond boiling – if that's possible – I reeled my imagination in and focused on the event at hand. Every moment was highlighted with the threat of a maddening frenzy that could easily knock us off our rocker – rickety chair, in our case. The crowds, the dancing, the music, ricocheted between purely beautiful and purely lethal. Frighteningly masked creatures strutted, pounded, and swirled about as a cacophony of whistles, drums, and ululating screams tore through the night. We broke out in a dizzying sweat. After a remarkable stretch of being tauntingly mesmerized by out-of-body fanatic displays and on-body ritual ceremony, we rose from our chairs with an assemblage of weak knees, pounding hearts, and blown minds. We departed the village with a singing escort and all the meat on our bones.

That night clued me in big time as to why many educated and devout Malawian Christians appeared unwilling, or unable, to totally break with the spirit world of their land: it wasn't worth the risk. After witnessing only a single Nyao ceremony on a single dark night, the native beliefs of the land appeared more credible and tangible to me than my own beliefs could ever be.

When dawn broke – so common, so calm – it was all we could do to believe that we hadn't dreamt up the night before. We regained our earthly balance over the next few days, relishing a more routine and sedate side of Likuni life. Then we headed off to sip Manhattans on the shores of Lake Malawi and chow down on Jackson's fried chambo. A bat in my mother's thatched hut caused a bit of a holy ruckus, but otherwise the lake time was mellow time. Next, we boarded a small plane aimed for Victoria Falls. Outside, the glorious misty spray of it doused our skin with exotic splendor, and inside, our semi-deluxe hotel offered a welcome sampling of American-like food. I felt like a tourist in Africa for the very first time. Returning from our pampered jaunt - there was even a casino - we loaded up the car for our safari to Luangwa Game Reserve.

A clear map to where we were heading was hard to find – the tourist brochure described the Zambian road to the reserve as "corrugated." As an experienced in the know driver, I stocked up on spare tires and extra petrol, preparing for no help along the way. Off we embarked on a seven – or who knew for sure how many – hour drive to witness animals living in the wild. My mother held close to zero affection for animals, harboring humongous fear of any and all types regardless of size or temperament. As for insects, she detested them at a percentage rate bordering the infinite. She braved coming to Africa for a glimpse of me, plain and simple. I couldn't for the life of me comprehend why she agreed to include a game reserve along with me. The touristy mind and pressure of an enthusiastic travel agent is all I could think of - unless, it was fear of disappointing me. I was arranging the adventure for them, but they might have been arranging it for me. Regardless, my mother's stoic bravery over the next few days ranked right up there with her long ago domestic bravery: getting out of bed each and every morning to face three children, alone. Alone was a different kind of beast, worse perhaps. You couldn't shoot it if you had to. In Africa I was proud of my mother's guts in a way that I didn't know enough to be in Erie, Pa.

Still driving, the sun began to sink while each of us silently feared that we would never reach our destination along the corrugated road that had eroded into much less than that. There were no signs anywhere – I felt so helplessly American expecting them. But we couldn't have been *lost* lost because it appeared that we were on the one and only road leading anywhere. Then, just like hard to find salvation, an all-too-easy-to-miss marker with the word "Luangwa" in small and chipped print peeked out from under a tree branch. A turn down a narrowing path, along with a few more miles, deposited us in front of a thatched structure serving as a dining hall for a dozen or more guests.

Despite the overhead fan, properly set tables, a bar with a minimum array of liquor bottles, and service-with-a-smile attendants, there was little visual doubt that we were in the thick of the animal kingdom. Confirmation sounded through guttural moans and shrieks cutting through the darkness, and with a troop of monkeys alternately lounging and banging on the rooftop and hood of our car parked alongside our sleeping bungalow.

At the cusp of dawn we rubbed our sleep crusted eyes, opening them to hippos – semi-submerged like perfectly spaced jumping rocks – bathing in the river running no more than twenty yards beyond us. We dressed quickly for our first open jeep excursion, though my mother had already witnessed enough wildlife to warrant heading straight back to the tamer fright of mission life in Likuni.

Jostling about in true safari-like fashion, we hit the bumps and battled the dust, aiming in the direction of an area best known for early morning lion spotting. One guide was armed with binoculars and the other with a rifle. We came to a stop and sat patiently and quietly behind tall grasses, looking and/or being looked at. *"There! Left, ahead!"* The driver gassed the jeep, taking a sharp and speedy turn over a tall bump that would have tossed me into the grass had not the arms of someone – or two – grabbed onto me with a grip like love. We hung tight as a family while chasing after lions.

After scouting about on the dry and open plains with limited success, we edged our way into denser territory, coming upon a herd of elephants blocking the two-tire trail before us. "Cool!!!" I let out excitedly, but our rifleman quieted me and turned all business. I thought that a good honk or two of the horn would encourage the herd to courteously divide – the parting of the elephants – making way for us to ride between them in all our white glory, waving, snapping photos, and oohing and aahing over the cuteness of the babes. Instead, we kept our distance and sat motionless, waiting frozen until the herd got around to budging their bulk in their own sweet lumbering time. A gun was positioned and ready, but the elephants called the shots. The largest elephant of the herd, lolling about dead center on our path, kept an ancient looking eye fixed on us, as the others chomped complacently on leaves from upper branches, daring us to move closer to the thick and wrinkled tonnage of any one of them. Once they ate the area clean, they moseyed on, as did we, heading back to a breakfast worthy of great white hunters. Later in the day, Karen and I the mounted the jeep for the dusk excursion, but my mother bowed out, opting for the gauzy protection of her mosquito net.

The second day's schedule was much like the first: animal spotting, I mean, attempted animal spotting. After breakfast on the third morning we cleared our windshield of monkey doo and drove out to connect with the corrugated road heading home. Since we were now aimed towards a town, as opposed to a game reserve, I circumvented any potential border problems by volunteering to cram the car full with Zambian or Malawian travelers hunting for a free lift to Lilongwe. It ranked as common courtesy to pick up travelers along the way, but under the circumstances I would've preferred to take a pass. But I didn't dare. So, on we rode, jostling about in cramped silence, our new passengers clearly wary of sharing a cage with a trio of dishwater blondes.

Unlike the customary slow moving pace of Malawian time, the family visit time seemed to speed by in a few blinks. Two going-away dinners were planned: one hosted by my mother in appreciation for the sisters' hospitality, and the other reversely hosted by my Likuni community in farewell. Mom treated a group totaling seven, including her and Karen, to dinner at Chang's, a Chinese restaurant situated among Lilongwe's main strip of shops. The seven of us spent giddy hours fumbling with chopsticks and sampling ongoing courses of food that threatened to never end. After multiple rounds of beer and sake, the bill was served up: under fifty bucks for the seven of us, including drinks and a sizable tip. Sooo cheap, my mother thought! "Ten months allowance," I gasped!

Our in-house farewell was orchestrated far more cheaply, but it was special, nonetheless, for we procured a chicken to wear the SHAKE 'N BAKE. Chicken rarely made it to our table. And, when we did get our hands on one, it often looked decrepit – barely capable of emitting anything resembling flavor from its aged out flesh. For this occasion, however, Sr. Annette managed to round up a rather feisty looking bird to bring home, chop its head off, pluck its feathers, gut it, and hack it into pieces. Then she turned it over to me to coat with the magic seasoning from afar. I did my job and set the tray of chicken pieces aside on the counter, all seasoned and ready for baking upon our return from Sunday Mass.

We walked to the mission church and entered in among throngs of parishioners, squeezing our rear ends onto hard plank benches spaced so closely together that bony kneecaps poked at our backs. No matter how many people settled snugly onto a bench, bottoms continued to inch in tighter and tighter to accommodate just one more, just one more. Many, if not most, women arrived with infants strapped to their backs, meaning, resting all but in the lap of the person directly behind. Flies outnumbered the congregants four to one, lighting on eyelids, nose tips, and ears as accustomed to their presence as to their own dark skin. Only we foreigners shooed them away like lunatics.

After the liturgy ended, I walked my family past the school for the last time, attempting to keep my thoughts focused on nothing heavier than SHAKE 'N BAKE. As I entered the back door to our matchbox-sized kitchen, I instantly noted the color change: the chicken pieces looked blackened! Comprehending immediately, I employed my body to shield the chicken from sight as I hustled my mother and sister into the next room. I hurried to dunk the chicken pieces in water and wash away the zillions of black ants feasting on imported spices. Lifting skin and wing folds, I eliminated as many clingy specks as I could in the few minutes given me before Karen walked in and spotted ants crawling up my arms. I released a quietly hysterical laugh and swore her to secrecy while continuing my ant picking. Around the dinner table everyone delivered bon voyage toasts and then delved into the chicken. My mother was quizzical as to the SHAKE 'N BAKE flavoring, but Karen and I said we tasted it just fine.

If you're thinking that it was dumb of me to have left the chicken on the counter in the first place - particularly after my Pogo experience - well, we commonly left food there. Our refrigerator was small, and the counter was, in fact, the only place in the kitchen where ants didn't tend to congregate. The allure of America was obviously too much for them.

By the time we arrived at the airport the following morning we were emotional basket cases woven taut in small talk and denial. Then…I broke…crying into my mother and she into me; tears from a complex mix of loss that had taken nine plus years to well up and spill over. We huddled together in an emotionally naked moment more foreign to us than all of Africa put together. It happened in the last three minutes of their two-week stay, just before they had to board the plane and fly away from me. Thank God it was in the last three minutes.

....

I wished that the plague of my body's desire could board a plane and fly away from me, along with that sinful, vile sounding word that summed up the act of pleasuring one's self. I couldn't take it any longer, living day in and day out burdened with the shame and temptation of my physical needs slowly eating away at me and rendering me unworthy of the life I professed to live - or so I believed. There was only one person I dared to confide such thoughts to: Sr. Felicia.

Mustering up all my courage, I told her that I needed to talk to her. I was overwrought. It was *urgent*! From the sound of my desperation she must have feared the worst – whatever that might've been – so her face reclined with sheer relief when the tepid nature of my sin poured forth. With reassuring calm and a twinkling kindness in her eyes she reiterated a variation of what she had said to me years ago when addressing my adoring crush on her: "You are fine. You are okay. You are normal." As before, her words stroked me with comfort, but they weren't strong enough to topple the menacing convictions built from the ground up upon the vibes of my mother, the death of my father, the taboos of the Catholic Church, and my conflicted mind – all housed in the shell of my shameful Polish self. When the door to understanding was cracked open for me, my private imprisonment slammed it shut.

In my fraught state of mind I struggled with meditation, turning it briefer and blanker; sometimes, I postponed the daily exercise to later in the day, and then feigned forgetfulness of the time owed. My prayer efforts grew lazy, succumbing to the more tactile allure and occupation of physical existence. And, while turmoil between faith and body threatened my Likuni paradise – like thunder on a sunny day – an additional wave of dark clouds formed in the distance and winds kicked up mightily blowing them my way.

Sr. Fernande, the school's Headmistress, had served as a beloved friend to me during our years together, but the school was due to switch over to African leadership; and, besides, Fernande's health needed attention. The combination ensured her a one-way ticket back to Canada and a prolonged absence from Africa. Fernande's departure from our tight and companionable living group was as subtle as an earthquake. The five of us lived life as equals, but four of us knew, even if she didn't, that Fernande was our mortar.

Ironically, the job would go to Sr. Perpetua – the one I had instructed so diligently on the ways of life in St. Louis – who was back in her homeland, all ready and willing to become Headmistress of the school. The giant spinning globe of my grade school world was looking more and more like a ping-pong ball in my present life. Though Perpetua's words were gracious and grateful in tone when officially assuming leadership of the school our congregation had run to date, her first official act launched like a spear aimed at my heart. We, our remaining community of four, could continue teaching at the school, but we could not continue to occupy housing among the Malawian faculty. There was no longer room for us. We had to move elsewhere, and there was no "elsewhere" in Likuni.

With her deep gratitude we were evicted. Two lumps of poverty rose in my throat: poverty of home and poverty of spirit. We had no choice but to move into the Provincial House in Lilongwe, where we were permitted to section off a small wing and maintain our independence as a mini-community within the larger community. From there I would commute to school – an inconvenient drive that wasn't so long as it was painful, a daily journey entailing a daily goodbye. Being uprooted from a home that was not mine, but *felt* like mine, wilted me to the core, unlike my other home departure. My transplant survival looked iffy to everyone who laid eyes on me.

As foreigners went, only Mrs. Babhuta, a veteran teacher from India, and yours truly wound up maintaining full-time teaching positions. The school would sway to rhythms that my hips – even swinging full steam ahead with effort – could not pretend to follow. Yes, gratitude existed for all the White Sisters had contributed over decades to establishing quality schooling within the country, but the past was past. Present focus rested on what the Malawians, themselves, could and would accomplish with pride moving ahead. The displaced feeling that I commuted with resulted, precisely, from our own proclaimed mission to work ourselves out of a job. I couldn't really blame anyone, so why did it feel so personal?...Why was I so miserable?...Was I just not up to swallowing the full price tag of poverty?...Chastity?...Obedience?

We established our displaced community in the right wing of the house. An interior wall and door were built into the corridor to section us off. An exterior door at the opposite end gave us access to the drive in front of the house. Behind these two defining doors I was in the throes of a private mini-breakdown that had puddled me into one massive glob of sadness. One night, while alone in our wing – the others were off on some sort of overnight business – I was awakened after midnight by a closing car door followed by an insistent rap on our outside door. Peeking out the kitchen window, charged with the type of fear that comes with nighttime knocking, I saw a moonlit Pierre. More knocking...more forceful. He was very nicely dressed. I suddenly remembered that some sort of embassy party was taking place in town that night. I felt that it might be for me – the knocking, I mean – but I didn't move, breathe, or swallow. Maybe he was banging from too much partying, too much wine, and all that. Maybe he was clueless as to the hour. Not until an engine roared and lurched away, did I dare to move an inch of me. Why was Pierre at the door? What could have compelled him to knock so hard and so late? In the daylight of our next encounter I never asked and he never offered. Even now, I still wonder. All I know for certain about that night is that I didn't dare crack open a door to the vulnerable mess of me.

....

Anyone who stepped into the main entrance of Likuni Hospital came face to face with a wall of brightly painted murals painted by, none other than, me. And anyone who walked into the lobby of the newly constructed hotel, situated in the newly developed government district of the capital city of Lilongwe, arrived face to face with a larger than life-size sculpture in plaster sculpted by, none other than, me. In the center of the school courtyard students daily milled around a three-piece stone carving carved by, yes, me. My footprints – executed in color, in plaster, in stone – were scattered about like an open diary of my presence on the land. All available space within our community wing acquiesced to accommodating dozens of wood and soapstone carvings chiseled and polished over my three years of life in Malawi.

While attending a July 4th celebration at the American Embassy, a distinguished looking man inquired about all this art of mine. Next thing I knew, I was orchestrating my first-ever solo exhibit to be held on the Embassy grounds. For weeks I rather pleasantly distracted my body and mind with polishing, waxing, titling, and pricing in Kwacha, each and every piece of my rather extensive body of work. Right in the midst of my exhibit preparations, Sr. Marie José D'or – still Mother Superior to our flock – arrived in Lilongwe to assess the scope of our mission work, and meet personally with each and every sister serving in the region. For me this equated to a one-on-one conference with God for the second time in my life. My mind and stomach churned in curdy anticipation, for I knew she'd want an answer as to why I hadn't formally requested to profess my final vows after so many years within the Congregation. You see, I'd been *renewing* my temporary vows annually for seven years now: a length of time considered to be beyond "temporary" - four years was about average for the term. While her eyes pinned me down, troublesome questions would surely pour out in beautifully accented tones, boiling down to, "*Why Sr. Gail? Why?*" And Amai Gailo would have no clear answer.

Sitting in front of her, once again in awe of every square inch of her Belgian frame, she threw me for a loop by opening her mouth to talk art. The subject shouldn't have struck me as sooo surprising given that she was the one who had steered me into it, but it was, nonetheless. She appeared genuinely impressed with the stockpile of work she'd seen lying about. She looked proud and satisfied – like she had bet on the right horse. There were other sisters within the Congregation who displayed a range of artistic abilities, but in her way of seeing and appraising, I exhibited a higher grade of talent, the sort of God-given gift that demanded being put to good use. Though far less convinced of her assessment, I inflated on the spot, filling with the lovely air of her belief in me. Before me sat my spiritual mother, all bent on praising my earthly talent.

Naturally, the topic of vows did come up, and when it did it became painfully clear that I had far less to say about vows than I did about art. Knocking me off kilter for a second time, Marie José threw out a completely unexpected proposal: participate in the Juniorate year scheduled to commence in Toulouse, France. The Juniorate was designed to provide a year of spiritual renewal to those nearing the decade mark in religious life. It was credited as a spiritual pick-me-up course for most, but in my case it would offer time to ponder and discern my future: God's will. The thought of departing Malawi for a year made her proposal land like a hammerhead on my soul. "Reflect on it," she said. But I knew that her suggestion was voiced as a plan. Obedience knocked. Again.

After her departure I semi-robotically carried on with the routine work of waxing and polishing my wares for their first ever showing. The exhibit was just around the corner so I was temporarily blinded to anything and everything else about me and around me. On the given day, the exhibit opened to a reception of Malawian and expatriate dignitaries strolling the lawns, nibbling hors d'oeuvres, sipping cocktails, and expressing approval – sometimes admiration for my accomplishments. Attending Malawians marveled that work exuding such African soul could have emanated from the all white hands of a young American woman. The pieces sold like candy, and given that my two suitcases could hold none of them, divesting myself in such grandiose fashion seemed acceptable. Until…I woke the next morning to the feeling of having been stark naked robbed the night before. I had nothing left to wax and polish, I had nothing left to show for myself, I had nothing left.

Logical and rational thinking seemed to have escaped through a hole in my head. I turned to desperate, begging prayer: "Give me the light of clarity, *please!*" Looking in the mirror I discovered a 29-year-old version of me worn thin from internal turmoil. Each day I woke with, and each day I ended with, *"Help me!"* glued like a prayer upon my lips. But I wasn't sure to whom I was praying anymore, who existed out there to help me? Maybe my plea was directed to everyone and anyone who had ever thought to love me. Maybe I was crying out to them. Maybe.

Then…I opened my eyes one morning to a vision of calm and irrefutable clarity rising before me. I hadn't made my final vows because I *couldn't* make my final vows. I *couldn't* make my final vows because my faith fell short in everything my beloved sisters so fervently believed in. Their minds and souls seemed able to navigate, or circumvent, doubt with a faith far more skilled and developed than mine. It was my relentless love for community life, my sisters, and the mission of the Congregation that anchored my dedication and devotion. It was not my faith. I was not married to God, I was married to them, and I didn't know how to reverse the order of my love.

It became crystal clear to me that I could not stand among women I respected with something close to adoration while being an inferior witness to their beliefs. I couldn't defile their purity of purpose by pretense; I couldn't be a phony among them. There was plenty that I considered impure about myself, but my love for them did not rank among that plenty. It was quite the opposite: my love for them ushered me to the door. Leaving them was the god-awful price I would have to pay for the clarity I had begged for.

It was to the beat of a death march that I, once again, made my way to Felicia's room. This time my words rang out with finality, they did not trickle out gingerly:

"I'm leaving the Congregation. I have to. Will you let Marie José know my decision?"

Felicia had a long history of reading me, at the sight of me, at the sound of me, she was convinced beyond a doubt that I *knew* what I knew. Over the next several days not one sister thought to challenge my decision, for everyone knew that the last thing on earth I wanted to do was leave them and leave Malawi. It was clear to all that only direct intervention from God could have led me to such a devastating plan of action.

My departure was arranged as quickly as possible, not to prolong the agony of it – as if speed and efficiency could do that. Students, teachers, and inquisitive others were left to believe that I was embarking on a year of study abroad; only my sisters knew the truth of it. Many of us were wept dry by the time Felicia and I headed for the airport on the very last of my last days. I walked out onto the tarmac runway and placed one foot on the bottom step of the plane's drop-down staircase – the second foot refused. I looked down at the dusty worn shoe cradling that second foot and wished it to stay put.

When the second foot finally lifted with the weight of the world from the ground of my heart, I thought I would die.

BOOK THREE

CHAPTER 12. LIFE B.C.

Life Beyond the Convent lingered at the threshold before crossing over. From Malawi I flew to Italy, making my way to the motherhouse in Frascati to finalize the details of my departure, but one look at me told anyone with seeing eyes that I could go no further. Not yet. I needed time to pull myself together in every way imaginable, so I paused there for two weeks in a comforting, yet almost pathetic state of clutching to the threads of everything I was about to forsake. I was still referred to as Sister and treated like a sister, but I didn't know how to act anymore, how to be. Tears were my normalcy: crying morning, noon, and night. The hearts of those around me ached at the sight of me, for each and every one of them had paid the price of the Lord's calling; they knew the wrenching cost of obedience and honesty. As women of great faith they believed for me and in me, assuring me that that I was walking in the light despite the darkness in my heart, for clarity lit my way no further than showing me the door.

In the presence of Sr. Marie José D'or – for the last time – I recounted for her the morning upon which I woke to the epiphany of my own departure. Marie José had no doubt that my crystallized awakening had come from a finger tap from God upon my shoulder, but she generously offered me an alternative hope to cling to: "Sister, if your path circles back to us, you will always be welcome." The word "welcome" hung in the air like a possibility in the face of my departure. Cradling that one word, I exited the room of the woman who had so thoughtfully guided my life, the woman I knew, only, as my superior caretaker.

Penniless, I could get nowhere, so I paid a visit to our Bursar's office. Sr. Bursar inquired as to what I thought my immediate needs might be? Her question left me bewildered by the word "need," and how it might translate into purely material terms. Noting the income generated from my recent sculpture sales at the American Embassy, she suggested turning the proceeds over to me for the start my new life. With approximately $1,800 and the word "welcome" banked in my heart, I ended a decade of life with the White Sisters of Africa and stepped out into the secular world.

....

I had written to my family informing them of my decision to leave the convent, but I shared nothing of my torturous decision-making process, offering up only that I was leaving because I didn't think I could pledge a lifetime to the cause. In pure Soliwoda fashion, no one probed any further. As well as believing that her prayers had *finally* been answered, my mother was beyond thrilled that I would return home in time for Tim's wedding. I arrived in Erie, Pa. to find my little brother 24 years old and more foreign than ever. However, the timing of his wedding turned out to be a serendipitous gift to me: it kept the focus off of me. The last thing I wanted were eyes directed at my phony smiling face.

Familiarity of place and family both offered tinges of comfort, but not enough to hold me for long. Before setting foot on Greengarden Blvd., I knew that I couldn't and wouldn't stay – Mongolia or Mars maybe, but not Erie, Pa. I made it perfectly clear upon my arrival that I was on a stopover visit. The full truth was that it was one more first aid station, but I stayed mum on that part. My stopover declaration implied that I had somewhere to go, which I didn't, so when pressed I was forced to improvise on the spot, concocting a destination. "St. Louis" rolled off my tongue, almost like a physical saint to the rescue. "Yeah…I'm returning to St. Louis to live…study, I mean…because…well, naturally, I want to continue with art." And I guessed on the spot that it was all true. What else was there to consider? My mother was sooooo happy to have me back safe and sound from the wiles of Africa that St. Louis sounded like no more than a hop across the boulevard. She was the only one who had planned for this day, having set up small bank accounts for both Karen and me in the event that we one day came to our senses and abandoned religious life for an earthly life. From her hope-filled account she handed me a check for $3,000 – an expression of her bankable love. Mentally, I allocated the money to my freshly conceived college fund. Fontbonne was starting an M.F.A. graduate program in another year. I could be first in line for an advance degree in sculpture. *Abracadabra!* I had a place to go and a path to follow.

My three weeks in Erie, Pa. entailed two things: 1. Faking happiness – a performance more exhausting than I remembered. (Though faking wasn't necessary when I set eyes on Grandma Stephanie; when she uttered "whichamacallit" I beamed!) 2. Contacting my old Fontbonne Professor, Mr. Torrini, and Annie, a college friend and classmate, to help me arrange the particulars of my new life. Annie offered me a room in her parents' house until I could get my feet planted, and Mr. T offered me use of the sculpture studio while waiting for the graduate program to start. With that sketchy outline of a future I headed west to St. Louis, Mo. – a secular pioneer this time, no missionary.

Culture shock attacked upon arrival. I hadn't suffered from it in Africa, but here, in supposed familiarity, it knocked my worn socks off. It surfaced like a quaking, widening split between my two feet, here and there, here and there. When my left foot adjusted, the gap followed; if I hopped back on the right foot, the gap hopped too – zigzag-zigzag – that's how I walked – zigzag-zigzag. Things were familiar to me, people were familiar…its just that I wasn't familiar to me. I was a zigzagging 29-year-old single woman. My last single woman steps had been taken when I was nineteen; my gait and my agility had atrophied. In the past decade, the majority of my high school friends had married, birthed children, bought homes, and joined PTA's; they were settled in that normal, accepted, and belonging sort of way. Their settling was likely prefaced with a period of freedom to experiment, date, party, and develop through trial and error into social and sexual adult beings. For the rewards of my own decade past, I had forsaken such a period. Now, I felt fearful that I was too old or crippled to achieve the mix of blending and belonging that they had earned for themselves. With so many cracks beneath my feet, much of all that I had buried soon rose to the surface in search of a fresh watering: patient, ever-green, and invasive choke weeds anxious to perform.

The culture shocked me with a different prick of pain when I spied excesses of material goods everywhere I turned. People had so much *stuff* and grocery stores had so much *food!* I took to strolling the aisles of a nearby grocery with my lips parted, taking in what I saw and feeling sated from the sight alone. The enormous variety was baffling and disturbing to me; the multitude of choices made me feel stupid again – out of my league in both familiarity and price. So, I bought corn. Also, I got a job there checking and bagging the parade of groceries, toiletries, cleaners, booze, cigarettes, etc. conveyed my way. I evaluated each customer by their purchases, speculating on everything from cavities to faith to alcoholism. Groups of jovial firemen frequently sauntered in, setting off heart-stopping alarms in only me.

After closing time on Friday and Saturday nights I worked late hours re-stocking, since I had no life waiting for me. The Saturday night shift offered the perk of radically discounted meat and produce, due to grocery stores being closed on Sundays. I could check out a giant bag of wilting greens and a jumbo pack of need-to-cook-in-a-hurry pork neck bones for next to nothing, leaving me enough money for a $2.99 gallon jug of Vintner's Choice wine to help quench my loneliness and usher me to a bed of dreams.

Thanks to Mr. T, who came to my rescue by co-signing a lease, I now inhabited my own matchbox-size apartment. Alone, I didn't have enough relevant financial history to begin to fill out an application. Folks were fascinated when I explained *why* so much was left blank on the application, but only that: fascinated. Rejection kept on coming until Mr. T came to the rescue.

Throughout the disheartening ordeal of apartment hunting, Grandpa Poplaski kept coming into my mind. How had he managed to make his way from Poland at 14 years of age all alone and with no one to turn to for any help whatsoever? How had he done it? I fell into a state of nostalgia at times, reminiscing over his late night slurred monologues and the smell of his boozy breath hovering over my very young cheeks. "You be a good gir!"

To fill my tiny apartment, I scavenged for concrete blocks and scrap wood to make shelves and tables. The contribution (from whom I don't remember) of a set of old twin beds, one to sleep on and the other to convert into a sofa, pretty much filled the place. The amount of stuff I managed to salvage in the alleys of St. Louis was mind-blowing. Draping a cloth chitenje (with the smiling face of Ngwazi Dr. H. Kamuzu Banda) over my makeshift kitchen tabletop saved me the cost of paint.

Resourcefulness came easily to me; piecing together a structure to call home was a project I could handle. More importantly, it kept me busy, which I desperately needed to be. Anyway, *things* weren't what I needed most.

When not at work at the grocery store, or outfitting my apartment, I hung out at the sculpture studio after classes vacated the space. Working by my lonesome, I attempted to give shape to images incubating in my mind, images that I couldn't find words for any more than I could find words for my own predicament. As before, female figures emerged from the explorations of my hands, but they surfaced fragmented, gashed at the breasts and abdomen, swollen in places, and disjointed in others – yet the heads remained mostly regal, close to African. Sunday mornings also found me in the studio, for I'd stopped going to Mass, although I wasn't entirely sure why. But, in my own way, I continued to pray because I needed to stay connected to the thought that what I was doing mirrored God's will and not some mortal mistake of my own doing. Though tender to the core, my divorce from the person of Jesus remained amicable; after all, there was nothing to fight over, no kids, no property, no cheating… just the hurt of rejection to cope with. Surely he could have spared me the necessary faith if he had *wanted* me! This rub of a notion sat on a back burner in me, until it eventually simmered into resentment, and then slow-boiled into a bubbling cynicism that came to permanently scar my thinking on the church, faith, and the all-around existence of God. Guess that's why I stopped going to church.

Stopping was no small thing, however. I had been raised on a steady diet of Catholic ritual. There were two Catholic Churches in the vicinity of Grandma and Grandpa Poplaski's house when I was growing up. When I woke at their house on a Sunday morning, Grandpa Alex often took me with him to the ten o'clock Mass at St. Patrick's, the farthest away of the two. He chose to go there because it was closest to the Polish Falcons club – a follow-up stop as routine as our Sunday devotions. Most of the men in the neighborhood belonged to the club. They gathered there to drink, play cards, and do whatever else they could do to relieve the monotonous stress of their work-a-day and home lives. From "Ite, Missa est" and "Deo Gratias" we made a beeline to the bar before noon. "Go, the Mass is ended" was not meant to direct us to the bar, but "Thanks be to God" was what we felt when entering the bar.

It was dim and laden with smoky air, the bar, rejecting the pure quality of Sunday morning light. Usually, only a handful of men gathered there at this early time of the day – I never saw another kid; "I" was, obviously, special. Grandpa propped me on a twirling barstool, my legs dangling free, as I ordered my standard: "Orange pop and popcorn, please." What a great moment! Almost in unison, the men about me would chime in: "Well, isn't she just the cutest…" They treated me like a princess and gazed at me with crinkled eyes of adoration, as if my presence forgave them for plopping themselves at a bar on a Sunday morning. Grandpa doted on me with boozy affection on these occasions, feeling even more redeemed than the others, since I belonged to him. He ordered a Seven & Seven, clinked glasses and declared: "Nosdrovia!" – cheers all around! Roundabout one o'clock, we meandered gaily back to the house in anticipation of a fine Sunday meal. But, catching sight of grandma's body language made me cringe and sober up - it was reddish hot and screaming, despite her icy silence. Grandpa and I clung to each other as we passed her by. We were a tight team on those Seven & Seven/orange pop Sunday mornings.

On weekend evenings Grandpa frequented the Polish Falcons with his friends, no me in tow. I, sometimes both my sister and I, stayed back at the house with Grandma. We made ourselves comfy in the living room, watching TV or playing a game of cards with Grandma – she loved to play cards. Later, Karen and I usually wound up dozing off on opposite ends of the sofa with the TV gone staticky for the night. Grandpa would return late in the night, or early in the morning, with a ruddy smile plastered on his face and a wobble to his step.

For a silent man with halting English, he turned talkative when he saw us, his angels, sound asleep on the sofa. Nudging us awake he beckoned us into his lap, which he collapsed into a stuffed armchair. A serious talk was in order right then and there, mindless of the hour or our tender age. His impromptu lecture was always the same: earnest words repeated and mixed with whiskey breath circling our captive sleepy faces. "You…must be good girl…must be good girl….no trouble…..no get in trouble…." We cuddled on his lap, but jerked our heads reflexively back when spit flew out, which it always did. Into the teary gaze of his reddened eyes, we pledged: "Yes Grandpa, we promise we'll be good girls."

Right about then, Grandma would appear on the creaky stairs in curlers and full fury, shouting out what must have been a stream of Polish swear words and yanking us away from the grip of his inebriation. I was never quite certain whether I wanted to be rescued or I wanted to stay swallowed up in the moment. Grandpa protested our abduction with hostile snarls directed like daggers at Grandma as she whisked us away under the clutch of her heavy wings.

And so it went – another sort of ritual. I would come again, and it would happen again. I would come again, and it would happen again. I did not find fault in my grandpa's behavior. Even if I had, I would have forgiven him, just like I had forgiven Grandma for hiding the letters to Grandpa. Fair is fair.

Grandma preferred going right around the corner to St. Hedwig's Church, and I accompanied her there at times, as well. We would attend an early morning service in Polish. Polish, Latin…no dif to me! It was mostly the heavy-duty smells of incense and the hocus-pocus stuff that captured my interest. I mimicked everyone devoutly: stand, kneel, the Sign of the Cross, closed eyes during a long sermon… However, Church with Grandma in the harsh cold of winter offered up the sensual satisfaction of snuggling close to fur, my hands busy pawing and petting my grandmother's coat rather than folded in prayer.

She had two furs: a full-length fur coat and a smallish shoulder fur. The shawl-like fur was made up of a combination of four critters – minks, I guess? The four little guys (or gals) were stitched and clipped together, each contributing to the length needed to wrap around a grown woman's shoulders and fasten into place, making a furry wrap with eyeballs and heads. Tiny snouts, previously effective choppers, were relegated to grabbers. *Press* and the jaw opened wide, latching onto another paw or tail. This is a pretty accurate description because Grandma's fur piece is sitting in my lap as I write about it; it's been tucked in my closet for close to 35 years now. I stopped petting it – her – long ago, but I can't let go of the critters…can't entirely let go of her.

In place of church, of Catholicism, I substituted Sculpturism: my own religion of form, ritual, and space. The only way I could survive the sea of my displacement was to lose myself in the search for a new creation, attempting to compose and assemble forms that aligned perfectly and beautifully – totally unlike myself. Dusting off my old art diaries, I found them scrawled full with images, thoughts, considerations, and desperate attempts at divining direction.

"Sever from the known form, but make it accepted and understood at

a glance. Recognition can be conveyed through an unknown form…it can identify itself by the *feeling* it conveys….like an awkward grace."
"The gesture must become a real figure and a figure must become a real gesture."
"Absolutely nothing must distract from the whole. The slightest thing must be essential….punctuate and clump forms into secondary areas serving the whole. Sacrifice *everything* for the whole."

My struggles and efforts continued to fall short, leaving me feeling destitute inside and out. My former high school confidante and friend – still a Sister of St. Joseph, though I now addressed her as Barbara – was studying in Chicago around this time. Hearing near despair in my voice over the phone, she intervened with a dose of her comforting presence. Again, I leaned on her for survival. I leaned and clung for all I was worth. Unknown to me, she'd voiced her concerns to my mother who, likewise, responded by hopping in the car and driving to St. Louis with my stepfather for a surprise visit to assess my condition with her very own eyes. My rooted instinct to protect her from all harm remained intact, so upon seeing the surprise of her face at my door, I flashed nothing but smiles and cheeriness, making her wonder what all the fuss was about. They drove down in Mom's old, gold Plymouth Valiant, having decided to leave it behind for me as a transportation consolation prize. After feeling assured of my mental health for a few days they flew home.

The gold Valiant served its purpose for roughly four months, until, idling at a red light one winter's day, the bottom dropped off (the axle was a big part of it) with a devastating metal "kerplunk!" The sound of it seriously freaked me out! Peering down at the slushy road beneath my suspended driver's foot, I broke into defeated sobs. The car's kerplunk felt so wretchedly personal – a symbol of so much more than ravenous rust.

With the aid of sympathetic bystanders, I maneuvered what remained of the car to the side of the road and walked home. The pot holed, icy and salted roads of Erie, Pa. had taken a toll on the car's frame, boring through it with rust hungry cancer – no one had suspected it had so little time left to it. With my fingers doing the walking, I found a cash-for-junk type of ad in the Yellow Pages, and with a phone call I exchanged my mother's consolation prize for $50 in cash. The cash got me a new pair of boots for walking my way through the remainder of a long and bleak winter and pocket change.

As the seasons weathered on in their orchestrated ways, the official start of the graduate program arrived, re-kindling in me the hope of belonging to some*thing*, if not some*one*. I finagled a teaching assistantship in drawing to contribute further to paying down my tuition. Between full-time classes, teaching, and checking groceries I had considerably less time left for lolling about on my dreary fire escape landing with a tall glass of my jug wine, morosely pining for Malawi and my White Sister family. Along with the welcome familiarity of studio classes, the intimidating, arrogant male of my Fontbonne undergrad past reappeared with an unwelcome familiarity. In déjà vu mode, he made a beeline for the sculpture studio he had previously reigned over. Following graduation, he'd gone off and married a fellow student, but according to him, they were now separated. She was in Hawaii, where they'd been living for the past year. He seemed back to roost.

One afternoon there was a startling and determined knock on my apartment door. The peephole configured none other than him in the circle with a chain saw in hand. True, there were times when I felt miserable enough to quit on life, but a chain saw ending troubled me. Though perpetually fierce looking in demeanor, he was a mumbler. He commenced to mumble something to the effect that he was there to lend me his saw; it might help with my latest woodcarving project. He guaranteed that it would save me tons of time and effort in the blocking-out stage of the carving process. This gesture was akin to the Lone Ranger lending Tonto, or Roy Rogers lending Trigger; a chain saw was personal to a sculptor, treasured. His massive man body coupled with the monster chain saw ate up the entire space of what I referred to as my living room. He insisted on demonstrating its use, but one lift of it from me confirmed that, even with my above-average female strength, I would quite likely kill myself with it. Blushing wildly, I thanked him for the kind offer and shooed him and his petrol-smelling tool out the door as fast as I could. He had a history of rattling me on the surface, but his stab at thoughtfulness extended it deeper.

With classes and such providing a meaningful reason to get out of bed in the morning, I eased my way into a more bearable, almost satisfying groove. My professors' yuckity-yuck nun jokes of years ago morphed into Polish jokes, the kind my mother could never really laugh at, but I could.

A Polish immigrant went to the Division of Motor Vehicles to apply for a driver's license. First, of course, he had to take an eyesight test. The optician showed him a card with the letters CZWIXNOSTACZ. "Can you read this?" the optician asked. "Read it?" the Polish guy replied, "I know the guy!"

....

One of my first bona fide social invitations was to attend Hank and Bonita's wedding reception – Hank was one of my past and present sculpture professors. Attending required that I mingle among an eclectic and artsy group of revelers. Some acquaintances of mine decided that the occasion provided the perfect opportunity for ex-Sister Gail to meet a nice fellow - "fixing up" the ex-nun was something worth taking bets on. So, that's how I met Joe: a witty, rather charming, intelligent teacher type. We chatted together while sipping a few plus drinks, and at the end of the reception he offered to drive me home. Though I wasn't quite sure how the heist would go, I suspected that in agreeing to the ride I was agreeing to lose my 29-year-old virginity that very night, on the lumpy twin bed in my matchbox apartment, to a man I had just met. At this point in my life virginity sat like a roadblock to being "like" other women my age. "Roadblock, be gone!" It felt crucial, in a life and death kind of way, that the roadblock be removed before I turned 30, but if I had thought to pre-arrange the heist, I would have been vomiting with apprehension. It was the spontaneity of it all, along with the cocktails, that tossed me into an "Oh, what the hell!" frame of mind that night. In the end, it didn't actually come off as robbery since Joe asked politely and I responded by nudging him towards my virgin bedroom.

The specifics of the act itself remain, gratefully, blurred and filed under "Lost" in my memory-bank. Whether I enjoyed it, studied it, or endured it, I don't recall for certain, but I choose to believe that I performed my part "well enough" because Joe remained clueless to the fact that he had bedded a virgin that night. I startled him with the news a couple of days later. Soon after, he appeared at my door with a quaint piece of jewelry in hand, though I wasn't sure how or if the gift was connected to the news. Anyway, we dated for a while, with sex becoming an automatic insert into the evening. Right there, at the very start of my dating career, is when I began to equate saying Yes to a date to saying Yes to sex. The two elements in what I thought to be an adult formula for socializing in the secular world of the late 70's. And, in my frugal way of thinking it made some sense, also, for I figured that if a guy was generous enough to buy me a meal (a very big deal on my budget, and usually enough for two meals thanks to doggy bags), then I should respond with generosity in-kind – the only kind I could afford to offer.

Moral browbeating, though dreadfully familiar to me, did not strike at my behavior, for my actions represented a cut and dry requirement for my career change: convent life required chastity – this life required sex. Besides, even if I wanted to say No, was it okay to say No? And what about the guy's feelings if I did say No? Would anyone ever ask me out again if word spread of my No? And would I even have the guts to say No? Yes, was just simpler. But, I did harbor resident hang-ups over the appearance of my naked Catholic body; so, if at all possible, I imbibed a Manhattan or two early on in the date to relax myself, you know, exude some confidence and professionalism. Most people wouldn't connect the word "professionalism" to dating skills, but I was forever wanting to be good at whatever I did – not inferior, stupid, and blah, blah, blah. In my case, the word fit.

Within the next year, I matter-of-factly went through a bus driver, a blacksmith, another teacher, a neighbor, a friend of a friend, and a dental student to whom I smiled engagingly while ringing up his groceries – all short, casual, and semi-sweet encounters that ended ultimately in tidy little friendships. Except for the dental student who appeared put off by my un-Catholic, loose, and professional ways. To him I seemed to classify as a cavity.

Why I carried on in the manner I did I can't fully explain, other than how I've tried. I guess my frankest excuse remains that I didn't know *how* to date. I had related to, connected with, and developed emotional intimacy and physical well being with women over the past ten years. It had been easy, natural, and affirming. Men came both clothed and naked in mystery – muscular, whiskered, hairy mystery. Other than sex, I was dumbfounded as to what men might need or expect, convinced that whatever it might be it originated from a planet unknown to me: Planet Penis, perhaps? The thought of a man ever loving me, and me him, forced the question: Wouldn't it be like living on the verge of a crushing loss waiting to land, all sudden and cruel? Opening myself to such assured devastation was such a threatening consideration that I thought it best to stick to sharing the easy stuff, the physical.

....

A part-time position opened up in the sculpture department of John Burroughs, a prestigious private high school located in an upper end wealthy part of town. A couple of my fellow students applied for the job, but I was focused on checking groceries and what not. Not being native to St. Louis – a city where what high school you attended matters throughout your life – I wasn't zeroed in on the school's clout or the golden opportunity at hand. Mr. T got on my case, insisting that I interview for the post with the head of the art department there, someone he knew personally. So, I went, feeling neither savvy, nor ambitious, nor professional. I interviewed in humble fashion, displaying my portfolio with lackluster enthusiasm. The interview took place in a contemporary glass enclosed Fine Arts Building, which housed an entire level dedicated to sculpture alone – quite some high school! Painting village huts, digging creek clay, boiling roots and leaves for glazes…seemed authentically primitive qualifications as I scanned the wealth of pottery wheels, kilns, welding equipment…at each and every student's disposal. However, my second interview with the school Headmaster proved me wrong. Supposedly, my exotic missionary background held a quirky value equated to a plus in the overall composite of the faculty profile. I was hired on for the part-time position.

Goodbye to memorized codes for bok choy, endive, ginger root, okra, shitakes….*Hello* to checking out intellect and wealth. The intellect portion applied to the faculty *and* the students, but the wealth portion rested mainly with the students and their affluent families. Lecturing one day on the works of painter sculptors such as Picasso, a slouching, half-yawning boy offered up, "Hey, we have a couple of those." No one raised an eyebrow except me. This high-end environment of privilege was a blend of misfit all together different from my Erie, Pa. misfit: I didn't feel pressure to run from it. In fact, I managed to navigate it with a semblance of ease, once I sagely came to value my unique decade of experience as my own measure of priceless wealth.

The artistic and academic camaraderie at the school was rewarding to me, as were the free lunches I gobbled up as my main meal for the day. In no time at all I found myself hanging out with (dating?) an adorably cute painting teacher who spoke with a hint of honey southern drawl, and becoming quick best friends with Debbie, a new hire in the painting department. Debbie arrived in St. Louis with her soon-to-be-husband, John, a talented and relatively successful potter. Miraculously – like manna from the sky – I found myself nestled in a close-to-my-age, foot-loose-and-fancy-free group of bohemian types ready to party; I belonged socially and professionally; I could mouth with credibility that I was a "teacher," a respected member of society. My convent life continued to inhabit my dreams, but upon waking the habit of the night would vanish as soon as I peered in the bathroom mirror, for my hair was permed and curly, thanks to my mom doing it up tight and frizzy on one of her visits. On top of that I'd hi-lighted the curls with sun-blonde streaks. But I didn't resort to any other fussiness in sculpting a new image of me, no make-up or such.

Continuing on with faculty members, after the painting teacher, a poetry loving English teacher, best physically defined as an all-around catch, corralled my interest. He was nuts about hiking and I was eager and willing to follow. One balmy autumn weekend we ventured off together to hike, camp, and romanticize in step with nature. Back at school on Monday morning I discovered a page of tender, hand-penned verse in my mail cubicle in the teachers' lounge. Reading his poetry made me break out in the hot blush of a 16 year old. I found myself teetering on the edge of falling in love. A formidable obstacle, however, intervened to break my fall. Let me call that obstacle Chainsaw for the time being - I trust that you know who I mean. His re-insertion in my life, likewise, managed to induce blushing, but not from poetry.

Here's what happened.

Back on campus, I had taken a curious interest in observing Chainsaw as he turned on the charm with a smattering of female students inhabiting the sculpture studio. One tall, ivory colored gal in particular caught his fancy. I witnessed him driving off with her on more than one occasion. It bothered me…I mean…he was still married and all…even if separated, or whatever. Certainly, cruising off with a pretty thing tucked close could never help salvage his marriage. Was it the residual nun-social worker in me that wanted to save him from himself, or just the residual Catholic? Talking was something he and I had done little of because despite his blustering arrogance, he was awkward with his words (on top of mumbling). Though he intimidated me to the core, I decided that, indeed, a talking to was in order. Someone had to step forward and flash a caution sign in front of his face. Bolstering myself with a pseudo air of authority and righteousness, I garnered the courage to corner him alone in the studio one afternoon. There, I laid out my concerns in a motherly manner, ending with an authenticating touch to his cheek. He stared down at me through the piercing slits of his blackish eyes; I fidgeted but held my ground. And then, without a blink of warning, he took a step towards me, set his calloused hands upon my face, and kissed me smack on the lips. If forbidden came in a flavor, I'd just tasted it. My wide blue eyes held to the darkness of his for the most imperceptible measure of time before breaking away. I was stricken! He turned and walked out of the studio with his swagger in tact, leaving me to nearly wet my Goodwill pants.

That's what happened.

The studio incident fired the starting gun to an obstacle course that hindered more than one relationship from progressing in my life. My do-good lecture and its resulting kiss led me down a road defined with euphoric peaks and anxious valleys. I tried to stay focused on my teaching, my sculpture, my other friends, but the double-whammy of his look and lips distracted me senseless. It was with anticipation and terror that I ventured towards the studio a few days later day. With freshly smitten looks we faced each other. Chainsaw ushered me towards privacy, enfolded me in his arms, and again put his lips to mine – this time we both kissed.

We battled (half-heartedly) for the next few months to reign in our inclinations and carry on with others in our lives, but the effort at restraint only led to clandestine outbreaks of a pawing nature. Toying with our dangerously addictive game left me hooked on the taste of his forbidden allure. My friends warned me away from him, for there was something in his demeanor that made people wary and uncertain of him; his intensity radiated at the level of unnerving. Turned to mush as I was, I interpreted his threatening air as nothing more than a brusque façade over shyness and insecurity, for I, more than most, could fathom the urge to disguise ones' vulnerabilities – that, we had in common. My schedule didn't easily allow time for this teasing and testing preoccupation with Chainsaw. I was working hard to finance a return trip to my beloved Malawi.

Once my graduate work was completed, I added to my high school income by teaching summer classes at Fontbonne; my earnings combined with occasional gifts of cash from my mother and grandmother, and frugal living allowed me to save for a trip that needed taking. On the frugal front, I baked my own bread, and made my own marmalade and yogurt. My staple menu was comprised of these three homemade items between date meals and free school lunches.

Sr. Cephas (remember the tiny, elderly Canadian sister with whom I traveled the highways and byways begging for money for the missions?) visited me in St. Louis while on collection rounds in the Midwest. She brought with her a culture from a long-running production of homemade yogurt – a housewarming gift with history. Touching a creamy spoonful of it to the tip of my tongue was like daily communion with the White Sister family. Other sisters dropped in to visit, as well, whenever they passed through St. Louis – each of them continuing to treat me like nothing less than one of them. The name White Sisters, however, had fallen by the wayside; now, the Congregation was referred to as Missionary Sisters of Our Lady of Africa.

Besides visits, I received letters from Fernande, back in Malawi, and Gyslaine, still in Burundi, each stamped with the exotic postage of my past. These far reaching threads of love stitched the "welcome" I had carried away with me in place for life. But, even with that soft comforter, I still felt the compelling need to again set foot on African soil. The ground of it no longer represented my future, but a sizable chunk of it wedged in me in a way that obstructed my growing space. It had to be loosened before I could live peacefully with my past and productively with my present. Nighttime dreams frequently carried me there, but I needed one more goodbye in broad daylight.

I invited Barbara to travel with me; we stretched dollars, rather miraculously, to fund the trip for two. We were set to go, but before our departure date, the Chainsaw affair reached the point of reckoning.

It happened on a gorgeous summer day, a day on which I was cajoled into abandoning my activities for canoeing on the Meramec River - Chainsaw's most cherished outdoor activity. He was adamant about being the first to unveil the meandering river to me, with its treasure of terra cotta and bluish gray colored bluffs and mossy verdant banks. (I later came to discover that he had exerted this adamancy with a number of women). The felt obligation of conversing in a car for the one and a half hour drive to the canoe rental was sticky for us. I babbled on like a broken Chatty Cathy doll to keep awkwardness at bay, and to keep myself from becoming carsick from nerve fumes. This trip, I knew, was about more than floating down the river. I had already reasoned with myself that by allowing to happen what was likely to happen once and for all, could amount to liberation for both of us – for I highly suspected that his interest in me was primarily rooted in the fantasy of seducing Sr. Gail, not me, per se. If so, it was best to get it over with. The End. A logical solution to a prickly situation. Right?

Upon arriving at the bank of the river and settling ourselves into the canoe, I stripped down to my bathing suit, tackling my first fear. My suit was a floral two-piece number sewn by yours truly after cutting a homemade pattern off an old pair of dissected undies. To my mind, the combo turned out quite swimmingly, but I knew that my standards for such things were not particularly refined. The top piece equated to two triangular patches tied in place, which was sufficient back then because my breasts, though floppy, demanded little else. According to self-critique, my breasts were lacking aesthetically. With his trademark sly and sideways glare, Chainsaw eyed me up and down as I exposed my suited body. I pretended to be uncaring, unnoticing.

The river sparkled in silver and multi-hued greens, breaking into foamy white whenever the current sped it around and over rock and wood tangles along the way. With every sip of my cocktail (he packed Manhattans) the liquid of it, like the liquid of the river, carried me along idyllically, rhythmically, and effortlessly. Calm ruptured when Chainsaw started slapping the paddle to splash, and rocking the canoe to tip, carrying on like a 12-year- old – an age he boasted reluctantcy to abandon. After a few hours of hip hopping between playful merriment and drifting serenity, we spotted an invitingly secluded area and paddled towards it. He made a small campfire, though heat was not called for, a romantic torch or touch, I suppose. After spreading our blanket, he produced fancy nibbles to feast on. Chainsaw was not unlike Grandma Stephanie in embodying both a slip-shod manner and a refined taste. For our day-long canoe trip he went all out, packing a selection of perfectly ripened strawberries, a softened triangle of Brie, a wedge of pâté, a fresh loaf of crusty on the outside (like he liked) and squishy on the inside (like I liked) bread, and my favorite cocktail – long-stemmed cherries and all. Dessert, I suspected, would present itself off the menu.

Chainsaw took a great interest in trees, naturally. He pointed out fine specimens with smooth bark and wide lower trunks, angled just so. After feasting, he took my hand and led me to one such tree, stretched a towel against the trunk of it, leaned my back against the towel, and pressed in on me, sandwiching me between two erect forces of nature. The triangle patches fell first, and then the floral undies slipped from my hips and caught on my ankles. *Oh, Lord, this was it!* When his own swimsuit dropped my eyes bulged at the sight of his ardor. The bent tree stood rooted and quiet as the two of us straddled and writhed against it, groping to consummate the crazy desire that had exploded between us. When we could no longer remain upright, and both our backs bore the deep markings of bark, Chainsaw circled my legs around his waist and with clumsy steps carried me back towards the blanket. As we neared the fire he lost his balance and the two of us rolled into what was left of it, him taking the brunt of the singe. Since our very first kiss, I had come to fear falling into a fire with him, and here we were. Our passionate moment turned comically befuddled, so we charged to the river to wash off our silly embarrassment and cool our skin. I doubt that any other of his river companions fell into a fire, literally, but I would wager money that each and every one of them wound up baring the markings of a fine bent tree. The fire, quite memorably, was all mine.

It was with the added baggage of this episode on the Meramec River – which, of course, resulted in fueling rather than dampening our relationship – that I flew off to Africa with the hope of reining in a different sort of burning desire. I was quite the fireman's daughter.

....

More than three years had passed since I'd left Africa with a heart more broken than beating. My existence had changed dramatically, but as I set my eager, anxious eyes upon Malawi, I observed it as unchanged from my memory: everywhere, dark glistening faces smiling in greeting; everywhere, the melodious sounds of Chichewa humming; everywhere, the patterned colors of women's chitenje's swelling with babes wrapped on the back, on the side, in the belly; everywhere, the scent of sweat, smoke, earth.

Arriving at my former home in Lilongwe, Felicia stood framed in the doorway so familiarly that it felt, for a moment, as if I was returning from no more than a day of teaching in Likuni. Choking back a river of emotion, I kissed her warm cheeks, moving on to those of other beloved faces lined up in greeting. As reliable as the soft cheeks felt, I half believed that I was placing my lips upon the flesh of ghosts; the murkiness in between living and dreaming never looked and felt so opaque. It took me a couple of days of staring hard at my former comrades eating and drinking, praying and laughing, before I was certain that both they and I existed, real and together again on planet Earth.

Barbara and I spent our time taking in the town, the villages, the market, and, of course, the school where my stone carving remained situated in the heart of the courtyard. Sr. Perpetua, still Headmistress, greeted me like a long lost friend and I her, having forgiven her for breaking my heart with her eviction. The school appeared to be sailing on smooth waters, staffed and directed 100 percent by Malawians. It was the type of missionary victory that qualified as undeniable success in the books, despite the tears shed over it.

Though rock solid familiarity and love filled the days of my visit, I knew, nonetheless, that I was severed from the source of it. Upon entering the chapel and sitting among my sisters, my communion remained with them alone: my inner tabernacle remained empty.

Mlendo ndi mame – a visitor is like the dew. I departed like the dew. My second departure came without sobs and hysterics, my foot lifted with only a pause of nostalgic reluctance. My return was like a healing ointment massaged lovingly onto the recovering body of my loss and longing. The trip validated my past and the fullness of my memories, while resolving the ache of my wondering. I departed Malawi with the gift of certainty: I had made the right decision.

....

With a home waiting for me, albeit a match-sized apartment, I was ready, eager even, to return to life in St. Louis.

Having drifted into my early thirties, the reality of my single state suddenly burdened me with new draft of considerations regarding purpose and fulfillment. And, though I don't recall setting it, the alarm on my biological clock rang loud with shrill demand – snooze time was officially over. I hadn't left the convent in order to marry, or to have children. I left because I *had* to. But now, after three years of puzzling myself together as a single woman, I felt it was time to partner and create a family from the matter of my own flesh and blood. The light turned green.

As I mentioned, my "let's get it over and be done with it" approach to Chainsaw failed abysmally: he was waiting for me upon my return. I worked on convincing him, and myself, that nothing could or should come from our unlikely pairing, but it didn't stop either of us from sporadically igniting our emotionally dizzying affair. His state of marital separation appeared to be progressing towards divorce, driven by its own dynamic, but even his close to "officially available" status didn't stop me from trying to free myself from the lion's den.

I tried to divert his attention by hooking him up with other women, while seeking out safer sorts of guys for myself. It was for the best, I assured him. Chainsaw and I met for *one last time* so frequently that it became a regular occasion to meet – every breakup more wrought with emotion than the previous one. A couple of times we managed to back off for longer stretches, until he roared back - quite literally one time on his motorcycle.

It was after midnight, an artist acquaintance and I were keeping each other company on my brand new double mattress, when an unmistakable rumble of exhaust exploded up my driveway, filling us with images of massacre. Chainsaw had a solid reputation for getting what he wanted, when he wanted it, and how he wanted it. Boundaries did not apply to him, nor did stop signs or red lights, if ill timed. My terrified companion rolled off the bed - like in a combat maneuver - and crawled along the floor butt naked in a search for his clothing – he preferred to face his demise with pants on. There was beating on my door timed precisely to a pounding in my heart. Pulling back the curtain covering a tiny glass pane in the door, I starred into a pair of forlorn and beseeching eyes – eyes yet unaware of my trembling houseguest cowering none too bravely. What my own eyes revealed I couldn't imagine, but my lips mouthed the words, "I'm not alone."

I held my breath…his jaw tightened and ground back and forth…he was visibly deliberating between bold revenge (tearing the door down) vs. wounded hurt (driving away spurned). The in between seconds before he turned away, revved his motorcycle, and sped away were nothing short of eternal. My companion and I slid back into bed for a dreadful night, grateful. Early in the morning, I was the one beating at Chainsaw's door eager to apologize – his look of hurt and rejection from the night before was simply too much for me to bear. In minutes we were together again, all lovey-dovey.

These shenanigans dragged on for a couple of years, eventually leading us to consider the seemingly remote possibility that we *were* meant to be, that we *were* soul-mates pre-ordained to exist as one. Moving in together might actually make sense, you know, give us a real shot at something together, figure it all out once and for all. I pulled out a Malawian souvenir, an empty composition book from Likuni School that I had possessively hoarded, and began filling it with letters: A love letter, A fear letter, A letter about Me letter, A baby letter. Rereading the letters now, so many years later, blushes me with ripe embarrassment. A shared sampling, however, reveals just how thorough I was in my considerations, and just how absorbed I was with my decision.

> *You fear that marriage would be the death of all, and I'm afraid you are so geared towards that way of thinking that you would take all of the little routine, everyday situations that people inevitably fall into as being bad...that you wouldn't be able to do the practical everyday things that keep relationships alive...your preference for big dramatic gestures being the only proof of life and love. I fear that you will think of my need for schedules and order as being destructive to your spontaneity, even though I believe that a certain amount of that is important in a relationship....*

> *I'm not sure about your feelings for me as an equal; I know you have some incredible ideas and hang-ups concerning women. I fear that you might never consider my dreams and needs to be as real and urgent as your own.....*

> *You seem supportive of my sculpture now, but I fear that eventually you would want me to give it all up. Creating is personally and deeply important to me and I need to be able to continue to do it...*

> *I have great fears concerning your hang-ups about aging and maturity – fear that if you don't get a handle on those things they will forever keep you disgruntled and acting like a perpetual adolescent....*

> *I don't know if you'll ever understand how my ten years in the convent made me who I am, and how I continue to be affected by them. My fear of rejection may be greater than average because I feel I've already had my world pulled from under my feet and my heart taken with it....The impact of what I feel to be rejection in that situation remains a wound and it has been a threat in my life to dare to love again.....*

> *I feel deeply that something great would be lost if I don't have a child...that there is something that I and another person (you) have to give to another...every urge in me leans there, and that's a lot of urge.*

There is plenty more penned about friendships, moodiness, the meaning of love, my insecurities...enough downright navel-gazing to gag a full-grown horse! But, at the time, these considerations were deathly serious to me, every aspect of every issue pondered ad nauseum. The writing exercises served to clear the air for me, but I can't recall whether or not they did anything at all for him. I wanted our partnership to start immediately and I expected it to last forever. I terminated my lease, sold off whatever was saleable of my make-do furnishings, and moved in with Chainsaw. The move was into a distressed and semi-abandoned historic area of the city; into a house he'd been restoring to accommodate living and studio space. Rehabbing severely maimed properties on the cheap had become an added obsession for him over the years, fueling his entrepreneurial spirit and profitably engaging his crafty and clever skill set.

Well...oh well...so much for the clarity of my letter writing...so much for readiness and preparation...baaarely moved in, in a matter of months I was moving out, abruptly uninvited due to a change of heart ensuing from last minute pangs of remorse over his pending divorce. His feet turned cold and he felt guilty. In his suffering mind divorce dealt a terminal loss of innocence, the end of all fairy tales - just the sort of reality vs. fantasy notion that habitually left him flip-flopping. For me, his change of heart (another eviction) dealt one more traumatic appearance on the doorsteps of friends, and another round of apartment hunting. Chainsaw aided in the hunt – out of a twin round of guilt, no doubt. Guilt was another thing we seriously shared in common: the communion of wayward Catholics.

Pangs of guilt, loss of innocence, or whatever the rub, it's still nearly impossible to stay apart when you're crazy-like-mad-drawn-to-each-other and mouthing phrases like "tragic soul-mates," but, we exerted effort once again, trying to run like nuts from the cursed blessing of each other. Concerned friends bent on rescuing me introduced me to an adorable, pony-tailed drummer in a blues band. Interest ignited between us and a spark of long-term potential surged through me. With my new interest absorbing my interest, I remained free of Chainsaw for some months before he spotted me at a party, smiling prettily and convincingly on the arm and to the charms of another. Sizing up the handsome threat at my side as major, he was punched in the gut with the possibility of losing me forever. He had booted me out, but he still wanted me...didn't he?... did he? Such flip-flops. He loves me, he loves me not...The motion of a spastic yoyo comes to mind, and as for sound, toss in a passionate aria and the pummel of rap overlapping each other. Yikes!

The topic of males continued to be a rather all-consuming distraction in my life, but the travel bug made an appearance, as well, placing China on my horizon of things to do. Under the guidance of a personable history teacher at the high school who conducted such excursions annually, I signed on with a small tribe of fellow travelers. Ever since my original departure from Erie, Pa., wanderlust had taken to flowing steadily in my veins. It now pumped a vision into my mind of China as a land of incomprehensible beauty. I envisioned it stretching, cascading, and mounting as gracefully and mysteriously as the poetic arc of its calligraphy. I craved to see it in the flesh – one more need to satisfy. While readying myself to drive to school early one afternoon to place my passport directly into the hands of our tour guide – the day was the deadline for submitting visa applications – I was diverted by the ringing phone: Chainsaw dialing up trouble. He begged me to meet with him (briefly, he promised) in a nearby park, and I (no surprise) agreed, despite the urgency of the errand at hand. We sat next to each other in the grass talking, while my passport sat exposed alongside me like another layer of goodbye. Planned or impulse I'm not sure, but in a split second he grabbed it, darted to his motorcycle, and zoomed off. Screaming, I set off in pursuit (I now owned a whole car) but I knew my chase would be futile. I considered calling the police, but I was too upset and didn't have the courage – policemen scared me, probably because I always felt guilty. Stewing in my own predicament, rage grew as I witnessed China slipping into the misty category of unfulfilled dreams. Mostly, I fumed at myself for having carried on with such a madman in the first place. Friends had warned me, but I'd ignored their warnings, acting out, as if in revolt, against my May Queen persona and a decade's worth of good Catholic behavior.

About 24 hours later, the thief appeared at my door with an apologetic bearing and a manila envelope in hand. My passport was inside, but there was something else: a velvety box slid out, and within that box a raspberry hued ruby ring nestled in creamy satin. The sparkling ring spoke *engagement*. "Forget China and travel the world with me, it will be our honeymoon," he said. Honeymoon first and marriage later - that was the gist of it. His plan congealed on the spot with more impulsivity than even his ring purchase. With great enthusiasm he proposed an exotic journey to mark our new beginning. Only my "yes" and plane tickets were lacking.

Consider for a minute how my life had changed: from the serenity and rock solid structure of religious life and dedication to others, I had lapsed into passionate chaos, indulging myself in the self-absorbed madness one stereotypically associates, precisely, with loony artist types. The notion of a bohemian existence had tempted me earlier in my life, but now I caved to it; both feet were in. I said, "Yes." We were down to plane tickets.

I tried to pin down the marriage part, but he wanted to talk only of the trip part and how we ASAP needed to shop around for the cheapest around-the-world airline tickets available. He had to scout for cash even harder than I, given that he adamantly refused to be employed by anyone other than himself. Naturally, there would be no itinerary, no hotel reservations, nothing to limit possibility, whim, or desire. A long and unrestricted adventure before settling down and starting a family sounded deliriously exciting. I couldn't deny it. Our non-plan entailed being gone for a few months – maybe more, maybe less. I suggested a small wedding ceremony in the chapel of Fontbonne College, just family and friends. He said that he longed to visit Nepal and scour the skies in the early morning dawn for the tip of Mt. Everest. If he couldn't handle the chapel part, then maybe a simple ceremony at the house, followed by a gathering of friends. "India most definitely," he chimed in: "The Taj Mahal, Old Delhi, and Varanasi on the Ganges." I needed to focus on tickets.

....

With nothing but bulging backpacks we took off for Japan – Kyoto first, checking into a ryokan to experience the simplicity of authentic accommodations. We strolled through mazes of meticulously clean streets and giggled at window presentations of glossy plastic food choices made easy to order with the point of a finger. In Hong Kong we were enraptured by the sight of the haunting harbor, and struck by the phenomenal beauty of the cosmopolitan blend of women adorning bustling streets. Succumbing to the seductive allure of Hong Kong's commerce I took to the streets to shop, buying a feather light, white cotton layered skirt, matched with a ruffled sleeveless top. I framed it as my wedding outfit. When I modeled the ensemble for Chainsaw at the hotel, nearly blushing like a certified bride, I was rewarded with nothing more than a reserved nod.

Whenever it was time to catch a plane to our next destination, we found ourselves trapped in a long wait in the wee hours of morning for the only flight available to those with discounted, open-ended tickets around-the-world like ours. Landing in Thailand, we spent our first night in a Bangkok dive dense with travel weary, semi-intoxicated European adventurers. We slept in a concrete block room, more like a cell, with musty polyester sheets on the bed and hard humps considered pillows. After a few days of over-dosing on museums and temples, along with polluted air, we bused to the resort town of Pattaya – a place noted for beaches, bars, and exotic Thai prostitutes.

There we got into a heavy argument triggered by jealousy, my jealousy. It was roused all slimy and green by Chainsaw's manly inclination to eye up and down the two-legged offerings readily available in the tawdry bars lining both sides of the streets. It wasn't the first time that jealousy got the better of me. To calm my feathers we settled down side-by-side on our hotel double bed and indulged in simultaneous one-hour massages for two bucks apiece. A pair of Thai woman straddled us, working us hard and deep. It was clear (even to me) that the women came prepared to offer additional services for no more than a generous tip. Pattaya was more body than place.

Boarding another bus, this time north to Chiang Mai, we rented a motorcycle upon arrival and lost ourselves among lush and terraced hillsides and quaint villages. We cruised past fields plowed by the heft of water buffalo leashed to the slight frame of man. We ate along the way (with only a token of caution) for nickels and dimes at non-touristy hole-in-the-wall restaurants and food stands - a decision costing bouts of gripping stomach cramps and diarrhea that left either, or both of us, uncompanionable at different points in time.

We motor biked to an area where elephants were trained to become a herd of laborers. Though I'd spent time elephant watching in a game reserve, I'd never had occasion to witness a full-blown elephant erection before - the fact that one particular elephant dangled his monstrous wand of masculinity *every* time I approached was (I'm reluctant to admit) deviantly flattering. With my maturity level registering at an all time low, I studied the erection long and hard, like revenge for Chainsaw's up and down prostitute gazing. It made me feel even. The lion's share of our moody spats and travel tiffs were settled with sex, cutting a pattern for what became an non-verbal solution to almost any and every problem that arose between us.

On to India. Once in Delhi, we made our way to the gates of Old Delhi, stepping through them and instantaneously falling behind in time. Sacred cows, goats, and bicycles littered the narrow paths, while hordes of inquisitive dark eyes zeroed in on my peachy female skin and my blonde curly hair. Feeling overly accosted by humanity, we remained in Delhi only a few days before boarding a stifling hot bus heading to the ancient city of Agra. The Taj Mahal rose into view like a heavenly apparition – though commonly referred to as a mere wonder of the world. What a testament to undying love, I thought, and what a dreadful occasion for Chainsaw to act as if he wanted to soak it all in alone, meaning by himself, not like "us" alone. He was besieged with a bout of moodiness that spread over me like black cloud. The day should have risen to the romantic height of our trip, but, instead, it fell into a patch of sulky brooding halfway around the world. It was pitiful how we managed to domestically wallow before the resplendency of the Taj Mahal.

Taking off for Nepal, we landed in Katmandu and spent the night at a rest house charging only $8 for the two of us – actually expensive compared to the four-dollar-a-night accommodations we found the next day. The chaos and hustle of India were mercifully behind us, but within the lush calm of this new terrain we walked past a burning wood pile with two feet extending straight out from under it – a startling slap to the face on day one. Our Nepal time alternated between low walking hikes and high motorcycle excursions over curved and terraced foothills sculpting the earth.

One day we ventured up a long, steep winding road to Nagarkot and spontaneously decided to stay overnight at a remote, bare bones guesthouse nestled in the high hills. We huddled in the candlelit space of it, along with another pair of adventuresome travelers, sipping tea and partaking in a Nepalese meal served by a capable six-year-old boy precious enough for us to entertain stowing him away on our return trip home. At 5 a.m. we woke with the clouds and the world below us, as if we had dreamed our way upward through sleep. The tiny group of us hiked in silence to a nearby ridge to perch and wait for morning's veil to lift, hopeful for a clear sighting of Mount Everest. Magically, as if out of the void of nowhere, a white glistening cap emerged looming higher than I ever thought possible. The sight of it stole my cold breath away. Heaven could not have been much higher. When the majesty of the moment clouded over and released us from its spell, we uncraned our necks and marched back towards the guesthouse for hot tea and porridge before descending to our Katmandu base.

Chainsaw's physical ailments peaked in Nepal with a prolonged attack of dysentery that accompanied him all the way home like a souvenir from hell. While his fiery fever raged and his bowels erupted ceaselessly, the unresolved topic of marriage growled in my under belly with a cramping annoyance of an all-together different nature. It was being fed daily by his stonewalling. Each day we drew closer to the precipice of a major meltdown. In this splendid frame of mind and body we crossed back into India and aimed straight for the ancient city of Varanasi: a Hindu pilgrimage site situated on the banks of the Ganges. As curious tourists short on holiness, and living in sin, we were a far cry from pilgrim material. On the golden purple dawn of our first day, we took a rickshaw ride to the river's shores, already flooded in the early hours with masses of people celebrating the Brother Sister Festival. In routine harmony people bathed and worshiped, yogi's contorted their bodies in astounding figurations, and bodies burned: just another festive day on the Ganges.

In Varanasi it was my turn to succumb to fever and wrenching stomach attacks. In my case, however, we believed that I'd been intentionally food poisoned at our hotel for the sole purpose of delaying our departure, thus guaranteeing more rupees in the hand of the hotel proprietor. Feeling miserably ill, disgruntled, and captive we impulsively packed our things one morning and snuck out of the hotel, hoping to squeeze ourselves onto a flight back to Delhi. By now, both our money and our mutual fondness were bottoming out. Our quarrelling subsided for the simple reason that we weren't speaking. There was zero chance of reconnecting via sex due to illness. It was time to return home. Yes, it was time.

Back in Delhi, I phoned the airline from our hotel and asked to be booked on the first available flight back to the U.S. In a thick and spicy accent the agent replied that all U.S. bound flights qualifying for our discounted open tickets were fully booked for the next two months. I *couldn't* have heard her correctly! When she repeated the information employing every English word available to her to say the same thing, I felt faint. The clear truth was that in another couple of days we could no longer afford a hotel. We had to leave. The only alternative was to head to the airport, put our name on a wait list, and wait.

At two in the morning the airport ticket counters were crammed deep, mostly with thin and feisty Indian males pushing, shouting, and vying for any available standby spots. Chainsaw reclined against a column on the airport floor and lost himself in a novel while I, still green around the gills, battled the crowd, shoving and pushing to get ahead as if my life depended upon it, which it seemed to. After hours of manhandling, I was awarded the very last two seats on a plane heading to the U.S. via Istanbul. The flight included a substantial layover in Istanbul, enough of a stretch to squeeze in a touristy sight if so inclined, but we chose to stay glued to our seats. We didn't dare chance getting bumped. We didn't dare risk prolonging the agony of our exotic, once in a lifetime, honeymoon.

And so it was…with approximately $14 remaining between us and zero talk of marriage we landed back in St. Louis. Off we went on our separate ways, wanting nothing more than to be apart after our three-month odyssey, our fresh beginning.

CHAPTER 13. WATER FOUNTAIN PROMISE

As if trying to avoid a pesky germ, we stayed hermetically sealed from each other for several weeks, but that was it: we were too hopelessly infected with each other to hold out any longer - for a second time I moved in with Chainsaw. I still got nowhere, however, on the notion of a chapel wedding at our college alma mater, nowhere on the idea of a simple ceremony at the house, and nowhere on setting a date to wear my Hong Kong wedding ensemble. The arrival of frosty cold winter ruined the sheer cotton possibility of the outfit anyway. Despite the burst bubbles of my wedding visions, one day we agreed upon a plan. On a non-descript Tuesday afternoon we journeyed one and a half miles up the street to City Hall to apply for a marriage license. The clerk asked Chainsaw to spell Soliwoda and he stumbled after S. She looked up quizzically and asked him how well he *knew* the woman he planned on marrying. He mumble-stumbled on that question, as well.

The following Thursday afternoon, January 13, 1983, I salvaged a sliver of wedding pomp and circumstance by playing Pachelbel's Canon in D while we dressed for the occasion of our wedding: me in tweed knickers (back in style) and an ecru satin blouse (purchased by him), and he in a standard blue oxford shirt and his snug fitting sport coat (past gifts from his mother who proudly compared her firstborn to Adonis in looks and Michelangelo in talent). With an air of secrecy usually associated with crime, we made our way back to City Hall where a minister typically hung out, all ready and eager to tie a simple civil knot with no more than a handful of binding words. Up the steps and barely through the door of the formidable looking building, the portly, elderly Reverend Theotrice Woods approached all snug and shiny in a worn black suit, a carnation in his lapel, and a ready-to-go witness by his side, offering us all but the convenience of a drive thru MasterCard wedding.

The workings of City Hall revolved around a musty and cavernous core of old and cold marble dim with a yellowing, depressing light. Exhibiting the longevity and wear of a lasting marriage, it appears the same today, decades later. The Reverend Woods suggested that we might care to pronounce our vows perched atop the grand central staircase, being that it was little trafficked at that time of the day, but my spouse-to-be declined. At the base of the stairs, slightly off to the side, an ancient looking ornate bronze, wall-mounted water fountain caught Chainsaw's attention: *"How about there? Right in front of that beautiful water fountain!"*

Theotrice looked perplexed but relieved to be spared the effort of hoisting himself up the marble mountain of stairs. And I? After the long and tumultuous journey leading to this long awaited moment in time, I prostrated my will before the water fountain, our sacred altar. He spoke his "I do" almost inaudibly; I spoke mine while a trickling of tears watered my cheeks. After pronouncing our vows, Theotrice announced that he had a few words to share with the newlyweds. They were fewer and louder than we could have imagined. **"Just remember folks, into every life some rain must fall. God Bless! You may now pay the minister."**

Exiting the plaque-coated light of City Hall, we squinted from the clear blueness awaiting us. Suddenly, I remembered the camera, turning back to ask the Reverend if he could snap a couple of wedding shots for us. Like a legit Mr. and Mrs. we posed snuggled close, camera smiles plastered on our faces for a pained length of time while the Reverend fiddled with the camera, hands trembling and his body slightly rocking. Click...Click... formalities over.

The first photo captured me, the bride, from mid-thigh knickers to the top of my permed head; it caught the groom from kneecap to the bridge of his nose, emphasizing the reddish tinged beard he had grown. The second photo caught only the grainy fingerprint of the Reverend Theotrice Woods. But, nonetheless, we were married. I married Bob - such a ridiculously ubiquitous name for such a complex soul, so in romance

I called him Roberto, in reprimand I called him Robert, in public, day-to-day I called him Bob, but in memory he remained Chainsaw, the man with the clear cut power over me.

Though City Hall was ever so close to home we headed elsewhere for the night, a wedding bone so to speak, adding a touch of credibility to the afternoon's doings. We paid for a one-night wedding package at a nearby downtown hotel – meaning a room hosting a bottle of champagne upon arrival and breakfast in bed the following morning. We acted out our newlywed roles with conviction: sipping champagne in bed, sex, sharing a romantic dinner, sex, munching on toast in bed, sex… then the one and a half mile drive home.

Having made the leap *at last*, I'm not precisely sure what I expected to change on a daily basis, but I certainly expected that we would *tell* people that we were now husband and wife. Bob, however, showed no inclination to mention the change in status to family or to friends. To put it mildly, his reluctance made me testy, so I resorted to a method of action that effectively guaranteed favorable results: I withheld affection. Presto! The news was out. My mother had been informed of bits and pieces of my tumultuous and adventurous history with Bob, but she kept on hoping for a tamer, Erie-like future for me with a generic Erie-like boy. When I told her, after the fact, that we'd married in City Hall, she again swallowed hard on my stubborn reluctance to conform to her Erie, Pa. standards. She took comfort, however, in her belief that the act of marriage, itself, would afford me some form of protection and security. Despite the bruising reality of her own personal horror, oddly enough, she still believed this. At 36 she had become a widow. At 35 I became a wife.

As a married couple we bounced back and forth like fresh racquetballs – on court and off court – scoring points with passionate gusto on one day and diving into the hard corner wall of daily expectations on another. My husband found the name Gail a little rough on the ear: the hard G sounded like a gag. He preferred YaYa, the childhood name Tim had coined for me decades earlier; it sounded sweet and playful, which was mostly what he wanted from me. Carrying the rhyming theme to a goofy-in-love extreme, he came up with BaBa for himself. BaBa and YaYa became our pet labels: names for the best of times, the most playful of times.

I never called my husband Chainsaw in real life, it's a book name only, but BaBa was as real as faith for believers. Those two names, however, sit rather well as bookends anchoring a whole lot of everything in between. I may not have made it clear enough that my husband was a seductively attractive man when we married in both a Chainsaw and a BaBa way: he could be heart-stoppingly terrifying *and* heart-warmingly charming seconds apart. I've seen women disintegrate before him, torched by his notorious up and down physical appraisals; I've seen women lose sight of their faithful, loving (but boring) mates, overcome by desire for a spark of Chainsaw/BaBa madness in their lives; I've seen women glare at me with eyes of envy and livid jealousy; and I've seen women look upon me with sincere and heartfelt pity.

BaBa was inclined to workaholic hyper states of activity. Once married, he charged ahead with transforming a section of the house into a gallery/ studio area to accommodate the sizable inventory of our combined sculpted goods. Keeping super busy helped him rein in the residential demons of his temperamental nature: shadowy thoughts, which could send him spiraling into dark, hostile, and depressive moodiness with little or no notice. My own moodiness arrived with the clockwork of a womanly, monthly schedule. We both knew precisely what time of month I might take to the neighborhood alleyways howling at the moon when I'd finished howling at him. Baba's insatiable need to be fully and creatively absorbed and charged at all times was both a certified blessing and a curse. If project satisfaction could've been purchased in capsule form, I would have stockpiled prescription bottles full of rainbow colored pills to induce shades of relief from his compulsive tempests of activity; I would have ground the pills into his morning oatmeal, or sprinkled them into his cinnamon flavored ice coffee. Baba, by his own admission, was anti-mediocre, anti-average, anti-rules, anti…He rebelled against the likes of everyday expectations, the need to plan, and the benefits of organization; he idolized opportunity and spontaneity. I was in a bit of a pickle!

Other than pure, honest, and crazy love, I was motivated to marry in order to settle into a suitably traditional and acceptable family life – the kind that had been taken from me at the age of 11, the kind I thought I needed to feel whole. But I was no stuffed shirt, mind you. Most of the time I went along with any number of my husband's zany escapades, triggering both thrills and chills up my spine. Living on the edge is where he chose to be, so, if I wanted to stand beside him as his wife, then, I'd have to venture out on the ledge with him. I had broken the confines of my own mold by venturing off to Africa, but Bob pushed me further in daring and devilish ways, wakening me to a cornucopia of possibilities that had lain buried under the weight of religious life.

I kept on with the regularity and normalcy of my teaching job, but more and more every minute and every thought of mine wrapped tight around my husband and his reality. With my eyes focused on my students' needs my mind could still manage to flit off in his direction with twinkling preoccupation.

BaBa pressed me into participating actively in his work, expounding over the beauty of harmonious partnering – working in sync, just like our pet names. But there was more to it than that. His pressure came with a measure of shrewdness tucked in, manipulation even. He counted on my entanglement as a method of securing my blessing and permission for whatever his projects might come to demand of both of us. With veins pumped full of artistic and entrepreneurial ambition, he was ill suited to tolerate obstacles of any kind, including that of a wife.

For me, being on board with him was a way of securing my existence – I wanted to matter. I tended to beat up on myself because I lacked the fire of his ambitious drive; I judged myself harshly, the way I feared he might. Whenever I headed down such a path I tripped up over a mound of insecurity, for the project that captured *my* deepest interest was that of building a home and a family. I didn't associate that kind of passion and desire with ambition. Perhaps, I had satisfied my life's share of raw ambition by leaving Erie, Pa., joining the Missionary Sisters of Our Lady of Africa, and accomplishing a mission in Africa. Compared to the domestic drive of nesting and nurturing that I was experiencing, ambition such as his was not a priority for me.

BaBa was ready to bust out and YaYa was ready to settle in. For him family could wait and for me it could not. He proposed holding off two years before even attempting to conceive children. From my 35-year-old perspective I already feared being too poached for the task, but looking out from his freshly divorced and newly married perspective, he needed a breath of time to acclimate. *"Look at you!"* he said incredulously, *"Anyone can tell that you're fertile! We can wait!"*

Comments like these always threw me for a loop and sent me reeling off in private to analyze my female persona and try to decipher exactly which parts of me looked so assuredly fertile and which parts did not. I wanted to be the type of female that he adored, lusted after, and cherished, although I was not at all certain as to what type of female I actually was, could be, or should be. He was my six-foot-two-inch male measuring stick. Taking his exterior appraisals deep, deep, deep to heart, I aspired to be the embodiment of what he wanted to see in me. From his every look I guess-measured his pleasure or displeasure, scrutinizing my every surface with a brutally critical eye – surfaces being of great importance in a sculptor's world – and fretting over the slightest nibble of age.

On occasion I attempted to point out to Bob the pitfalls in judging others by appearance alone. My counsel brought no more than a guilty shrug conceding shallowness on the point. So…I remained preoccupied with my own exterior, devaluing my interior side and re-focusing my worth on thin-skinned wrapping and curly blonde hair. Immeasurably influenced by the power of Bob's masculine demeanor and control – which I aided in ceding to him – I surmised that *all men* viewed women in similar fashion. He became my norm for male behavior. He became my definition of the word "male." But I can't blame him solely for the ruts I steered myself into. Eleanor Roosevelt had it right when she said: "Remember, no one can make you feel inferior without your consent."

For the majority of our evenings at home we settled onto cushions positioned side by side on the living room floor with our backs resting against the sofa, in front of a blazing fire in our oval fireplace, and a drift of classical music encompassing our ears. Bob had crafted a narrow, low to the ground table under which our legs tucked perfectly. Upon the table, before the fire, to the music, we shared dinner: a gourmet meal prepared by me and accompanied by liberal pours of a full and buttery Chardonnay.

At times, the Better Homes and Gardens setting succumbed to the pressing distraction of our bodies, so warm, so tight, and we tumbled over and let the food turn cold. At other times, however, when the wine glasses sat emptied and smudged, the mood abruptly clouded over – as if someone flushed a toilet bowl directly over the fire. On these occasions the black smoking differences in our needs curled up around us as we choked out horrible words to each other, slammed dishes and doors, and utterly lost sight of the picture perfect moment ago.

These upsets could be brutal, fueled by the same alcoholic mix capable of mellowing us into kittens. Bob tended to view these eruptions of fury as signs of well being in our relationship, wholesome, vented sparks of vitality. He reasoned that our ability to arouse such passionate fireworks proved that our temperatures continued to burn hot and heavy for each other - always a good sign. These fiery outbursts were best resolved with a physical remedy, not the tepid resolve of piddley make-up words. Our reunions were affected quickly, passionately, wordlessly – usually consummated in the early hours before dawn so that we could wake reunited. I was susceptible to both his reasoning and his resolution, though I occasionally turned back to letter writing, mostly as an exercise for clearing my own head, but I hoped, nonetheless, that my written words might sink in and help him better understand me. I hoped that he wanted to understand me.

We put honest effort into the formidable task of balancing our needs, knowing full well that each of us was poised to benefit by the other's happiness. Together we started a business, our own company, officially joining the forces of our artistic abilities, his entrepreneurial savvy, and my secretarial know how. The business initially focused on architectural reproduction and restoration. St. Louis was, after all, a candy bag full of deteriorating architectural delights: in other words, opportunity.

We moved a hefty concrete mixer into our large and vacuous basement, set up a fiberglass casting booth, and hired our first two employees, learning together by trial and error how to actually fabricate the things Bob had smooth-talked clients into believing we could make. Artistically we were more than up to the task, but the tedious drill of mass production and durability required a thing called consistency: a boring and cumbersome prerequisite to success. We cranked out any number of cracked, crumbled, shrunken, warped, and otherwise defective architectural products while experimenting our way to success with concrete, resins, latex, and urethane materials.

God-awful clouds of concrete dust and intoxicating fumes poured out from our basement garage door into the back alley and settled around our neighbors' homes and yards. After a series of complaints, and one near physical altercation, we were forced to abandon our basement shop and set up production elsewhere. Bob's willingness to take a shot at creating just about anything that a developer or restorationist might need, soon cemented us in with a curios reputation and income in relatively quickset fashion. The combination of his unrestrained enthusiasm and no-challenge-is-too-great ability, along with my tempered caution, practicality, and attention to detail, produced a set of convincingly balanced wheels rolling forward: BaBa and YaYa, BaBa and YaYa…

Sticking to the area we lived in, we purchased an empty one-story warehouse style building on the cheap and began renovating the façade, approaching it like a billboard parading our arrival and our intent. My husband was, of course, the master creator and I was, of course, the master paper pusher, though, when production called for second opinions, quality control, and fine finishing, I shuttled back to the workshop, blending in compatibly among the guys. I didn't have the luxury of Bob's single-mindedness, for there were other demands tugging on me: teaching, my own studio time, and the wifely duties I felt compelled to exercise, like improving the condition of our slip-shod household and preparing nightly feasts for my beloved Roberto. At times, balancing the above produced a cloud of brooding resentment, for I wanted Bob to openly acknowledge and value the timely demands of my multiple duties. He was good at tossing out compliments from time to time, which promoted domestic peace, but my perky ears – ridiculously fine tuned to any slight – sometimes detected a calculated indulgence in both his tone and his timing.

But, even when his love rang pure and adoring, as was often the case during this stage of our lives, I found myself questioning, "How could *he* love *me?*" My nagging sense of inferiority persisted. And it didn't help knowing, beyond a doubt, that the core of his existence revolved primarily around the fiery mania of his creative mind: it was who he was. At times, I saw myself as nothing more than a shelved project, a mission accomplished, a human nuisance secondary to cornices, lintels, dormer tops, gateposts, and spandrels – the *things* of his current interest. Growing success only made the competition fiercer, adding a fill of large sculptural creatures like gargoyles and lions to confront me on all sides.

The combination of being madly in love and desperate to matter had a way of making me feel as needy as a fatherless child.

Soon, a relentless baby alarm chimed in, driving me close to nutty – a full moon and werewolf kind of nutty. A solid year before the end of the two-year wait desired by my husband, with no disclosure I stopped using birth control. I was convinced that pregnancy would, in fact, take time and effort. His eyebrows rose at my increasingly voracious appetite for sex – almost blinking red at nymphomaniac levels. He didn't catch on.

I attempted to gauge the best moments for coupling, figuring that if the old-fashioned calendar method was the Catholic way of things, I should be blessed enough, due to time served, to hit it on the nose eventually.

Months of futile sexual trickery passed before I confessed my deception, desperation, and fear. He sympathized with me and hopped on board. From then on we coupled with purpose as well as passion, frequently and innovatively. But success continued to elude us and gradually we wearied, arriving at the point of dreading the chore of fertilization. What used to pass as raw and lusty passion between us became about as interesting as clothes tumbling in a dryer. And that's how I felt: dried up.

Initially, fertility tests revealed nothing but the need for additional testing. Delving further into the *why* of my vacant womb, I submitted to a diagnostic laparoscopy; it showed multiple adhesions obscuring the ends of my fallopian tubes, perhaps from a low grade infection long left untended. My doctor assured me that with surgery he could remove the scared wads of roadblock and open my tubes to traffic. I made eggs okay.

His confidence bolstered my hope. I envisioned a family right around the bend of this minor plumbing clog. During the operation, after clearing away the adhesions, my oh-so-confident doctor discovered that my tubes had clubbed ends, as well, not the open ends he optimistically expected to find. The tubes offered zero chance of delivering pregnancy in such a hobbled state. The scope of my surgery grew as he took to reconstructing the ends and testing that they were good to flow before stitching me up.

I woke to a long and nasty bikini line incision (like a C-section) stitched across me in black coarse thread, and to the news that my chances for success had plummeted from 85 percent to 50 due to the unexpected complications. Physically, I felt as if someone had rummaged through my insides with a plunger, but mentally I chose to view my condition like a glass half-full, or one-tube-able. Surely ten years in the convent qualified me for heavenly odds.

Six weeks later I returned for a supposedly simple, but excruciating as it turned out, procedure to confirm that my tubes were, indeed, open and ready for business. My doctor was youngish, almost cocky in his assuredness, but as I groaned away I noticed sweat beads multiplying on his upper lip and across his brow. I noticed his silence. I noticed his humbling. The ends of both tubes had curled back in on themselves – they were as clubbed as before. The surgery had affected not even one clear shot at delivering life. All it got me was a rough and red scar testifying to A in effort. The Erie, Pa. curses that had been playing hide and seek with me appeared to bloat my empty womb with nothing but remorse and more damned guilt. My past tracked me down – my shame wasn't over. The no longer cocky doctor informed me that I was severely prone to scarring. Such a revelation.

My clubbed tubes couldn't perform their sacred duty, but they functioned well enough to beat on my head like drumsticks, further knocking about my already muddled notions of womanhood and femininity. I was thoroughly depressed by my malfunction, my inability to procreate for BaBa and YaYa. He, on the other hand, tried to console me by telling me that it wasn't that big a deal for him. He was okay with it, fine with it. His words helped to keep my shame from flushing me down the toilet whole, regardless of whether or not he was being truthful.

Stubbornness can be a virtue. I refused to be left childless. Debating all possible options, we considered traveling to England for invitro fertilization; the success rate there was higher than in the U.S. at the time. My doctor was confident again, back into assurances: he *assured* me that his in-depth letter of introduction to the best doctor in the field would testify to my suitability as a candidate and earn me a coveted spot on the list of slim chances. But the invitro avenue would require my spending months in England, months apart from BaBa, so in the end we scratched it. The option was too painful.

On to adoption. Both of us were open to welcoming an American or a foreign born baby into our home. I scoured the shelves of the public library obsessively for all information related to the process of adoption – particularly agency lists and requirements. Charging ahead like a crusader fueled with a belly full of determination, I rapid dialed calls to agency after agency, deducing in seconds whether to rank them as friend or foe. I had my questions down pat, but my queries led to the discovery of more things wrong with us than I could have ever imagined: too old, wrong religion, not married long enough, no divorcees…And for the agencies for whom we *weren't* too old, by the time our name reached the top of their list – a good five to seven years in some cases – we *would be* too old. Considering the option of private adoption, I contacted lawyers, doctors, friends of lawyers and doctors…scouting out any and all opportunities and getting the word out. I even ran an ad in the paper, something subtle, I'm sure, like: **DESPERATE TO ADOPT!!!**

While crusading for my cause, our cause, I learned of a local Christian agency claiming only a two-year wait for a healthy newborn. Filling in the application papers pronto we advanced through the stages of health exams, interviews, reference letters, and home visits. For this last item we spiffed ourselves up along with the house, fabricated plans for cutting into studio space to accommodate a baby's room, and coordinated our answers to thorny questions aimed at stability, religious beliefs, and so on… Ozzie and Harriet we weren't, but we got the equivalent of frequent flyer mileage out of my convent years. That disclosure alone made us appear sufficiently religious and holy acceptable. We dodged a bullet all right!

While my best thirty-something-year-old friends began to pop expansive bellies and sport the glow of an occupied womb rosily upon their cheeks, I resigned myself, pale and slender, to being a number on a two-year wait list. And so, I waited.

CHAPTER 14. A COMPLETE FAMILY

With our names secured to a list, I attempted to lose both myself and time in my studio working with clay, plaster, or any willing and able material I could get my hands on to mimic life. My studio space served as a pseudo womb of fertility. Bob tried to bolster my spirits (he didn't like mopers, even justified ones) by pointing out that we'd just been awarded bonus time to luxuriate in ourselves – maybe another travel adventure! "How about Egypt? Let's go to Egypt!" he offered.

Before I could seriously consider camels and deserts, the agency phoned – meaning, the adoption agency, not the travel agency. A prospective birth mother with a long list of criteria for the adoptive parents had dropped in their office unexpectedly. After scrolling down… and down on their wait list, our names popped up as the closest available match to her wishes, even though we were near dead bottom on the list. The young woman was due to give birth in about four weeks, sooo…were we willing to sign an agreement, pay the deposit, and commit immediately? *Four weeks! A baby! Four weeks! A baby! Four weeks! A baby!* It seemed as if I was still in God's favor, even though he had directly ushered my Polish ass out the convent door. Our two-year wait evaporated into no wait at all.

For the next few days I sang out in joyous exultation: *Four weeks! A baby! Four weeks! A baby! Oh, my God! Oh, my God! A baby!* But a phone call sliced into my jubilation: seems the choosy birth mother chose to change her mind. She wanted to *keep* the baby. While I was tumbling off a cliff in slow motion with the phone still attached to my ear, the agency director was explaining that our signed contract entitled us to automatically jump skip to the number one spot on the wait list. In other words, the *next* available child would be ours. Her words began to soak in, halting my mid-air tumble and intercepting a horrid fall. I reached out for a ledge, climbed back to solid ground, and reset my Wait button as if it had the power to generate babies.

Two months passed before the next call came informing us that in approximately six to eight weeks a certain pregnant teen would birth a baby destined as ours forever – another round of paperwork was in order. Strangely enough, these teetering and tottering waiting periods had the unforeseen effect of instilling newborn fear onto our anticipation – fear that our personal freedom verged, irrevocably this time, on domestic lock-up for life. It's not that we were wavering on the baby front – I certainly wasn't – it's just that, suddenly, we experienced a tangible urge to plunge head first into the waters of our freedom one last time for old times' sake. With that urge guiding us we dusted off our backpacks and headed straight for Egypt.

Upon arrival, the land and the people of Egypt appeared so vastly different from the Africa I had known that it felt like a virgin encounter with a new continent. For two weeks we traveled in standard tourist mode: absorbing the raw and thrilling sensations of Cairo, exploring claustrophobic mazes meandering deep to royal tombs, riding through the desert on humpy camels, climbing on mega-sized pyramid stones, and cruising along the mystic Nile. I indulged my senses as fully as I could on the grandeur of Egypt, but my mind and heart kept flitting back to domestic shores offering a promise of permanent nesting. Keeping my daytime thoughts on the exotic occasion at hand proved difficult; my night dreams were consistently domestic. There's no sense in going on about the particulars of the trip for towards the end of it all I wanted to do was soar like a bird from the top of a sand dune and fly straight towards a future of lost freedom.

Upon our return, I waited through time with an air of contentment, focusing my attention on a checklist of last minute baby to-dos. The news finally arrived via one of those heart-stopping-in-the-middle-of-the-night phone calls: *"Congratulations! You're parents to a healthy baby boy!"* It was November 8, 1985 and the darkness outside lifted hours before dawn.

Gender selection was never an option with this particular agency, we didn't know until that very phone call whether we would be parents to a boy or a girl – which is why I prepared for the baby's coming in ambidextrous primary colors. Besides, with artistic reputations to maintain we needed to stay clear of mass mentality choices like baby blue and pretty pink. Though, somehow, in one of his earliest photos our son stared up at us in a light (almost pink) raspberry colored sleeper, or was it mauve?

Our ears having absorbed the news, we were dying to set eyes on our precious bundle, however, the birth mom was beset with health complications and the baby could not be released from the hospital before she was. Over the next several days she was tested for an array of potentially alarming diseases. Though not alarming, she even had her wisdom teeth extracted – a diagnosed necessity that I could never quite associate with birthing complications, but who cared? I would've gladly paid for a full set of veneers by this time. Anything at all to get to my baby!

We were instructed to stay clear of the hospital while she was still a patient, but knowing that our baby was visible behind the glass wall of the nursery drove us from temptation into action. Feeling as guilty as thieves, we snuck in late one night for a peek. There, among the pink-tagged girls with their family names clearly visible, were two blue-tagged boys, one with a name on his tag and one without. The name tagged baby had a peachy complexion and golf ball sized blue eyes – an alert beauty ready to roll. The name free bundle was pinkish, prune crinkled, and hairy. We paused tactfully before speaking. In the world of art, when a creation presents itself as distinctly off-putting it can, ironically, exude a rare shade of perfection at the same time – one that successfully challenges conventional notions of beauty. With eyes alighted on such a creation, we set to cooing over the nameless bundle we presumed to be ours, now wailing purple and fussing mightily behind the glass. As for coming up with a nametag, we had officially decided – as if by the bang of a gavel – that if a boy, we would call him "Max."

Why this mattered so much I'm not sure, but I couldn't decide what to wear on the day we were finally able to collect our baby and bring him home. I didn't normally dress like a mother because I never had to dress like a mother because I never was a mother. And, in any event, I didn't exactly know how a mother-to-be would dress for such an occasion, period. All I knew was that I wanted to look *somewhat* like a mother, because I didn't want the agency reps to suspect that I was anything less than perfectly tailored for the job. And, for the baby's sake, I wanted what I was clothed in to be soft. I didn't have a set of pillowy engorged breasts upon which to lay his head, so the softest of fabrics would have to do.

As to color, I ruled out black. There was significance, I felt, in our son cuddling onto color from the get-go – even if his eyes were still dialed in to black and white. Most of all, I wanted to reflect myself as a bright spot in his life: a vibrant color like love. After much consideration, I settled on a boldly colored skirt and a striped jersey top. The top had some thin black stripes on it, but they were totally secondary to the broad hot pink and electric blue ones that would pattern across my welcoming bosom.

Entering the dimly lit hospital chapel – whose smells transferred me back to Blessed Sacrament Church – we encountered two familiar adult faces. The head of the adoption agency cradled a bundled baby in her arms, while her assistant occupied herself full-time with smiles. I was in a dazed and dreamy state when the blanket was pulled back from the bundle, revealing a face lit like a light bulb and a teeny curled body. My foggy senses were mightily jolted when I realized that I was gazing into the sparkling golf ball sized eyes of a peachy-faced beauty being handed my way – our nameless blue-tagged assumption had been totally incorrect.

My arms reached out automatically, firmly, as if backed by my entire existence for the work of supporting new life. Nothing, however, in my wide world of experience could have prepared me for the godly surge of possessive warmth that accompanied seven pounds and two ounces of flesh when pressed into mine for keeps. I would protect him. I would defend him. I would roar like a lioness for him. I would die for him. The second our bodies traded heat, my heart brimmed full of Max. He did not exit my body – he entered it.

Arriving home we all but fought over who would hold Max first, resolving it by snuggling together on the sofa and sharing approximately three and a half pounds each. Our heavenly bliss was soon disrupted by a red-faced grunt and smothered by a putrid smell emanating from our bundle of joy. We hadn't attended much in the way of baby training classes…actually, nothing at all. I had done a fair amount of reading, posting notes here and there of things to remember, but no hands-on experience to speak of. And, despite the heft of the cumulative years between us, neither Bob nor I had *ever* changed a baby's loaded diaper. Aware that my mother-in-law was en route, I chose smell over action and waited for her guidance. We opted for cotton diapers and safety pins – as if the choice reflected old-fashioned purity and stability on our part. But after turning my fingers tips into pincushions, I found myself lusting after Pampers as I wheeled my grocery cart past their pop appeal and practical convenience.

Born with an ever-cheerful disposition, Max seemed oblivious to our lack of parenting skills. His accommodating nature bathed us in unearned rewards night and day. We were a picture of family contentment. There was no doubt in our minds that the world at large, with every person in it, would feel as crazy about Max as we did, so we took him everywhere: work, grocery shopping, restaurants, weddings, movies, Erie, Pa. – even to Puerto Rico and a small island resort in Vieques that publicized a "No Children Allowed" policy. Somehow we missed that little tidbit in the travel brochure, or thought that Max clearly classified as an exception. In the end it didn't matter, the owners and the guests did fall in love with Max. He charmed the flip-flops off of them. It was right around this time, when our son was only three months old, that my name officially changed to "Max's Mom."

I bid farewell to my high school teaching career with nothing but relief and a sigh of gratitude and transitioned into a stay at home/studio Mom, tackling shop assignments when office matters called or Bob desired. Max became a permanent fixture both in my studio and among the expanding crew of guys working for us at the shop. Before taking his own first steps he followed in his parents' footsteps by placing his tiny fingers to work in wet clay on a regular basis. In fact, he became overly resourceful with pliable materials.

Technical gadgetry has always boggled my brain. Even today, it's all I can do to turn the television on - picking up the remote raises my blood pressure. Anyway, that's why it took such courage on my part to go out and purchase a video camera to record Max's growth – one of the expensive clunker models to first hit the market some two decades plus ago. I battled my natural incompetence until I was close to certain that I was capable of recording my first footage of Max. The end of his noon nap presented the perfect time, the time when he was always, and I mean *always*, clinging to and peering through the bars of his crib with a grin on his face as joyous and content as that of a Buddhist monk.

Expecting to find him in that exact state of grace, I tip-toed into his room, my eye glued to the camera lens and my voice chirping a sing-songie, "Oh, Maxie…Maxieeee…" My timing was dead on, he was… wait a sec… "Oh, shit!" I recorded. Lowering the clunky gadget, my eyes confirmed what my nose already detected. He sat diaperless – brown grin, brown hands, brown walls, brown crib bars – creating with the only pliable material at hand. Digesting the shock of it, I raised the camera and proceeded to document the potent, raw, artistic moment. The cleanup was dreadful, but the video footage was like securing a trophy to share with his wife-to-be, and on down the line to his children's children. Parents, of course, are known to relish their kid's most candid and embarrassing moments; they regard them as treasure and value them like gold. I turned into one of those parents overnight. Ironically, I wound up embarrassing no one but myself by recording right over the poopapolozza the very next time I attempted to use the camera. Damn those gadgets!

....

The problem with having one child, particularly an easy-going adorable one, is that it makes you want another one. Multiples had not been a topic of discussion between us, but now, the possibility boiled over in me like another rush of all devouring need. All I could do was blurt it out: I WANT a girl! I mean, how could I *not* want a sister for "Maxie Boy," as his daddy affectionately called him? You can't believe the number of people who confided in me that the surest way to get pregnant was to adopt. It appeared as if I was the only woman standing to have failed this sure proof method of conception.

Coincidentally, Max resembled me, so when people discovered that he was adopted I was subjected to comments such as, "*Oh, Really*! I thought he was *Yours*!" "Listen birdbrain, he IS mine!" I wanted to snap back. But didn't. The truth is that some individuals seem incapable of comprehending that Max was as much mine as if I had spread my legs, crouched, and birthed him on the spot – afterbirth and all that mess as a puddle of proof.

Bob was so enamored with his son that it turned out to be surprisingly easy to nudge him towards the notion that Max deserved a sibling, and I deserved a girl. Making the girl happen was delegated to my "To Do" list - just like before. He was increasingly occupied with an array of sculptural commissions offering far more challenge and satisfaction than the bread and butter mass production fare of our start up days. His kind-of-sort-of game plan for success was showing signs of progress: wedge a foot in the door, steadily press your weight against it, and then bulldoze 'em! Extreme tactics such as fabricating a sculpture of a 4000-pound, 24-foot-tall Praying Mantis and erecting it on the rooftop of our shop building generated the sort of hype he favored: BIG and **Bold!**

With career and family life both swinging upbeat, he pecked my cheek and Max's lovingly each morning and dashed off to build castles. Though I had so looooonged to be tied to the apron strings of motherhood, I couldn't help but envy his continued freedom to come and go, the massively engaging proportions of his feats, the luxury to create at will. Absolutely everything about the scale and scope of his day threatened to erase the significance of my domestic ambitions; thus, the significance of me.

Our former adoption agency refused to bend on permitting gender selection, so I scratched them from immediate consideration. Once again demonstrating a frenzy of diligent research, I unearthed an international adoption agency offering as little as a six-month wait for a Korean infant boy *or* girl. Conquering the mountain of international paperwork, however, required super-human patience and commitment. Fortunately, I had honed both during my convent decade. After passing muster on our home visit and completing a daylong seminar on issues relating to cross-cultural adoption, we relaxed into a short wait for Lily. I'd already named her Lily – wherever she was, *if* she yet was – she would be Lily. Unfortunately, the speedy process slowed to a near halt almost before the ink of our names dried. The Korean government began taking steps to rein in the growing number of out-of-country adoptions by investigating more thoroughly the circumstances of each and every child being considered for adoption, searching long and deep for in-the-country relatives willing to raise the child. Due to their efforts more than a year passed. Lily played on in my dreams. I phoned obsessively for updates, only to be met with the words "Very Soon."

"Very Soon" lasted two years before turning into "Next." The *next* baby girl scheduled to arrive in St. Louis would be ours: Lily would join us in approximately two months. Less than a week after hearing the hopeful word, the agency phoned - the *other* adoption agency, our previous agency. Seems that I hadn't "officially" scratched our names from their wait list (Wink! Wink!). While I'd been impatiently waiting on Lily, our names had patiently been crawling up their list. A young woman close to full term arrived – again unexpectedly – at the agency wishing to place her unborn child up for adoption. "Are you interested in adopting the baby?" they asked over the phone. "Is it a girl?" I asked back. If they knew, they wouldn't say – we had 24 hours to reply to their question. Wait… wait…wait…then bam! A choice! A god-awful choice! Maybe not… maybe both…I thought! Hyperventilating, I shared the choice dilemma with Baba. He registered calm to my storm, spouting out the old adage, "A bird in the hand is worth two in the bush" – or nest, or whatever. His advice was to commit to the bird in hand. "So what if it's another boy? Lily might never come for all we know."

Nearly torn in two, I flailed about in bed that night wide-eyed and sleepless. Was there a Devil God out there toying with me? Was there a right choice and a wrong choice? At the age of 41 I questioned whether or not I could sane-fully handle two infants and a toddler at the same time; I reconstructed scenarios of possibilities all night long. At dawn I resigned myself to a blind leap of faith and, as if still bound by the vow of poverty, I acquiesced to dispossessing myself of Lily, my hope, my girl. With red and bleary eyes I squinted into the morning light, shuffled to the phone, and dialed "Yes" to the bird in hand.

Unlike Max's name, which felt pre-ordained, the task of selecting a second boy's name seemed daunting: no name emerged from the mighty shadow of Max. Axle, Hardy, Oliver…all came up for discussion without consensus. Yes, there remained a 50-50 chance that a girl might appear, but I reconfigured the odds at about 98-to-2 against it for psychological cushioning. Nevertheless, in the event of an odds defying upset, we needed to have a girl's name tucked away as well. Lily was out because in my mind the name was forever taken. Scratching my head led me back to a vacation trip we had taken with Max to the Virgin Islands the year before. There, we befriended a vibrant young woman from Chicago named Daisy. The sweet sound of her name struck a sunny wholesome note in our ears. It wasn't that I was hung up on flower names; I was hung up on a name that would pluck at my heartstrings. "Daisy" did exactly that, so I held it close to my chest.

Antsy, yet again, to divest myself of waiting, I went back to losing time in my studio. For some odd reason that antsy frame of mind made me insanely prolific. Working away one day, finely dusted over in clay and struggling knee-deep through heady sculptural dilemmas – roughly ten days after the "You have 24 hours to decide" phone call – my studio phone rang with the announcement: "*God heard your prayers! You have a beautiful daughter!*" It was February 28, 1989, and I was as dumbstruck as the Virgin Mary must have been when the Angel Gabriel first announced that she would birth Jesus, the Savior of the world. But she pulled it together enough to blurt out the Magnificat – I remained dumbstruck. When any sort of blessing came my way I tended to react with a bellyache of disbelief and a surge of unworthiness. I hadn't even prayed for a girl, not in a standard way to a traditional God. Typically I expressed my pleas by turning my eyes skyward, watching birds soar, and acknowledging all that was greater than me and beyond me. If that classifies as prayer, then I prayed.

Two days before we were due to bring Daisy home from the hospital, I went on a bubble gum pink shopping spree, even though I was opposed to such gender coloring. My opposition was mowed over by baby girl euphoria flashing its fave color directly in my face. Piling no less than 15 to 20 pink everythings for newborns on the counter, the saleswoman asked, " And which ones did you decide upon?"

"All of them."

"You certainly like pink."

"I certainly do!"

On the appointed day I alone was permitted to set foot in a special section of the hospital's nursery where Daisy was being held. Bob and Max trailed me by squishing their beamingly curious faces onto the door's 8" x 12" windowpane. There were four newborns positioned throughout the small area. My feet seemed set in concrete, incapable of moving in a right or wrong direction. It was my eyes that traveled, resting on a tiny beauty nesting off in one direction. Absolutely certain that I should direct my glance elsewhere, I turned away. Then, "Here she is!" a nurse announced from that very spot of beauty. My feet edged towards the ivory doll, her body was bundled but her head was uncovered exposing feathery black wisps of hair. She looked up at me through near slits of dark eyes set on a petite-sized face accentuated by a daintily pointed chin. Regarding her more closely, I was certain that she would come with chopsticks. I gingerly lifted the slightness of her and aimed her in the direction of the father & son faces stamped on glass. Right on queue my heart began thumping with the familiar and ferocious pride of a lioness. My girl was coming home. Our family was certified picture perfect complete.

Daisy wasn't a bit Asian, but as a newborn she appeared convincingly so. When my mother-in-law got her first peek she exclaimed, "Oh my, she *almost* looks American!" We hadn't informed people of the last minute flower swap. Everyone was perennially confused when I introduced Daisy as Daisy, not Lily.

For all Max's chattiness, Daisy was quietness itself. The only thing she offered up on a regular basis was puke when her daddy, after feeding her a bottle, playfully hoisted her over his head like a Raggedy Ann doll. After repeat deposits of regurgitated formula smack dab on top the thinning hair on his head, he took to extending her at arms length and carrying her like a serving platter. As for Max, when his goo-goo-gaga face wasn't glued within an inch of hers, he shoved toys there insisting that she play with them – as if her face could play. She tolerated Max's smothering affection, eventually rewarding him with her first authentic giggle. Encouraged by the sound of success, Max took on the challenge of making his subdued baby sister laugh out loud on a daily basis.

As a mother, I harbored an intuitive sense that Daisy was observing and willfully testing us to see if our love registered for keeps before she dared to commit herself to us. Though it was odd to link such suspicion to an infant, it was obvious to me from the start that Daisy did not possess Max's trusting nature. I believed that I would have to earn her trust and I understood why. Had I left a natural womb for the arms of a stranger, I, too, would have held onto my heart with a grip of caution.

Despite the talk of two kids being easier than one due to their ability to keep each other amused, in my opinion such talk ranked as theory without wings. I became consumed more than ever with the mundane chores and daily demands of family life. Occasions for involvement in my husband's schemes and dreams fell more regularly to the growing mound of paperwork he amassed and less to the hand-dirtying fun of sculpting side by side. Our marital highway gradually divided up the middle into his and her parallel roads dotted along the way with intersections: binding and significant intersects, but fewer than before. His side of the road was paved with ever-evolving grand plans and complex schemes, each absorbing him like a giant sponge with a monster thirst – or was *he* the giant sponge with the monster thirst?

In my mind, a road beset with too many diversions can equate to a road full of excuses for not arriving at the agreed upon intersection on time. His creative preoccupation held a relentless air of life and death urgency that excused and extended his away time with something close to regularity. How could I compete with such urgency? How could the domestic commonality of a wife cooking dinner with two tots underfoot be as compelling as the stimulating thrill of sculpting a great white shark or a tentacled giant squid – only two examples of the formidable commissions now coming his way from big time clients such as zoos, botanical gardens, and theme parks that had come to discover his fierce talent? I began to think of his projects as mistresses, love affairs: Madam Shark, Madam Squid…each one more titillating and seductive then the next, each one beckoning him away…away…

And he had other compulsions, other mistresses as well, like real estate. Bob had an appetite and a knack for real estate development, introducing additional brick and mortar demands on his time and affection. With so many desires pulling at him, we became increasingly engaged in our own tug of war over balancing priorities: family vs. work and work vs. family. It was not so much spoken as implied that his projects and interests merited greater consideration, outweighing mine both in measure and significance, and I understood that they always would. I understood his nature. I understood the differences between us. My interests currently revolved around the behind the scenes demands of a growing family – nothing particularly tempting or sexy to a thrill seeking husband. But they were like mortar to brick, just different. The thorn in my foot was not over placing his projects first, it was in believing that I sufficiently mattered to him when it so often felt like my role did not. My tug of war was over mattering.

....

But I waged another war, a much more private one. I'd like to ignore it and steer clear of it all together but that would be like trying to avoid mountains in the Himalayas. Further tiptoeing around it will only hinder the chapters of this story from maintaining their truthful soul. I can't jeopardize that, so I'll share with you the truth you might already know. But let me lean for a moment upon a cushion of excuses – for excuses are a mighty fine symptom of the problem.

Artists types tend to drink a lot, lonely types too, insecure types too, shy types as well…got it? I drank a lot. I've described my teenage self being heaved through the front door of 3304 Greengarden Blvd., and I've confessed to being an inebriated May Queen, nearly botching the crowning of the Virgin Mary statue, but teenagers do those sorts of things, right? *Right?* The convent intervened to restrain me from myself, and after that, being short on cash took a shot at it. Hallelujah! For Vintner's Choice at only $2.99 a gallon - lowbrow liquid companionship that even I could afford. I'd developed a taste, however, for the highbrow companionship of a Manhattan cocktail. I loved the syrupy golden color of it and the plump maraschino cherry that bobbed about, stem and all. To me, a Manhattan represented far more than liquid magic triggering relief and good cheer: it represented a glass of beauty worthy of love at first sip. Cradling the beguiling blend in one of Grandma Stephanie's fine crystal stemmed glasses was like holding onto visual and liquid salvation combined.

Pouring myself a full glass of something or other came to mark the start of a sacred ritual timed to my workday's end. The ritual transformed me into a witty and social being, a me free of inhibitions. Besides lugging around the baggage of so many blah-blah-blah past issues, I was additionally burdened with an introverted shyness. Oh, I could perform on command and fool audiences any time called upon, but performing was all it amounted to. Drinking, however, made my performance real to me. Drinking made *me* real. On dating occasions I drank to calm my insecurities and ready myself for the bodily act of sharing I thought compulsory at date's end. And when it came to my rough-riding Chainsaw courtship, drinking was downright essential to survival. And, naturally, I needed to drink to celebrate my marriage; definitely, I needed it at romantic dinners and after nasty quarrels; desperately, I needed it when my sculpture fell into a funk; and certainly, naturally, definitely, and desperately, I needed it when I was told that I couldn't bear children. I just *needed* it. Experiencing the urge to escape or alter myself, whichever was called for, usually both, I poured a drink – I poured a solution. Both in ounces and in need, I came to exceed the classification of a casual drinker: one who indulges in occasional swallows of cheer or escape. But I never felt the urge to drink in the daytime; it never crossed my mind to compromise responsibilities associated with the light of day. Discipline ruled where duty was concerned. I functioned like a steadily ticking clock. Reward time arrived when the day's work was done, and a reward is exactly how I viewed alcohol in my life: not only did I need it, I deserved it. Yes, indeed, I *deserved* it.

Deep down in my gut, however, in the bowels of where truth attacked the tomfoolery of disguise and excuse, I wallowed in a far different assessment of my drinking life: it was a dark and loathsome scar on my being. It was not an honest reward, and I did not deserve it.

I tried bringing in the troops, dragging in my Polish ancestry to justify my bent and assuage my guilt. Hell, everyone knows Pollacks are natural born drinkers! Grandpa Poplaski was an early example to me of how alcohol released inhibitions and inspired free-flowing talk – sermons, in his case. No one in our family identified Grandpa's behavior out loud with the A-word, at least not in English. My mother succeeded in attaching the A-word to her father through her tight lips, prickly glares, and an overall absence of affection. She was ashamed of it, of him. Grandpa continued to drink his Seven & Seven's despite the fact that alcohol was engaged in a deadly dance with his bleeding ulcers. In the end, his death came from complications: drinking being the biggest among them. Drinking behavior displayed itself on the Soliwoda family tree, as well. We were a two-trunk family of drinkers.

After Dad died, Grandpa took up the habit of driving his impeccably clean 1950's blue Oldsmobile to our house for impromptu visits. He parked his car in our driveway, entered through the back door, set himself down on a stool in the kitchen, and… sat. He had little to say without being fueled by alcohol, but his silence spoke to his purpose: he was there to fill a space. For three years he continued to drive up and sit – continuing even when my sister and I acted as if we had far more important teenage interests to tend to than to keep him company while he kept us company.

My most favorite lunch, when I was left to fend for myself, was egg salad plastered thick on both sides of a white hard roll, accompanied by an icy cold bottle of Coke. I loved the fleshy bite in the hard boiled white of the egg and the pasty mush of its yoke. It was a feast of texture. Returning from Teresa's Delicatessen early one afternoon with my purchase of hard roll and Coke, I proceeded to lather the roll with homemade egg salad. I was in mid-drool when the phone rang: my mother's voice was on the other end of it telling that Grandpa had just died during surgery – the surgery that was supposed to fix his ulcers and bring him relief. His heart stopped in the middle of it and stayed that way. High-pitched cries and a litany of Polish sounds squeezed through from behind my mother's voice: my grandmother grieving her husband's silence.

What was it with all this sudden death business? What the hell was it? I had enough of it! Searching for a new method of coping, I came up with six thoughts to help make my grandfather's death seem "okay" in the scheme of things, six things to quiet my heart and mind: 1. Mom's disappointment with him might now soften. 2. His 66 years of old age wouldn't age anymore. 3. Grandma's bickering with him would cease. 4. His bleeding ulcers would stop bleeding. 5. He wouldn't have to make the heroic effort to stop drinking. 6. He wouldn't have to live without alcohol.

I suspect that he wouldn't have wanted to live without drinking. And I understood why.

....

Back to mattering. Spring weather – of all things – offered me a real occasion to matter.

A blossomy spring day rang out like the sound of the sirens in Bob's ears, a hypnotic call luring him away from projects, urgent or not. *Nothing* was more seductive than gorgeous spring weather, another type of demanding mistress. When the call came to him he insisted that I drop whatever I was doing – how important could that be anyway, right? – and take off canoeing or hiking to wherever the budding sunny skies might lead us. Such a day revolved around intoxicating weather and zeroed in on romance: it was a day for us, a BaBa-YaYa day. Quite honestly though, I preferred planning for such occasions: I liked to feel the worth of being penciled in, I liked squeezing pleasure out of anticipation, I benefited by having time to adjust my schedule and arrange in advance for a baby sitter and all that pesky practical nonsense. Nonetheless, I won't deny the sweet perks of his springtime whims: on those sugarcoated days I felt as if my role mattered mightily.

Bob shocked me well beyond the norm one fine specimen of a spring day by taking it upon himself to purchase a hundred or so acres of land roughly 40 miles from the city limits. He punctuated the factual news with: it was *beautiful*, I would *love* it, it was the *perfect* location for a regular family get-away. The purchase was directly related to his impulse to play in nature's dirt – escape might be the better word – for it struck a mere two months after Daisy's birth. Trudging through muddy eroded land and shrubby fields scattered with car and refrigerator shells, I came face to face with a smallish, rusted tin roof 1880's farm cottage ("cottage" being a charitable descriptor). Beautiful eluded me at every turn. With sweepingly enthusiastic gestures, Bob pointed to future pond and lake sites, patio and barbecue areas, cedar groves, terraced slopes, and curving dams and drives. Upon hearing his crystal clear vision for the sad and sorry looking acreage we now owned, all I could muster in response was doubt-ridden acquiescence and sorely strained eyeballs.

Over the following months, when the children and I regularly visited him at the site, we were treated to field fires blazing, chain saws buzzing, and bulldozers repeatedly shifting mounds of earth – pure hot and noisy fury directed at damming up a serenely sculpted five-acre crib of land to cradle water. Each week brought further shades of transformation. I began to picture, to see, the actualization of exactly what Bob's gesturing arms had defined and promised. By summer's end the five-acre lake held six feet of runoff rainwater, well on its way to filling to the 25-foot level it still maintains today, 23 years later.

Predictably, after several months of compulsively re-sculpting the face of our promised land, Bob's mind drifted back to the mega-projects he'd left idling in various states of execution back in the city. His waning seasonal interest sounded like a bugle call for the changing of the guard: my turn to swing into action – BaBa The Starter and YaYa The Finisher. Feeding my own hardy appetite for king size projects (for I did have one), I planted flowers, modestly at first, but gradually disregarding of borders and directed with abandon; I crouched low in a tiny BaBa-made pond, with my mouth registering barely above the murky color of it, to root water lilies and then I gilded the pond with richly colored carp; I painted the insides of the wee cottage and added the elements of domesticity needed for weekend living at the farm (as we came to call it); I learned to drive a 1948 Ford tractor and to grade the road and brush hog the fields – nearly annihilating the tractor and myself in several mishaps caused by brakes that didn't always brake; I cleared rocky fields by hand and seeded acres and acres of grass and, then, upon success, I mowed it all until I was green in the face, annually. I loved farm work.

There were times when our individual pet projects, wherever they might be, led to aesthetic collisions: just about the worst kind for a duo of fussy artists. A particularly brutal collision occurred right at our, intended to be, quaint and peaceful family farm. My husband planted close to a dozen sycamore saplings alongside the house, in front of the house…just *absolutely* all around the house and then some. My increasingly elaborate gardening binge called for flowers alongside the house, in front of the house…just *absolutely* all around the house. My colorful, painstakingly nurtured flowers required full rays of sunshine, and trees, obviously, delivered shade, the enemy. We fought so constantly and furiously over sun and shade that some farm weekends turned near deadly. Had anyone ever filed for divorce over irreconcilable sycamores? If not, we verged on being the first.

Mother Nature mercifully came to our rescue by eliminating a few shady saplings on her own call, and over time I shrewdly negotiated trades for the intentional demise of others: sexual favors, Mother's day indulgences, and the like. I had learned all kinds of tools of the trade from my husband. By hook or by crook, the garden of my need would flourish, and that was that! I had needed to leave Erie, Pa. I had needed to go to Africa. I had needed to marry. I had needed children. And now, I needed flowers. There was no cap on need.

CHAPTER 15. LIFE'S DAILY BEAT

Back in the city – before Daisy, and the farm, and the sycamores – friendship took root between Greta and me soon after she moved into the neighborhood. Greta wasn't her actual name, but she looked like a Greta in my way of seeing: blonde straight bangs, sometime pigtails, sturdy frame…so Greta. She arrived with a husband and a young daughter about six months older than Max's two years. Spotting another rambunctious tot on our sparsely child-inhabited street, both of us felt like PLAYMATE lottery winners. We weren't as dialed in, at first, to our own co-existing desires for a certain type of grown-up playmate: a playmate experienced enough to appreciate and validate the challenges of day-to-day domestic life.

When I first met Greta it was with the cumbersome bulk of a cast attached to my left leg and a crutch under my armpit – souvenirs of fresh surgery. I'd like to boast that my ligaments snapped while hot-dogging down ski slopes at Park City, Utah, for I'd taken up skiing in my early thirties; it did occur skiing, but it happened with little fanfare on the first run of the first day of a five-day ski trip with Bob. Skiing almost as cautiously as I now walked, I was about 30 yards down the slope when my ski tips crossed in a poorly executed turn and my legs stretched in a grossly unnatural spread until I heard more than felt the ligaments go *POP* in my left knee. What a devious little ambush in the midst of a mountainous winter wonderland! My body tumbled over with the *POP* and my spirit with humiliation.

With my pride shattered beyond repair, I encouraged Bob to stay and ski the trip out while I flew back to St. Louis for ligament surgery. I couldn't shoulder the burden of ruining his adventure on the slopes, as well as my own. The dandy little mess that I found myself in was in was far worse than that of a previous skiing incident involving humiliation alone. On that occasion I took one of my graceless splats while skiing directly under an ascending ski lift full of spectators. In my tumbling-bumbling fall I lost not only a ski, but also the boot fastened to it. While lying there like a mogul, my ski and boot cruised straight down to the very foot of the mountain. I was left with no choice but to alternate between hobbling on one foot and sliding on my butt all the way to the base of the mountain.

"Loser!" I grumbled to myself all the way down, "You are *such* a loser!" Skiing was in some obscure way tied to my Erie, Pa. Polish inferiority complex. Vacationing at a ski resort resonated with a tony, upper crust vibe – so not like the vibe I was born into. It was bad enough that I viewed *myself* as a wannabe – my performance on the slopes broadcast it for all to see. The visible assurance that hordes of other skiers also engaged in spectacular and not so spectacular spills, and that I was not the only one to descend the mountain strapped to a rescue sled, did nothing to hearten my spirits the day my ligaments popped. And even after 20 plus years of relatively incident free ski trips with Max and Daisy barreling by and flouring me in white powder, I've never seen another ski sail to the bottom of the mountain with only a boot along for the ride.

Meeting Greta was perfectly timed to recovering from my ski accident. Bob actually went out of his way to initiate our meeting, for the thought of playing nursemaid and housemate to me had to have made his skin crawl. In barely no time at all, Greta and I came to share our lives with an ease common to breathing. Personality wise she was outgoing, chatty, curious, and bubbly with enthusiasm. I was introverted, quiet, and corked (except when drinking) – gurgling brook meets still waters. With a spread of consistency that felt thin in my marriage, I mattered in her daily life and she mattered in mine. Her everyday friendship made me feel good about myself in a way I hadn't experienced before. While our children played themselves out, we talked ourselves out, and while our husbands turned towards their work for reward, we turned towards each other.

We lived close enough to sip a morning cup of coffee together, baby-sit on a second's notice, share grocery runs, stroll the kids through the park on sunny and gray days, unwind with a Manhattan when our husbands worked late, laugh generously and cry liberally, whichever was called for. While I waited impatiently through Lily's arrival and then Daisy's, Greta's belly rounded, as if for both of us, to a nine-month peak. And as if scheduled from on high, she delivered a daughter a mere 13 hours after I received the studio phone call announcing the birth of my own daughter. Our girls arrived home from different hospitals on the very same day, destined for a lifetime of friendship. We celebrated the double miracle – the cruelest of miracles, as it turned out.

Arriving home one afternoon, I came upon the heart-palpitating sight of an ambulance parked in front of Greta's house. Rushing in, I found her crouched at the top of the second floor landing, wailing and rocking, wailing and rocking. Greta's precious baby had refused to wake from her afternoon nap on that sunny afternoon suddenly felled by darkness. A mere two months of nestling, cooing, and sucking, and her body lay still from Sudden Infant Death Syndrome (SIDS). There was no warning that day, or the day before, or the day before that…no chance for goodbye – *sudden* struck a blow as wicked and heartless as ever. Witnessing my friend's ruptured heart was near unbearable. Adding to her agony of the heart were two engorged breasts screaming for release, aching to be suckled.

Time itself inflicted its own torture by crawling at a funeral pace. Nearby families gasped in horror at the news of the infant death in our midst. The extended neighborhood experienced labored breathing for days…weeks; minds and hearts bogged themselves down in the unfairness of it all, the wrongness, the utter cruelty – none, perhaps, more than mine. How could I, why could I, cradle Daisy in my arms while Greta's arms hung empty? When would I stop feeling such wretched guilt over Daisy's still-beating heart? Why did I think that it would've been fairer to happen to my child and not to hers? Was it because her baby had grown so visibly from inside?…because Greta had waddled from the actual belly weight of her?…because she had screamed out loud with her legs spread? I could not hold Daisy in my arms for a time. I called upon Bob to do it. I could not allow myself to take comfort in the soft heat of her body. It felt wrong for me to find comfort.

Acting as if Daisy amounted to stolen goods, I concealed her as best I could from Greta over the next several days, prescribing her absence as medicine for Greta's healing. But Greta entered my house one afternoon while I was in my back studio working and came upon Daisy napping in the living room. As soon as I detected the sound of footsteps I knew that I was too late: Greta was face to face with Daisy. My own face broke out in a pained grimace and my stomach swirled in nauseous dread. Quietly, I peered around the corner expecting the god-awful worst from the moment at hand. What I saw was Greta's arms filled with Daisy – what I saw was Greta finding comfort. Daisy became solace for Greta in the throes of her grief. Slowly, we reclaimed life by sharing the single gift of Daisy.

Beyond what I now thought of as my own complete family – a girl, a boy, a husband, a me – there remained the rest of my family. Visits to Erie, Pa. fell into the annual category of family expectations, though everything about the visits and the place felt remarkably daily, even annually. Time spent there was anything but stimulating for my action-driven husband, but he dutifully made the best of his three or four day obligatory visits. Scenery wise, he took great pleasure in surveying the multitude of the city's majestic trees, some with enticingly bent trunks – a preference of his, you may recall. They lined the street curbs of the older parts of town and reigned over the front yards of even the most decrepit of homes, conferring natural treasure to near blight. And, of course, there was summer's pleasure of cruising along the peninsula to one of my favorite Lake Erie beaches with the free smell of char-grilled hot dogs scenting the way. On the beach he skipped rocks and built sand castles with the kids, the trio of them action figures for a Norman Rockwell painting. When such wholesome behavior turned dull for him, he concocted mini-thrills for himself by demonstrating to Max and Daisy the mischievous act of tossing bread crumbs onto the blanket edges of vain and unsuspecting sunbathers, chuckling with devilish glee as flocks of seagulls swooped down in a cacophony of startling disruption. While he beamed at the rewarding chaos, the kids and I scolded him in unison. The line delineating parent and child behavior was not always clear for Bob or our children.

Trees and seagulls aside, the main purpose of our Erie visit was to be among family. My brother Tim and his wife Diane topped me in the grandchild count by producing three: Brian, Steven, and Stacey. His family had moved away from Erie, so they made an annual visit as well. Sometimes our visits overlapped, totaling a happy mess of family for my mother. Though our visits appeared focused on bringing outside joy to those still living in Erie, Pa., I welcomed them for purposes of my own. I wanted my entire family to love Max and Daisy as much as I did. I wanted to observe my mother holding them, playing with them, indulging them – gestures I had forgotten or blanked-out from my own young life. I wanted a chance to catch a glimpse of her through their eyes. And I wanted her to catch a glimpse of me through theirs.

Max has no memory of the two occasions upon which he met his Great Grandma Stephanie Poplaski, my mom's Mom, before she died the year before Daisy's birth. His second visit took place in a wired and beeping room in the intensive care unit of St. Vincent's Hospital where my grandma clung stubbornly to the thin thread of life left within her. Over the years she had fallen victim to diabetes, high blood pressure, and debilitating arthritis. They struck like ruthless bandits, eventually robbing her of her east side home and her beloved gardens and landing her in a senior citizens apartment before demoting her even further to the confines of a nursing home. As she lay stretched out at death's door, I wished with all my might that she would open her eyes just a sliver, just wide enough to feast on the beauty of Max – one last delight as sweet as buttered lobster – before closing them forever. *Whichamacallit!* She opened them and she saw. I believe she saw. On April 13, 1988 she died at age 85. Despite her many ills, she was neither willing nor ready to die. She would never have conceded to either.

Max and Daisy both suffered through the horrors of nursing home visits to Grandma Smieciuich. Despite their wary puckered faces, I dragged them along out of a sense of unflinching devotion to my father. I was certain that he would expect it of me. Outliving both of her husbands by decades, in her early eighties she was moved to a nursing home by her eldest son. The move appeared premature, for from what I gathered she still had the ability to manage her house and mow her postage stamp size front yard with a push mower. Despite the formidable wall of her will, somehow it happened. Relegated to the boarding house of death – as I considered it – she aged into a stooping fixture, then progressed, with the help of arthritically deformed joints, into a crippled and bed-ridden body of misery. She shrank dramatically and shriveled to resemble a plucked emaciated bird, like so many lackadaisical others tucked into their final nest. She lived like that for ridiculously close to two decades.

The hallways of her so-called "home" were lined daily with rows of wheel chairs and gurneys packed with propped up and strapped in rheumy-eyed, drooling, white-haired or no haired residents – all unidentifiable crumpled up shells of their former selves. A visit to the boarding house of death fell under the category of "hair-raising," but it escalated to "especially hair-raising" the time we found Grandma Smieciuich on the floor of her room flailing about and emitting bird-like screeches to no avail. Despite observing such horrors, Max and Daisy marched in for their visits like tiny troopers set on performing their inherited duty for their near octogenarian great-grandmother.

A brief twinkle flickered across Grandma's narrow eyes when my children entered her shared room. Upon seeing them she squawked in her own manner of English, "Kum ere gev granma kiz," a gnarled hand beckoning. Color rose on their soft cheeks as they approached her bedside to kiss a pruned up cheek and observe up close a near-fossilized body. Max, born with a sensitivity in tune with mine, lingered near her to trace the purpley veins in her twig like arms and touch the bulbous knuckles of her hands, while a wide-eyed Daisy retreated for cover behind my legs. The room's window ledge held crocheted doilies hosting a smattering of knick-knacks, a few small stuffed animals, and her rosary beads – everything lined up single file, doing all it could to represent her fading identity. Curiously, as if she still entertained regularly, she consistently managed to have a small box of chocolates tucked away in a drawer. "Kandie, tek kandie," she urged, though they weren't chocolate covered cherries.

Even after reaching the venerable age of 100, Grandma exhibited little wisdom regarding conversational boundaries. I scolded her when she asked Max directly: "So whu yu like betr yer mommie or yer daddie?" With an angelic smile across his face, Max replied, "I like them both the same." Grandma Smieciuich looked genuinely disappointed, as if she had hoped to set off a round of family fireworks to spark up her dull existence. On another occasion, directly in front of my husband she asked me, "Yer huzben dreeenk? He big dreeenker?" "No Grandma, he's not a big drinker." Upon which he chimed in, "*She's* the drinker!"– pointing a long thick finger my way. The little bird cackled at his joke.

These nursing home visits made a lasting impression on my children. They held onto the trinkets she gifted them from her window ledge as if they were ancient and magical charms. When I shared with them the news of her death at 101, their eyes lowered with a befuddled sadness. Daisy retreated to her room and wrote the following:

Dear Smieciuich

By Daisy Gail Cassilly

I not tryng to be mean but I am glad you are DEAD because you don't safercate in the holspt and be DEAD in front of every baty else and thay will not no that you DEAD in the holspt and no one would cry a lot in front of you.

One thing I am sad about is that you are DEAD and I herd about it on Thuseday night instead on Monday night and I stile have your tetey bear you gave to me and the neklise you gave to me and Max still has your hert you gave him but he lost it but he will have to find it.

Daisy and Grandma Smieciuich spoke the same language.

....

My mother and stepfather were in the midst of enjoying life together: vacationing with friends, driving east for visits with my stepfather's family in New Jersey, and west to my family in St. Louis. Their life drifted at a calm and pleasurable pace, until the tremor in Bob's hand could no longer be ignored or controlled. The tremulous hand interfered with the precision required for TV repair work, forcing him into an early retirement from RCA and separation from the fine-wired electronics that he loved.

My mother held firmly to the hope of retiring to Florida with him, far away from the wintry weather she so hated and closer to basking among the privileged. It was her "wannabe" dream – her vision of escape. Bob, however, wasn't particularly keen on the notion of Florida, so her dream dulled and then faded away all together. In my mind, she failed herself by not exerting sufficient effort and resourcefulness into turning her husband around to her way of dreaming (i.e. my sycamore battles). If she really wanted it she should have tried harder. She should have pressed and shoved. She should have demanded it. She should have made it happen. Instead, she settled into a disgruntled state of feeling cheated by the physical collapse of two husbands. As his Parkinson's disease worsened, so did her resentment, followed by anger at herself for being resentful – she knew that he outranked her in the victim category. And in true Catholic fashion, she felt thoroughly guilty over the absolute mess of her conflicted feelings.

Towering over almost every other aspect of my stepfather's persona was his private dignified nature. It was deeply humiliating for him to witness loss of control over what had been his tall and sturdy and reliable frame. Then his speech slurred…then his vision blurred. Left intact and at his disposal were his mind, his hearing, and his appetite. To the sounds of his favorite classical music spinning on vinyl – mostly piano concertos, having played himself for years – tears were prone to trickling down his cheeks. He made no effort to wipe them away. Perhaps he couldn't. They were not, they were never, tears of self-pity. They issued to the sounds of beauty, to the poignantly composed notes of music that he loved and could still cherish.

At age seven Max started piano lessons, so on consequent family visits he delivered fresh and youthful notes directly to his grandpa's appreciative ears. Arriving at the blonde brick house on Greengarden Blvd., Max darted down to the basement to perform on his grandpa's old piano, which was still stored there. Max's tongue stuck out, curling to one side in his trademark gesture of concentration as he powered through his repertoire of kid's ditties with gusto: Cuckoo, Oom-Pa-Pa, Music Box Rock, Tumbalalaika, Popcorn… When Max performed in his first group recital I taped it and mailed it off to his grandpa, and during the long in-betweens of our Erie visits, Max's newest melodies sailed through the telephone receiver that I held in the air to capture them. Some notes arrived too quickly, some too slow, some were forgotten, some landed perfectly.

After 18 years of convent life with the Sisters of St. Joseph, Karen decided to call it quits, effecting a pitch perfect re-entry into the family. Her return made a world of difference as my mother's world began to revolve around the daily caretaking needs of an invalid husband. My mother had undoubtedly over the years, longed for, maybe prayed for, the day she could say to her firstborn, " I knew it was a mistake." But 18 years of commitment hardly qualified for an I-told-you-so lecture – even my mother couldn't cough one up. She settled for being overjoyed. And *why* did Karen leave the convent? I know you are wondering. Well, her answer is somewhat opaque, like mine – I can tell you that much – but the rest is uniquely hers to share, or not. Translating my own why into words has taxed my brain enough.

Having spent years teaching at all levels in parochial schools, Karen

SALTWATER

returned to secular life more than qualified to jump into the public school system for her bread and butter. Securing employment was a breeze compared to living life in a new skin – a lesson I'd already learned. Once gainfully employed it wasn't long before she climbed the established ladder of success, becoming an Erie, Pa. homeowner right on the divide between the east and west sides of town. She settled for good (as of this writing anyway) into a single lifestyle – not counting the pampered dogs and birds (and current cat) she has taken in with unconditional love over the years.

With Tim and I gone, Karen shouldered the responsibility of keeping my mother and stepfather up and running on Greengarden Blvd. She plugged the expanding gap in all realms of home maintenance, an area my mother had ascribed solely to the man of the house. My mother expended her energy on chauffeuring, struggling with all her slender might to transport her husband's uncooperative frame to never-ending doctor appointments in a quest for the newest and best drugs available to tame the Parkinson's beast. The disease afflicted him for 20 years of his life, the later of which were mostly swallowed by sleep. On our visits we usually encountered him sitting upright and rigid on the sofa in what long ago served as Tim's walk-through bedroom/den, shuttered eyes and a lax, drooping jaw doling out sleep.

Around the clock the house exuded the end-of-the-road hush of a funeral parlor – a maddening, shrieking silence. My mother felt like she was being buried alive. This woman who had all but resurrected herself from the dead decades ago because three young sets of eyes demanded it of her, was now worn out and depressed from years of adult caretaking: her mother, her brother, and now her second husband. With relentless effort she and Karen struggled to keep Bob at home where he begged to be – the one and only thing he asked for – but even with the aid of outside help they couldn't support the needs of his collapsing body.

When my mother finally caved and placed him, still with his pencil sharp mind, in a full-time care facility she was laid low by her betrayal of his one and only request. A few months later, just days after the world rang in a new millennium, he died for he had no will to live where he was. My stepfather's appreciative ears missed out on hearing Max's first solo piano recital during which he manipulated the keys with finesse and nuance to the compositions of Kabalevesky, Schuman, Khachaturian, and Liszt. It was a debut performance that would have resounded angelically in his well-tuned ears and released a waterfall of pride from the crinkled corners of his dimly lit eyes.

With decades of care giving behind her, I saw my mother as perfectly poised to bounce back into life – maybe even hobnob in the Florida sunshine. My stepfather had invested shrewdly over the years, leaving her adequately secured in green as she entered her golden years. "Move to Florida Mom, do it!" we encouraged. She ventured there on a couple of short jaunts to visit friends, but she no longer appeared to have it in her – if she ever truly did – to move from the place she was born to, the familiarity she lived by, and the ground her loved ones were buried in. Perhaps it was the fearful sting of aloneness and/or newness that immobilized her, though I'm guessing it was more the massive disruption involved in realizing her dream that kept her seated. The energy requiring such a feat had expired in her. She had lived too long in the shadows of death. But I could be all wrong. Maybe she had simply arrived at a point of full acceptance of who she was and where she was: **I am Irene Poplaski Soliwoda Siry and I belong in Erie, Pa.**

Regardless of her bouts of simmering resentment over the cards she had been dealt, my mother remained consistently grateful for her three children and the fact that we were thoughtful, or lucky enough, not to have posed any certifiable reasons for severe worry (that she knew of), though she worried anyway. As far as kids were concerned, she considered herself a blessed woman.

There came a St. Louis visit, however, during which I managed to set off an alarm that sliced through years of silence and choked up dust balls from the buried past. Her visit coincided with a vulnerable time for me, a time during which the rolling rhythm of BaBa and YaYa had skipped out of sync – a disruption I tried to conceal from her and myself through Manhattans. Her visit added strain to stress. One night, after the kids had gone to bed and she had retired to the guest room, I knocked on her door with a drunken kind of nerve. Entering, I immediately collapsed into blithering sobs and a long-running litany of questions: *"Why didn't you talk more about what happened to Dad? Why didn't you help me? Tell me exactly what happened that night? Did he love me? Are you proud of me? Why don't I ever feel good enough? What's wrong with me?"*

After years on end of convincingly playing the role of "the dimpled everything is fine child," my mother sat stunned by my total breakdown - as did I. She found her words, a few: *"I did the best I could back then. I had to make myself forget. Why bring up what happened nearly 40 years ago? How can it help anything?"* I couldn't soberly explain how the long ago past still clung to me, to my marriage, to my future…I couldn't bring clarity to my boggled need for and fear of men in my life. In a kind and concerned way she told me that I shouldn't drink so much. I denied it being a problem, denied the emotional trigger attached to it. I framed drinking as my salvation, not my undoing. Usually the bombs of my buried past only detonated when I was off alone wandering the farm after sunset with a couple of cocktails tucked away, freed to exhibit my morose slobbering self to Mother Nature. This outburst, in the presence of my mother, was pathetically embarrassing and grossly awkward, yet, oddly relieving. My mom continued to talk to me with a gentle tenderness – as if I were 11 again – sharing with me how much my daddy adored me, how I was the apple of his eye, how he loved to crack jokes, how he disrupted hushed movie theaters with his poorly-timed laughter, how he did this and how he did that… She swore to me that *nothing* would have mattered more to him than the happiness of his children. Sitting upon the edge of her bed, I had a crazy urge to move closer and nuzzle my head against her chest, but that went too far beyond the words I had already risked. Even alcohol couldn't land me in her arms. We were too much who we were.

Despite my disturbing surprise attack on my mother's peace of mind, the next few years deposited tiny packages of enjoyment at her feet: she could come and go as she pleased, cook or not cook, open the living room curtains wide to allow daylight to pour in unfiltered by the needs of diseased eyes. She spent countless hours at the mall rummaging through sales racks and collecting bargains, which she phoned to boast about, but wound up returning once the glow of the hunt faded and she realized she had little actual use for the bargain. My mother was consistently and stylishly well put together – pulling it off was the closest thing she had to a hobby.

Karen continued to be key to my mother's management plan inside and out on Greengarden Blvd., for it was my mother's turn to insist on staying put, even though she had talked a steady stream the last couple of years about moving into a condo. She now clung to her blonde brick house with a last stand ferocity, as if it were her everything. And increasingly it was, for despite her well-earned freedom she leaned towards becoming more reclusive than social, to duck from life rather than embrace it. Unlike her husband's body my mother's body remained healthy and fit, but her mind began to dabble in treachery, first revealing itself through slips and slides on basic and simple domestic chores. Then, her prideful sense of style began to give way to mismatched combinations totally foreign on her body. She exhibited less and less desire, or interest – ability as it turned out – to engage in daily conversation. Progressively, she abandoned all interest in the present and the future, becoming stuck like glue to her past until even that betrayed her. The brick house was her hold on reality – the home Salty had built for her.

....

Back in the Midwest, Greta and I spent a fair amount of time at the farm with our children in tow. Sharing Daisy amounted to one and a half kids apiece for each of us before Greta became pregnant again, and then again, delivering a healthy boy on each occasion. And two legged creatures weren't the only ones sprouting. Greta framed a picture in my head of sheep roaming the greened out pastures of our farmland. They would add a wooly and blissful touch to the pastoral landscape. Within her colorful past she had had some experience raising sheep, thus she assured me that we could easily handle the endeavor: the vaccinating, the breeding, the lambing…no problem! Sheep…I pictured and pondered… how marvelously quaint! And lambs…how ridiculously sweet!

Two weeks later I found myself behind the wheel of a borrowed truck with Greta sitting next to me and a husky, Cadillac quality, silver fleeced ram's head squeezed through the cab's rear window pumping hot and heavy breath in my ear throughout our two-and-a-half-hour drive. Four bargain basement ewes tumbled about in the back of the truck, along with the rest of the ram's handsome body. I shelled out bigger bucks for the ram because I was told that investment in the male was the trick to better breeding. Through mating his greatness would dominate over the insufficiencies of the dowdy ewes. By the time we turned down the gravel road to the farm I was fairly ram-smitten, affectionately naming the creature nibbling at my ear "Salty." The breeder made a point of telling me to never – as in capital N-E-V-E-R – befriend a ram, for they tend towards a territorial disposition best handled by aloofness on the part of humans.

Well, being named Salty and all, I figured that my ram was an exception. He ate corn and oats out of my hand and I held out fresh slices of Wonder Bread to him while scratching long and hard behind his ears and under his jaw. We had a loving relationship, until his ram-ness surfaced and got the better of him. After that, whenever I paid any form of attention to the nickel & dime ewes – Iris in particular, the scrawniest one who'd established herself as ewe leader – Salty reacted with what could best be described as a fit of jealousy. On his first attack he charged and butted me with a resounding *thwack!* to the thigh, and then a second *thwack!* to the back of the knee when I tried to run. Though shocked and limping, I offered him the benefit of the doubt: he was just in a temperamental snit. But his territorial charges and thwackings became so frequent that entering the pastoral field was like entering a bullring. We fell from the heights of love to the lows of utter disappointment in each other.

With our premiere lambing season at hand, I couldn't help but feel a tad nervous about Greta's animal husbandry skills. She bought a copy of the latest "How To" manual for up-to-date guidelines on when and how to assist in the lambing process, and when and how to neuter male lambs, since one virile male was all that was required for a small flock of ewes. We readied ourselves by preparing a birthing bucket: rubber gloves in case we (Greta) had to delve inside to assist, needles, syringes, antibiotics, vitamins, molasses to boost the mother's energy level, scissors to cut the cord, powdered colostrum, and baby bottles with jumbo sized nipples, in the event an ewe mom died on us during or after delivery. Given that sheep roam freely and deal with birthing quite naturally in numerous countries and environments, the emergency bucket seemed more for our nerves than our sheep.

With all four of our ewes ripely impregnated by Salty, we expected anywhere between four to seven lambs given that twinning is common. Well…it was more like popcorn popping when quads erupted out of one ewe, triplets out of another, and twins out of the remaining two: 11 lambs total! It became quickly apparent that the quad mom couldn't and wouldn't handle the nursing demands of four: she systematically rejected the same lamb over and over as it attempted hungrily to nurse. Congratulations! I became mother to a pink nosed rejected lamb named Tulip – so many flower names spouted from me that I suspected my brain had become permanently grafted to a bulb.

Tulip returned to the city with us and commenced life in a penned up area in the basement. As for a newborn, I established a four-hour bottle-feeding schedule, rising in the middle of the night to perform my ewe-like duties until Tulip could make it through six and then eight hours without raising a baaaa-ing ruckus for our neighbors to question. For fresh air we put her on a leash and walked her in Lafayette Square Park, generating double takes among dog walkers and dogs alike. Outfitted in pampers, Max and Daisy each took a turn at bringing Tulip to school for Show & Tell, skillfully demonstrating to their classmates the proper method for bottle-feeding a lamb. Tulip grew like a weed and her size, along with the deepening tone of BAAA's escaping from the walls of our house, signaled time to return her to the flock.

I was prepared for the territorial ones in the flock to butt her around a bit before accepting her back into the fold, but I wasn't prepared to wake one morning to find her dead for no apparent reason after only a two week return to what resembled heaven on earth for sheep. The untimely demise of that precious bottle fed lamb was the most personally devastating casualty over what was to become two decades worth of sheep succumbing to the inevitability of old age, the vicious sport of wild dogs, the bug of disease, and, as was likely in Tulip's case, an excess of human bonding.

Greta was a mother earth type overtly nurturing and comfortably disposed to engaging our combined lot of children with crafts, cookie baking, nature walks, and homespun adventure stories, while I indulged them in lawn mower rides and tended to farm chores that Bob had rather permanently strayed from. In the division of labor, I felt like I had a wife. Greta and I often felt as if we added up to more of a fair and square unified family than we did in our respective homes with our respective spouses. Her marriage, a long-standing, troubled one on many fronts for many reasons, was limping along on two bum legs.

And in my home, with life's daily beat striking its demanding but monotonous pace, complacency crept in and nibbled at its core – its fireplace. My husband didn't have much interest in routine maintenance, routine family life; he hated mediocrity and household expectations reeked, in his nostrils, of precisely that. There were times when it seemed like the only way I could garner his full attention was to jump on his back and harp at him, which repelled him as much as mediocrity. My frustration over the urgent litany of his *just one more time* excuses, coupled with the short life span of his promises, coupled with feeling like the contributions I poured into our partnership amounted to little in his measuring cup, grew and grew until my face looked permanently stung by resentment – resentment being a bug that festers ever so well on daily doses of perceived slights. The nasty bug of it even proved resistant to our make-up sex, for make-up sex in essence functioned more like a band-aid than a cure.

Standing back from his entourage of project-mistresses, he eventually took the time to take clear measure of the depth of the all around intimacy that Greta and I had developed over years of sharing daily life as equals. At the sight of the formidable bond formed between us – a connection only strengthened by the ghastly blow of infant death – jealousy stirred in him. In my analysis, he coveted the relationship he witnessed and wished for one equal to it in richness, but the daily cost of acquiring such treasure appeared to be more than his budgeted time could afford. He was driven in multiple directions on most days – dedication was iffy. He was who he was. And so, with a long history of insufficient self-worth strapped to my shoulder, I leaned in the direction of the bird in hand – just as he had taught me. I leaned towards my reliable friend for the bulk of the confirmation and companionship I craved.

As marriages stretch in length more is demanded of them, not less; here we both stumbled over excuses… so much love and all.

SALTWATER

CHAPTER 16. RISKING A FIX

Snip…snip…snip…
"More."

Snip…snip…

They fell like confetti curlicues sprawled about me, the permed locks upon which I had relied to secure my female identity for nearly 18 years. From time to time, I had considered tackling life without them, but I always wound up chickening out for there was grave danger and severe consequence tied to such risky foolishness. Example: I feared that my husband might reject me outright without them, or that whatever womanly charm I possessed would vanish in thin air, or worse, that the entire realm of my worth would be trimmed to non-existent.

My presence at the salon that day was an intense distraction for stylists and clients alike – especially for Roc, my forever long stylist. Year after year I had asked and paid for the same treatment: perm, hi-lights, trim, perm, hi-lights, trim… Uncertain as to the full nature of my why and why now, I nonetheless arrived there one day fully open to change: "I want a new color… red, I think…deep terracotta red."

That's why the clipped curlicues dusting my feet an hour later were the color of brick. My color transformation alone ranked breathtakingly sufficient as real change, but I was on a hot gambling streak so I wagered everything: "Now cut!" Even the walls of the salon seemed to catch their breath at the sound of my daring, an order that sentenced me to either a new beginning or the end of me all together. After a tensely nervous Roc finished the cut with an audible sigh of relief, I gazed into the mirror from all angles, viewing a short punked-out lush red do long on attitude. Coordinating the do with a slightly browner shade of dyed eyebrows, I strode out of the salon feeling as free as if I'd been released from Alcatraz – as if oppression exhaled right off the top of my liberated head. My skull tingled with a feathery freshness. Oh, I could skip! Oh, I could sing! You see, my appointment dealt with hair, but my decision to change dealt with courage.

When dropping the kids off to school that morning I gave them a wee heads up, saying that I might look a tad different by day's end – a courtesy I did not extend to my husband or Greta. Their shock was factored into the courageous merit of my act. Decked out in dark shades, tight black jeans, a black tank top, I sashayed into our place of business knowing that I'd find my husband and his crew there busy at work. Strutting down the red carpet of my imagination, I moved across the long stretch of warehouse space leading towards the smelly fabrication area where they were gathered. As if intuitively sensing eau de female, Bob's head lifted while I was yet a distance away, and without a hint of recognition I heard him mutter conspiratorially to the others, "Check it out guys!"

A small tribe of heads popped up from tasks at hand and lips curled in sly and manly ways. Bob's eyes stayed riveted upon me with a predatory focus and I knew in a flash that I was experiencing first-hand how he scoured and devoured the sight of attractive females when I was out of sight. I was on parade before his eyes, but he was the one standing naked before mine. With the dueling impulses of a stroked ego and a jealous heart, I faced him up close. "Can I help you?" he asked. A game and flirtatious smile shaped my lips before answering back, "Well, I don't know, *can you?*" At the sound of my voice, color erupted on his cheeks, speeding crazily up his forehead and down his bull neck; his eyes held the epitome of startled, with a spark of fear tossed in. "*It's you!*" is all he could muster.

Those few moments of his utter incapacitation are what I remember most, the seconds during which he was rendered vulnerable and uncertain, the brief time during which I stood more like him and he stood more like me. He claimed to love and crave spontaneity, but he preferred his own whims to dictate the when, the how, and the where of it. That day they didn't.

I was at the corner waiting when my carpool alternate dropped the kids off. Max appeared not to recognize me at first, but Daisy, with her eagle eyes, spotted my artsy belt buckle and acknowledged me as her mother based on that assurance alone. They both stared up at me with lips curiously gapped, as I assured them with my motherly voice and touch that nothing had changed but my hair – the honest truth regarding the outside of me.

I lingered in front of my house, waiting purposefully for Greta to return from picking up her own kids from a different school. Spying an apparent stranger idling about in front of my house, Greta fell for the bait; she got out of her car, approached, and asked me the same question my husband had, "Can I help you?" True to her nature, her eyeballs bulged past enormous when they came around to discovering me, and she unleashed a screech of disbelief followed by gushing words of praise for my outrageous act. It took a week for her to settle down and treat me confidently like me.

My very first night as a redhead my husband attempted to get back on top of things by luring me to bed and vigorously seducing my newness. The "new woman in the bedroom" fantasy spiced up our sex life quite nicely, but the change in me delved far deeper than sex could reach. Gambling with my hair ultimately rewarded me with a jackpot of self-confidence, effectively shaking up and enlivening the routine of my day-to-day existence. Just how I could feel so absolutely "born again" by the superficial effect of color and cut, I can't really explain, but I did. Perhaps it was the part related to conquering fear that left me so proud and delighted with my spunky new self.

....

My husband took the next shot at orchestrating a risky move of an all-together different nature – his move as grandiose in nature as mine was personal.

Bob's eyes gravitated magnetically towards more attractive women, they also zeroed in on unwanted buildings, mostly commercial ones floating in a sea of bargain basement prices like damsels in distress. He displayed a clever knack for climbing the real estate ladder by purchasing in our name – thus rescuing – one such neglected building and resourcefully transforming it into an income generating opportunity for us before selling it off and using the proceeds to rescue a broader, full-bodied damsel in distress, and so on. Any failure to successfully acquire the most current object of his heart's desire often led to a serious bout of despondency, from which he had to be coaxed out with tender care and assured promises of greater opportunities yet to come.

His brick and mortar transformations were actualized through the renaissance-like magic of a creative mind, brute manpower, and quality (though salvaged) materials. Additionally, Bob was close to clairvoyant in pinpointing a deplorable site with the potential of one day evolving into a must-have-site for a nearby business or institution caught on the upswing with no space to expand. That's precisely how the sale of approximately 60,000 square feet of filthy, sooty, contaminated, oil-saturated foundry space catapulted us into downtown St. Louis real estate entrepreneurs. The gi-normous profit on the sale of this suddenly "must-have-to-expand land" sent him on a merry and grand scale shopping spree along a fairly derelict stretch of downtown's Washington Avenue: a thoroughfare of partially abandoned, architecturally significant buildings that had once housed a reputation for thriving commerce in shoes and garments. The International Shoe Co., at one time the world's largest shoemaker, had built its headquarters there, establishing itself as one foot of the old triangular St. Louis expression: "First in shoes, first in booze, and last in the American League." The grand building, designed by architect Theodore Link and opened for business in 1910, was up for sale. It had been sitting on the market for quite some time, for in 1993 no one was gobbling up property in this semi-blighted neck of the woods. Bob's friends advised him to buy small in the area or not buy at all - advice falling on deaf ears. Giddy with cash in hand, he (we) made an insanely low offer on the giant two-building edifice, and, astonishingly, it was accepted. We acquired title to 700,000 square feet of space, more space than we ever dreamed of owning – more than *I* ever dreamed of owning, I should correct.

Along with the vast hulk of it came a smattering of paying tenants occupying space in the rear factory/warehouse portion of the building where, supposedly, Tennessee Williams had once been employed. The architectural gem of the front office building facing Washington Avenue with its stone façade and ornate detail, however, was entirely empty and in dire need of an infusion of tender loving care that could only be dispensed with cash: "credit" as we came to call it. Empty space wound up being our most demanding and costly tenant: "opportunity" as Bob called it.

As with prior makeovers, we tackled the building's exterior first in hopes of generating a curious buzz throughout the weary area. The brick and stone were sandblasted clean of grime, broken windows were replaced, the urine tainted foyer was disinfected, waxed and buffed, the architectural motifs adorning the front were repaired or replaced, the sidewalks were cleared of trash on a daily basis, flower planters installed, and rows of trees were planted curbside. Most notably (crazily many thought), we erected a massive and long running concrete fence sculpted into the shape of an undulating serpent to enclose and define the back building's parking lot. The formidable serpentine fence all but guaranteed making the news in the same manner that the giant Praying Mantis erected on our shop rooftop had; after all, loonies erecting zany and costly extravagance in an off-the-beaten-path part of old downtown clearly classified as newsworthy. What's going on there? people wondered. We had no sensible answer.

The curious buzz magnified from then on, luring kindred spirit types willing to take a risk on those willing to take a risk. With the trickling in of new tenants came income, and income insured progress - every penny reaped was channeled right back into feeding our 700,000-square-foot monster of a pet. This may sound odd, but my hair episode (courage) prepared me, strengthened me in some bizarre fashion, to face down the fear inherent in our soaring level of financial risk taking: I had been more afraid of the color and cut.

Artist types are by disposition, and often by necessity, resourceful people, and as such they gravitate towards similarly wired brethren like architectural preservationists and scavengers, people obsessed with authentic quality and beauty. Such bands of noble ones seek to salvage and restore threatened objects of distinction and materials of value for the purest of reasons, as well as for naked financial survival. St. Louis houses a vast network of these like-minded ones insuring continuous rounds of eclectic and intense bartering, usually consummated with no more than an honorable handshake and a memory etched in granite. Exchanges are driven according to need - or whim and need - as in "one man's junk is another man's treasure."

Cheap and relatively easy access to a wide assortment of salvaged treasure resulted in the emergence of distinctly restored, yet originally crafted, square footage in our behemoth of space, which we made enticingly available for well below rental market prices. Our immediate goal was to secure a couple of long-term leases to halo our project with an aura of financial viability. And it worked like magic. Previously vaulted bank doors opened before our eyes and offered us the use of terrifying amounts of ready cash. We had skillfully avoided incurring debt at any frightening level until now. We were at a make or break moment. Despite increasing bouts of something gaseously similar to indigestion, I ranked among Bob's true believers; I wanted him to fulfill his dreams even though they never stayed put. So, for better or for worse I signed my name right alongside his. I believed. That's not to say that I didn't carry on with my role of devil's advocate, for I did: he needed one, whether he knew it or not, whether he appreciated it or not. I was a necessary evil. In my way of thinking, anything that could force thoughtful pause on the eruption of creative euphoria about to blow in him could only help in the long run. In his way of thinking, I was a party pooper.

Artistically, we agreed on most things, but we differed as artists. Creative fulfillment ranked mighty high on my own personal list of priorities, but relationships always ranked higher. Falling in love with a building did not come naturally to me, but, my oh my, Bob's brand of elation could be wildly contagious over time.

Our joint business venture of years ago had officially linked our names with an ampersand, but I never attempted to assume artistic credit for the creation of the Praying Mantis, or the serpentine fence, or a family of hippos, or a giant squid, or a giraffe tall enough to loom large over a Texas highway, or even a Texas-sized sculpture of Jesus, to name only a few works commissioned or non-commissioned. And I never claimed to possess real estate savvy or prescient timing or driving ambition. I only claimed, fair and square, to having partnered equally in risking reputation and financial well being in the pursuit of my husband's dreams. I only claimed to having contributed any and all talents and time at my disposal to satisfying the multiple demands of business life and family life with such a man. Wearing the mask of a behind the scenes partner, I focused on injecting stability into a day-to-day regime ripe with pandemonium. Participating in Bob's fearless exploits – in whatever capacity – served to broaden the brush strokes of my thinking and expand my own canvas of abilities and possibility. He was a harsh guru. He exerted an indelible influence on both my strengths and my weaknesses.

The ampersand in our business name and the one in our Mr. & Mrs. name did not insure fairness on either front. When it came to the question of what mattered most in our lives, the "we" implied in business and the "we" implied in marriage often butted heads, looking like no "we" at all. Weirdly enough, it was the humongous challenge of our new building that aligned our differences into a steady flow of teamed up efficiency for a significant stretch of time.

With space galore to spare, Bob marked out his personal territory, reserving about 115,000 square feet of the back building as birthing ground for his whimsical indulgence: space where he could run wild assembling the jigsaw puzzle pile of scavenged materials he had been accumulating to erect some kind of realized magic. Besides feeling the security of financial backing from tenants and banks, even some family members and friends stepped forward to invest in the pulsating mystery of what could not yet be defined. My mother and stepfather were among the first to gift and loan us money, demonstrating unblinking support in their quiet way for doings they were not wired to comprehend, like the construction of a colossal 35,000 gallon-fish tank in what once served as an indoor, oily surfaced first floor parking garage.

That just happened to be the first tangible inspiration to light in Bob's mind: building an aquarium. "Fish tank" was hardly an adequate term for describing the massive container of water he constructed and adorned with voluptuous mermaids, menacing sea creatures, and cascading water play. The ambitious aquarium idea proceeded to gobble up space, spreading upwards through the mouth of a 50-foot long bowhead whale sculpted in plaster and interiorly designed to serve as a ramp up to a mezzanine level overlooking the "fish tank." I spent months of a cold damp winter crouched in the bowels of that whale, plastering and sanding secret crawl spaces concocted for a future's worth of tiny and daring adventurers. Downwards, the project excavated its way under the building's loading docks to forge a twisted maze of underground caves designed to rival the skill of Mother Nature, herself. The caves were sculpted with no obvious relationship to the fish tank, which was…well…leaking…and there were those poor fish to consider!

Even with professional intervention they suffered considerably more from our grand scale folly than my big and wooly sheep ever suffered from my pure ignorance. Blimps of slippery fishy bodies languished then expired, necessitating more and more scaly recruits to test our watery formula for survival. Our colossal, florid fish tank was there to stay, thus the fish would have to learn to live on art's terms. Some species began to show signs of adjusting, and the turtles we tossed in seemed both content and amused by their opulent digs. But, just as the fish started to swim about with a splash of spunk, Bob's original aquarium idea went belly up in his own mind. Maintaining living things involved too much care to qualify as fun on a daily basis, best to restrict them, best to limit difficulties to one massive aquatic centerpiece and move on from there. We were stuck with it anyway.

After the tank, the walk-thru whale, and the cave, events spiraled out of control: magnificently so like fireworks with a band of fuses lit at once. Our private endeavor began to draw an audience of curious onlookers eager for a taste of something spicy enough to rattle the palate of the local community. The scope and the pace of our mystery project jumped by leaps and bounds as segments of the starving artist population signed on, and friends of friends filtered in to take a look – a look that usually led them to pick up broom or shovel and stay.

Bob led our buzzing army and every soldier among us guzzled the can-do euphoria of the sweet madness engulfing us. With the once abandoned block all but vibrating from the frenzy, we drew in other sorts of visitors, civic leaders and wealthy patrons who detected in our grassroots verve a potent source of energy for jumpstarting the revitalization of the area soon to be dubbed The Loft District. For many dusty years the main problem in the area had been one of life, not of space or of buildings, and here we were splattering life about in every which way but the ordinary. These connected groups and individuals offered to buy in to the momentum of our waves. They tossed the perks of cash and kudos at our feet and we succumbed to their lure.

Unfortunately, though naturally, the perks came with snagging hooks attached: we would have to define our enterprise, set a time table for completion, and develop a mission statement geared towards benefiting the local community at large, not just ourselves. We would have to become a not-for-profit entity and live by the rules of one. All of our projects tended to evolve from creative whim, challenge, and opportunity, leaving profit to cozy up with a question mark, so the bleak financial tone of "not-for-profit" didn't rattle us, and the social-minded overtone of a mission wasn't altogether unappealing – at least not to me. Primarily, it was the fear of restricting ourselves (Bob) by definition and the dread of being governed by, and held accountable to, an outside board of directors that brought chills and raised hairy goose bumps. Bob would be tethered: cash for cage.

Though the not-for-profit road appealed to my nature, I wore my devil's hot red cape and taunted Bob with repeated warnings about the pit-falls involved in relinquishing full control, and questioning head on his ability to play team sports and follow team rules. Having always functioned as his own boss, we debated long and hard over the pros and cons of hopping into bed with the establishment. The choice fell to him in the end; he was the only one who could make it. He opted for the cash, cash was the only way the project could keep up with itself and, true to form, he ignored the cage. With his decision our partnership revved up its engines and accelerated full-speed ahead: BaBa would get it made, and YaYa would get it opened.

At this stage we semi-guessed that we were well on the way to constructing a kid's version of wonderland, though aesthetic and sculptural design dominated to such an extent that we might've been in the middle of birthing a co-existing haven for art lovers, as well. Given all the recycled materials and architectural goodies being freshly incorporated into what now added up to three entire floors of the 10-story building, green-minded folks and preservationist types flocked to us as if we were in the midst of erecting a citadel of salvation. All types licked their lips and stared in astonishment at the spectacle taking shape.

How do you title that which defies definition on all fronts? Circling round and round, entertaining hilarious, outrageous, and moronic attempts at labeling, our brain-storming led us smack dab back to where our feet were planted and our work was focused: the city. Embracing a generic sense of freedom we named our enterprise "City Museum," trumpeting the word "city" as a thrumming hub of energy, a bustling center of activity, a diverse body of possibility infused with a touch of panic. As for the musty, stuffy word "museum," we leaned towards the long ago interpretations of "cabinets of curiosities" and "pleasure houses." We envisioned the whole of the building as one luscious muse: a lively spirit imbued with powers to generate life and inspiration. Combined, the word "city" and the word "museum" covered vast and vague territory. I recall being the one to coin and push for the name, but over the years I've heard others lay claim as well. Whoever, the name seemed perfect.

It was none other than my husband's idea that I, his wife, assume the role of Director of City Museum, and Greta seconded the motion. At first I balked for a full menu of reasons, foremost being my obvious lack of experience and knowledge of such things and places. Studying the reality of the situation, however, it became clear that the most significant credential called for was one of knowing how to manage Bob and his erratic ways. No one could hold a candle to me there; my resume was top-notch. I signed on for our wildest ride yet.

My ignorance liberated me in a kindly way. It left me void of the magnitude of information, the volumes of right and wrong traditionally shouldered by a certified museum director. Without such cumbersome baggage, I was free to conceive and construct a day-to-day administrative structure using the same craft and sensibility I employed sculpting figurative structures in life, ones that breathed. It felt like the only difference was the material at hand: City Museum was simply a new material to manipulate, no more no less.

Greta came on board. She served as my sidekick, enthusiastically assuming the role of Assistant Director and exhibiting flair all her own from the get go. Together we formed a tag team of talents and shortcomings. We began shimming to an increasingly convincing beat of authority. Getting our hands on a library book outlining the "How To" for starting up a not-for-profit organization, we discovered that, essentially, we had to read the book backwards to relate. Seems we had completed most of the final steps, but skipped nearly all of the preliminary ones. Nothing like a spontaneous jump off the high dive to get things in action.

In October of 1997 City Museum's doors opened to a media blitz orchestrated by one of our town's finest public relations gurus who, upon being brazenly contacted by my obviously naïve self, generously offered her services pro bono – a term that plastered a completely clueless look across my face upon first hearing it. On opening day media honchos came face to face with a jaw-dropping, mind-boggling, mish-mash of creative gusto that thwarted definition. The sea of wordsmiths stood speechless. Along with the fish tank, the walk-through whale, and the caves, the first floor was overlaid with elaborately designed tile patterns and massive structural columns were covered with mosaic mastery. A staircase creeping up the back of a sculpted brontosaurus led to the second floor and Art City, an area in which artisans demonstrated the crafts of weaving, pottery, glass blowing, and papermaking. Adjacent to Art City sat an assemblage of vintage shoelace making equipment that hummed a mating tune as neon colored threads twisted and tightened in embrace.

The third floor offered up desirable space to an eclectic group of artist-entrepreneurs, allowing them to establish venues hi-lighting their own talents and quirky obsessions. We bartered space for talent and stuff. A sizable chunk of the floor was dedicated to establishing an architectural museum devoted to exhibiting, thus preserving, the precious bounty of St. Louis's salvaged treasures. On the other side of it, waiting live and ready to roll, was The Everydaycircus, featuring a homespun acrobatic group of young performers trained to leap, tumble, and swing their bodies into action for audiences of museum goers clustered around the circus ring and munching on pop corn and peanuts. The Museum of Mirth, Mystery and Mayhem was housed next to the circus. Among a competitive spread of so-much-of- everything vying to be nominated as "most unique and indescribable" out of the whole of City Museum, perhaps nothing ranked higher than The Museum of Mirth, Mystery, and Mayhem. The name, itself, was sufficiently perplexing, but the dim and carnivalesque seediness permeating every square inch of its occupied space offered an honest-to-goodness glimpse into its soul. A global History of the Corn Dog was mounted in graphic display directly across from where – supposedly – the world's largest pair of men's jockey-style underwear hung. Further in, Elvis's retro trailer housed a fortuneteller willing to reveal all to you for next to nothing. You could pull up a chair in the down low funkiness of the place and enjoy a smoke – you could drink beer there, too, and play the jukebox, and there was so much more. The only thing missing was snake oil for sale.

I could go on and on describing the plethora of concoctions, activities, and exhibits, the wealth of both witty and fine sculpture incorporated into our museum, but it would take another book to do it justice. I was Director and spokesperson for years, but it never became easier to be clear and succinct when talking about City Museum.

During the media opening I delivered a short spiel from the top of the brontosaurus staircase, flanked by dozens of artists, employees, and supporters. Nearing the end of my extensive thank you list, my eyes turned misty and my voice choked as I addressed a deeply personal thanks to Max and Daisy, the tiny troopers who had paid the price of neglect during our long-running marathon towards opening day. For the life of me, I can neither recall nor imagine how I juggled their young needs with the relentless demands of our all-consuming muse – it couldn't have been anywhere near as well as they deserved.

In relatively little time, daily crowds began to swarm like bees to honey. Multi-generational families poured in, each generation succumbing to their own brand of elation. By the end of our first year somewhere in the astounding vicinity of 300,000 people had come through the doors, and we set out to get them back by a steady drum-roll of additions and changes, additions and changes. As time flew by, contributions grew, bills grew, attendance grew, vision grew. The noise of our unlikely success advanced toward the decibel range of phenomenal. People referred to us in terms such as: brilliant and irreverent, anarchists and saviors, rough gems and local treasure. We built it and they came.

The lioness's share of my time crept steadily in the direction of fund raising, saddling up with our board of directors to raise millions of dollars to feed two increasingly ravenous and competing appetites: 1. Bob's mega-vision and 2. The not-for-profit call for educational programs, community outreach, and such. This was far from my favorite part of my job, but I became a polished saleswoman capable of delivering impassioned and sincere pleas for support, even off-the-cuff. At times I felt like I was back in the pulpit with Sr. Cephas, all pumped up to play on the heartstrings of a captive audience. Dividing up the financial spoils among the dueling appetites, however, became one hellish job wrought with troubling domestic ramifications.

Far more pleasant was fielding phone calls from the eager-to-participate masses of people wanting to donate (re-cycle) things such as: the entire contents of their recently departed great aunt Nettie's attic, or the oddity of things such as thousands of cheap wrist watch bands, old crane parts and plane components, billboards, viaduct beams, miniature train collections, church pews, and store fronts – just about anything sitting idle and aging in uselessness. It wouldn't have surprised me to find a husband or a wife dropped on our doorstep for recycling. We had blessed *and* cursed ourselves by effectively broadcasting a scavenger persona and building wonders out of the most unseemly materials: hundreds of stainless steel steam table pans (employed as rodent housing at a medical school lab before heading our way for reincarnation into lavatory walls), expanses of conveyor belts once assigned to shuttling shoes throughout the warehouse, floor sweepings referred to as FOD (foreign objects of debris) from a Boeing aircraft facility, and shells from a few weeks worth of oyster consumption at a local bar - just to give you an idea.

The public fell in love with our clever and resourceful ways and they wanted to express their approval by sharing every bit of their – now thought to be precious – junk with us, no matter how lousy. Saying no was extremely hard for some in our merry band – need I single out our resourceful leader? Mounds of generous rainy day salvage piled up around the property, inside and out, resembling heaps of warty toads waiting to be transformed into princes.

....

While this wacky but happy type of chaos rumbled throughout the confines of the museum, a poisonous type rumbled inside me. The relatively insane pace of keeping up with our crowning accomplishment generated a tense fatigue, and the tense fatigue gravitated towards relief, and relief could be found in my liquid love, Manhattans – so full-bodied and sweet, so accessible, so soothing. I don't recall imbibing more than my large standard dose of evening comfort, but something began to swirl about viciously inside me with every nightly pour: hatred, I think. Hatred of myself for *needing* to drink; hatred of waking up every morning to the same futile promise of *Tonight I Will Not Drink*. It was an accumulation of this vile brew that spewed over in my office one unsuspecting morning.

Greta uncorked it with an administrative pop when she emphatically stated that we needed to have a serious conversation, right then and there on the spot. Behind her in-control demeanor I detected a touch of uncertainty – almost terror – circling her eyes. She proceeded with the silenced truth quickly after so many years…rather quickly. "You're an alcoholic, you need help." Just like that… rather quickly. She expected to be shutdown, expected an outburst of anger and denial. She didn't expect an on-the-spot sobbing breakdown. She didn't expect surrender. Neither did I.

And it's that feeling of surrender that I remember most. It stunned me! I would've assumed that within my jumbled lifetime of trial and error, faith and disbelief, the deepest bottom of the word surrender would have revealed itself to me. But the way the word settled on me at that moment – like an anchor tied to the bitterest truth of all – I realized that it hadn't. I felt the full dimensions of it, more raw and naked than even my departure from Malawi. Greta arrived at work that morning fully prepared in the event of a miracle: she did her homework, made the calls, and cleared my calendar. In the event of the miracle of willingness, all I had to do was show up the following day at a certain location and check myself in for a four-day in-patient treatment program.

As I experienced it, tomorrow sounded as far away as the moon. I had to go then and there, before my courage evaporated, before I was tempted with the sip of an unthinkable goodbye. I called Bob to come to the office. At the sorry sight of me his expression took on a sheen of panic, though his voice held steady with its everyday tone, "What's up?" He had touched on the drinking topic during our years together, accused me of it, particularly during arguments when both of us had had too much. On each occasion I'd firmly shut him down with irritable denials and rock-hard excuses. My about face stunned all three of us.

I'd like to believe that I effectively disguised my problem from just about everyone over the years, though I doubt I was that clever or lucky. I focused mostly on hiding my need and not my glass, though I did some of that too. Drinking was practically a bona fide requirement to qualifying as an authentic artist couple – nearly all the artist couples we knew testified to the truth of it. Alcohol played a role with fickle consequences in our lives: imbibing could make me just like Bob wanted me to be, or not, and it could make him just like I wanted him to be, or not.

Thanks to a decade of convent training, mustering the discipline to function daily at a high level of efficiency and delaying personal gratification until my duties were done came quite naturally to me. Arriving home from work, I made certain to attend to the kids' needs before allowing my reward to flow, but I obsessed on reaching that glorious moment from the time my morning alarm rang. There were a host of pleasures and challenges that filled my busy days with reward, but the sorry bottom line of it was that a day without a drink was a day lost in my book. And it's precisely that type of thinking that sentenced me to prison, a cell of solitary confinement infested with rotten, dirty, foul smelling shame.

When I had to attend an evening open house or school conference for the kids, I reluctantly pushed back my reward time to nine at night, or later – the remaining drinkable time barely qualified as sufficient, it was close to a day lost. When I had to help Max and Daisy with schoolwork – which was always – I insisted on tackling it early, so I could cozy up to the fading light with a crystal stemmed goblet (one of Grandma Poplaski's finest), filled with golden reward and adorned with a bobbing cherry. In a vague and fluffy cloud of passing time, the evening led to my eyelids drooping and bedtime. My drinking life all but strangled me with its addictive grip; I was hooked on precisely that which pained me the most. Sadly, my marriage increasingly reflected the same dynamic: not the strangled part, but the part about being hooked on what pained me.

Even after 13 years of sobriety, I'm still squeamish writing about a disease so frequently and coarsely wrapped in the stigma of a brown paper bag. It's hard for me to attach alcoholic to myself, hard to claim alcoholism as my own. Sharing this truth has felt like running down the street naked. I struggle to objectively list it in my mind among other certifiable diseases linked to the chain of heredity. I have to constantly fight the temptation to view it as a form of lowlife weakness dumped like a ton of bricks on top of the guilty-stupid-something's-wrong-with-me garbage pile I've been working to clear out of my life.

My departure line to the kids was that I was checking into the hospital for a few days of routine exams: the human version of oil and air filter changes, tire realignment, brake adjustment…While packing my suitcase, I fell to such a ground level of need that I asked Daisy to lend me one of her favorite dolls, Water Baby, to provide me with something to cuddle at night and to remind me of her. The doll was a rubbery thing filled with a cup or two of water to give it a semblance of human pliability. She, of course, said yes.

When I checked into the re-hab center, the attendants immediately confiscated my suitcase for inspection. I was startled by the notion of an "inspection," and truly mortified when they came upon Water Baby. "Ohhhh…that's my daughter's…she *begged* me to bring it along," I lied. I watched as they unplugged her and drained her right in front of my own draining face. Apparently, every trick in the book had been employed to smuggle in booze. Was it possible that there were more pathetic drinkers than I? The possibility consoled me.

It wasn't until the third day that I was permitted to receive visitors. Bob and Greta arrived together. I moved towards them with a re-hab hollowness that appeared to shrink me in size as well as spirit. They looked at me with trepidation, as if they were visiting an invalid in intensive care. The visit was awkward and strained for I was temporarily scared of everything and everyone; I had no idea who I would be when I checked-out of what felt like temporary safety.

Both of my visitors brought encouragement, gentleness, and sincerity with them. Bob, moved by the sight of me, said he would support my recovery 100 percent of the way; he said he would *never* hold my illness against me; *never* think ill of me for it; he said he was *proud* of me. He believed, and so did I, that self-improvement on my part would reap benefits for our entire family – it might even cure a partnership ailing from the perils hidden in success.

But, for my husband, there was a shady downside lurking in my recovery, for in some ways my alcoholism had provided him with both ammunition and cover. My self-improvement, my sobriety, would rob him of that. It had been convenient to point a finger to *my* problem as *the* problem increasingly festering between us. By doing my part and tackling my demons a dangling finger was left in the air, a finger reflecting no inclination to take a turn at pointing back in his own direction, as far as I could tell. For, from my vantage point, our giant leap towards success had altered the man I had married – fame and power had served his talent but not his person. Power, after all, carries an addictive urge to satisfy itself first, and fame comes with adulation.

When my in-patient treatment ended and I was released to home, I arrived on the doorstep of a harsh reality lined with question marks: How would I spend my evenings? How would I entertain and socialize among drinking friends? How would I wrestle myself free from the trappings of a shy nature without the support of a Manhattan? How would I swallow inferiority with a dry throat? What would reward me at day's end? How could I bear the sight of alcohol absolutely everywhere but in my hand? Minus alcohol the entirety of my life would have to change.

This struggle to re-focus and re-define my life was indescribably grueling and challenging. It required nothing less than a day-to-day miracle. Afloat on a raft of counseling and AA meetings, I made it to the seemingly unreachable 30-day mark…then to the 60-day mark…then six months…one year………13 years and counting.

Early on at my AA meetings, I stated quite adamantly through words and body language that I would **NEVER!** *be grateful* for not drinking. So many people used the word "gratitude" at AA meetings that I wanted to tear my hair out, storm out of the room, and drink! I sat glumly in a place where I felt cheated and deprived that I could not drink like other people – like practically *everyone* else it seemed. *Poor, poor me! Why me!* Even at "one day at a time" there were days that passed for years, and walking without a crutch to the tune of new purpose did not happen by just removing the bottle. Placing the bottle out of my line of vision simply cleared the way for me to see more of *everything* that needed fixing.

S l o w l y . . . .s l o o o o o w l y . . . on pace with an extremely old, arthritic turtle, I crawled ever so steadily over tender blades of grass until awakening one morning to find myself fully coated in the dew of pride. What a fresh and marvelous sensation! Pride at its purest, pride at its best! I felt so good about myself. The permed and golden curlicues were shorn from my head; the bottle was removed from my lips. I had nowhere left to hide - I had no more need to hide. In dispossessing myself, I came to possess myself. Luscious pride trickled in as venomous poison trickled out. I was transfused in mercy, and, lo and behold, I was grateful.

....

Back to work.

Two full years of City Museum being up and running netted us a wall of impressive awards and a forecast for bombastic expansion. Bob's drawing board was covered with the permanent scrawl of: *More! More! More!* He wielded the hammer of creative control, but given the not-for-profit way of things, he didn't get to nail down financial control. That thorny lack of control grew into an insurmountable obstacle – as I had feared it might from the start. I was yanked by the limbs trying to play fair with two masters, though I was certain that he viewed me squarely on the side of the enemy. His preference for spur-of-the-moment projects generated by nothing more than impulse, as opposed to the budget-plan-schedule variety called for by our administrative structure, pretty well doomed the team approach that he had signed onto in exchange for cash. Despite the museum's ongoing public success, the months leading into our third year met with rough sailing behind the scenes, and the months leading into our fourth were engulfed in stormy seas. It soon became painfully clear on multiple levels that ceding control to him on *all fronts* was his proposed way of moving ahead - his only way. His prior decision needed reversing and he was hell-bent on doing it.

It's difficult to fully explain in words how a mega-environment built and spirited forward with communal backbone and boundless goodwill could devolve into something resembling a calculated battlefield. Success, power, duty, direction, money, jealousy, desire…all turned into weapons. And, it's heartbreakingly painful to explain how nearly two decades of partnership – domestic *and* business – could crack and fall from the binding glue of oneness. My husband and I had engaged in rounds of counseling over the years, tackled sore spots, out-of-sync priorities, and personal hurts in the hopes of keeping our ship upright; we made efforts along the way. We both shouldered a share of guilt for betraying sworn fidelity, belying trust, and otherwise rocking the marital boat, each in our own ways. Neither of us wore a halo, and our ungluing did not happen overnight. Yet…it was as if I woke one day to morning's light and there it was: undone. Who actually pulled away first, and why, and how, and when? Who stopped caring? Had we stopped caring? Could we be re-glued? Did either of us want to be? Questions are late by the time you are able to clearly see that the foundation of love, trust, family, and home has begun to slide from under your feet at an unstoppable pace.

I could read my husband's black darting eyes and the set of his clenched jaw easier than I could read the alphabet: all it took was the nerve to look. The news I now read there was terminal, and about me. Six months of sobriety set me on the road to saving myself, but it couldn't accomplish the twosome work of saving us. Bob's excuses for missing dinner, then nights, sounded with hopeless clarity, though a breeze of lukewarm love sometimes wafted from him in passing. The kids stopped asking where their Dad was at suppertime – they knew I'd say no more than the customary he was working late on a special project, another special project. I hoped they believed it. We fell into associating like two people who work in the same building but have no reason to speak to one another, nothing to say that the other might actually want or care to hear. The chill between us spread with glacial consequences when he revealed that he had, in fact, rented a furnished apartment. All that remained to be stated in clearer terms than that were the ramifications of the word *separation*.

And what about our beautiful children? What about Max and Daisy? Would a parental breakup scar them for life? Every question relating to them viciously stabbed at my heart, and I felt deserving of every thrust. We sat them down on a hot summer's day, only a few days past the fourth of July fireworks, and I delivered another kind of blast as gently as I could: "Your dad and I have decided to try something different…we're going to experiment with living in two different places for awhile…we think it might help us…it has nothing to do with either of you…we both love you…you'll spend plenty of time with each of us….things will be fine… you'll see" - all the while knowing that we were tearing them up by the roots and shattering their young hearts. I felt like a murderer. Their dad chimed in with a diversionary ploy, trying to lift the mood by promising them each a cool bedroom to design in his new place. Daisy was 10, Max nearing 14. While I spoke, Daisy was masked in her own peculiar version of emotional blankness, while Max attempted a heroic smile that only served to highlight his hurt. We had just soft-pedaled our greatest failure as human beings directly at them, our innocent children. The camouflage of "things will be fine" couldn't begin to hide the catastrophe of it all.

It should have arrived surprise free, but the next day, the day of his departure, struck me like another round of sudden death. *"C'mon kids, let's go check out Daddy's new place!"* he cheerily bellowed. The kids were so used to "us" that they presumed I was included in his invitation. I assured them that I'd see it the next time. Instead, I entered our husband/wife bedroom and knelt on the floor in front of the family's laundry pile waiting to be sorted and folded: first his socks….then his tee-shirts… then his threadbare Fruit of the Loom briefs… He had removed next to nothing from the house. I heard him coming down the hallway, his large feet making their elephantine thud. He stood framed in our bedroom doorway to say that they were leaving, that he would drop the kids back later. I kept on folding. I couldn't look up. When the front door shut with their departure, I fell upon the laundry – *his* laundry – cradling it and sniffing it as guttural cries rose over the shredded fabric of us. This was not a separation, it was the end, and I knew it.

We managed a barely acceptable, mock stable front at work, that is, until the separation started gnawing on the brittle remains of us. I was saddled with the responsibility of reassuring many more than our two kids: there were the board of directors, hordes of employees and volunteers, and multiple business entities – not to mention keeping myself in an upright position. Despite witnessing my private and personal life turn into the gossipy public fodder of a soap opera, I was counted upon to walk tall, smile and greet, focus and direct, and act cool, for eyes were upon me. Other than the episode at the laundry pile, I succumbed to only one other massive private breakdown during the early months of our separation, it happened while showering.

I lapsed into envisioning Bob there, on the very spot where I stood under strands of falling water: the way he crossed his massive hands over his chest, lowered his chin, and swayed from the hips as water washed over the length of him, matting the darkening hairs on his body and jetting off the pinkish tip of his penis. My knees buckled at the sight of him, my body slid down the tile wall and laid there puddled in warm running water…eventually cold running water piercing my skin like ice daggers. Balled up in fetal incapacity, I shivered and let loose with gut wrenching wails over the loss of the man I loved, frozen to the bone by a coldness far more chilling than the water pouring over me.

When the word "separation" finally notched its way up to the word "divorce," speculation over it wreaked tumultuous havoc on the workings of the museum. The board of directors found themselves mired in a domestic cesspool; consensus grew that one of the two of us would have to go, though I kept hoping otherwise. Along with my marriage, my job sat on the brink. My soon to be ex-husband rather ruthlessly masterminded ways to stir up the mucky mess in such a way as to guarantee that I would be pushed out the door. His vision was viewed as integral to the museum's future, despite his exasperating and destructive behavior.

Talk of what had been *ours* turned into talk of what was *his*, reference to what *we* had accomplished reformatted itself into what *he* had accomplished. On both the wife front and on the job front I went up in smoke, just like that. Local newspapers offered accounts of the ruckus between spouses, board members, banks, donors… I'm loath to offer up the particulars of my actual departure, so I won't, except to say that stunning and uncalled for betrayals of intimacy occurred, and promises close to freshly hatched were shattered beyond belief. Even knotted in the wretched emotional state I was in, down deep I grasped the inevitability of my departure, but not one iota of me could comprehend the cruelty being employed to make it happen.

I often wondered - like a million times - how he could deal the final blows without appearing to suffer from them himself, for he walked about chillingly detached. Had he so thoroughly voided the entire slate of our fruitful past and purged me from his heart entirely? Or, had he intentionally blinded himself and padded himself by fabricating a dense and self-righteous coat of anger for the explicit purpose of protecting himself from blame and pain? Didn't he honestly know that he bore a mighty share of blame? Did the excruciating burden of loss and remorse fall entirely on me alone? Out of all, and I mean *all*, of the destruction strewn around me, it was the loss of that complete family picture – the mother, the father, the children – the crushing loss of a complete family that rose from the suffocated past to burn me raw all over again.

There might be good reason to revert back to the Chainsaw name at this sad point of the story; after all, the deeds done were effectively toppling. But, the fact is, those early Chainsaw years buzzed with passion and possibility, not annihilation. Now, it was protracted silence that deafened me: his silence. When we came together to meet for the final paperwork of divorce – after almost two years of separation – I sobbed out a litany of explanations, apologies, compromises, questions…for I suffered from wounds that I believed only he could heal. His cold guard dropped for a brief moment and a glimmer of tenderness registered in his eyes, but no "I'm sorry" made it to his lips. Absorbing my apologies as deserved, he never offered back the ones I deserved, the ones I waited for. His appraisal of the situation was bluntly pragmatic: 1. We had our time together. 2. Things were different now. 3. It was time to move on. Every tracking device out there indicated that I was stranded solo on the island of regret.

For many months, many years…I lived chained to the hope that he would one day call, or knock on my door, and voice pangs of remorse and loss, that he would feel an urge to reminisce, a need to validate our years together, a desire to acknowledge me in a loving way…. It's what I wished for the most on my birthday, Christmas, Mother's Day, our anniversary… every day, every year. But we weathered our divorce like sun and snow: never had the differences between us been so boldly distinct.

Having known him so well for so long, why on earth did I fall victim to surprise when he moved on swiftly and intact? He had done precisely that countless times out of boredom with old projects and excitement for new ones – even a change in weather could whisk him away without regret.

<hr />

Despite the tragedy of it, I breathed in an air of blessed relief when our divorce settled: layers of tension wafted out of my pores and out of the very house itself. As a husbandless woman in a fatherless house, I struggled to fill the gap by holding on to tradition, adding on to structure, and aiming forward. It was all I could think to do. The kids and I carried on with our annual ski trips and we forged new travel adventures to places like Peru and Costa Rica – places with jungle green powers to distract. Almost routinely, the three of us engaged in individual and family counseling. Weighted down by guilt over having stymied Max and Daisy's childhood, I was on a mission to, at the very least, minimize their scarring. I was a bit of a wobbly duck at it, but I tried my hardest.

Divorce for any reason tears upon the fabric of family and home. Even with warnings sounded and provisions made, the shelter of belonging flies off like a roof in a hurricane, leaving your home and your very person standing in rubble. Individuals absorb the aftermath of the storm's damage each in their own way, according to their own needs and ability. Some choose to walk away and not look back, while others choose to camp in it and rummage through the remains hunting for embers of life – a compulsion not altogether unlike kneeling over and clinging to the worn and scented laundry of one no longer there.

CHAPTER 17. FLYING SOLO

My studio had sat empty and cold for the last several years while I'd been hitched 24/7 to the dreams and schemes of my now ex of a husband. Never had I ignored my personal sanctuary for so long. Sensing my availability, the space of it seemed to reach out to me like a long lost friend eager to reconnect, a friend willing to move beyond the affront of having been cast aside thoughtlessly for so long. Propped in my favorite corner in my old plaster and resin splattered rolling chair, I observed the northern light as it poured in from generously-sized windows and settled on the plentiful contours of dusty sculpted figures – rounded asses, taut thighs, exaggerated cheekbones, heavy eyelids, pursed lips – touching them with a ray of clarity. There, in my corner, I felt similarly touched with the sureness of knowing that creating was the first and best step I could take towards reclaiming my soul.

Solitary studio life sounded like a version of heaven on earth. The danger of engaging in such a life long-term, however, is that it can lead you to become a little, or a lot, reclusive – even anti-social, cynical, and blunt. Your social skills can get abrasive. I already possessed a fairly blunt vocal hammer – which I wielded, most often, to conceal my homegrown inferiority – I didn't need more of the same. Drinking and employment in the public domain had previously insured and/or required that my introverted constitution be juiced enough or responsible enough to perform effectively in social and work situations. Without either of those demands, hardcore reclusion felt as tempting as retiring to my warm waterbed on a frigid night. For two years I took cover in my studio, immersing myself in sculpting a new body of work that I deemed worthy of exhibiting. The notion of exhibiting exhibited my first signs of healing.

As a result of no longer being a nun, a student, a teacher, a business partner, a museum director, a wife…when someone inquires as to *what it is I do*, I am forced to rely on a far more nebulous means of defining my existence: "I'm an artist," I whimper. For some reason it's a hard tag for me to get out. And it doesn't help a bit that 'fessing up to it frequently evokes the generically irritating response of: "Oh, inteeeressstinggg!" – usually accompanied by curious bobbing of the head and nothing more. Far worse than that reply, however, is the dreaded, gushy reply:

> *Oooohhh Reeeely!* My mother was an artist and I *soooo* wanted to be an artist but I don't think that I can even draw a measly stick figure anymore even though my grade school teacher Miss Cleverass thought I was real talented and she kept tellin' me to push myself push myself so I decided *what the heck* I'll try some pottery and I made some *real* cute things over the years mostly for Xmas presents *no money gosh no* but then I decided to try painting since I had a real natural *you know* feel for color and you just can't *believe* the things I made and makin' them made me feel like I was goin' somewhere fast but you know what I honest to goodness wanted to do was metal work doing jewelry and stuff like that because so many people *will buy* that kind of stuff *know what I mean*???? After all there's an artist deep down in everyone *isn't it God's truth*???

On such numbing occasions I pretend that I'm still in the convent. It's the only way I can control my mouth.

Though I made it to the studio most days, getting there wasn't the primary reason I hauled my body out of bed: I rose each and every morning because of Max and Daisy. I pledged, first and foremost, to center my life on their needs, no matter what state I woke in. My pledge may have originated from guilt, but I committed to it from love. Studio time was relegated to school day hours or their weekends with their father. It was obvious to me that hands-on responsibility for their daily needs, school or otherwise, fell on my side of the divorce – regardless of the official wording – just as it had fallen on my side of the marriage. I didn't dare gamble on assuming otherwise in a parental divide that looked to be one-sided on communication.

The lackluster academic performance of both kids called for a firm routine of assisting, prodding, and nagging served up as regularly as breakfast, lunch, and dinner. Though sufficiently capable when willing, neither seemed motivated, interested, or excited by the prospect of academic success. Having grown up in a highly unorthodox household brimming full of exceptions to the rules may have dulled the appeal of such routine standard fare. Their father had bragged openly to them about his skipping school exploits and graduating from high school with the lowest possible honors. Annual repeats of the school drill, badgering and all, bordered on torture over the years – mostly for me. Drawing closer and closer to my wits end year after year, I swear that if I could have forged or purchased their high school diplomas I would have.

That's the skinny on the academic front.

Though convinced that my eyes were fully open to their social comings and goings, both kids managed to pull off a complete array of teenage trickery. Blinded by their consistently sweet and loving demeanor, I was naïve to the hormonal call of nature and peer pressure to pull one over on Mom. They managed to pull off a lot more than one on me before I was mother-shocked awake with the full (?) discovery of their high school exploits. We experienced some rocky and trouble infested times while each of them learned to navigate their way through the temptation filled rivers of youth. Life calmed in my world, but they were in the throes of coming of age; they were sipping at the ocean of adulthood.

And, that's the skinny-skinny on the social front.

There is a bounty worth sharing about the character and lives of my beloved children. I have only sketched their outlines, not filled in their vivid colors. Their memories, their stories, are for them to write.

In the grieving cycle of divorce, I appeared to be both a slow-learner and an under-achiever. Meaning, I took longer than the three-to-five-year dose of time routinely prescribed for bouncing fully back into your being and forward after a marital collapse. Multiple years worth of counseling sessions resembled a parade of shovels heaving off scoop after scoop of dirt, until finally tapping upon the lid of my buried vault filled with the Polish thing, the Father thing, the Mother thing, the Catholic thing...

Upon cracking open the vault the work turned towards that of archeology: the thoughtful dusting off of brittle fragments and the re-piecing of history. Dots connected into lines and lines connected into shapes and shapes connected into understanding. As my misconstrued past righted itself, the cure of it inched towards my present body and commenced massaging the more recent scar tissue of divorce. But the dual challenge of healing my past and my present met with obstacles as well. I was vulnerable to setbacks along the way. When Bob proceeded, after a long round of sampling, to marry a much younger woman and father a child, as well as adopting her first child, the news hit me with the force of a charging bull. It wasn't that I wanted him back. It's just that I didn't want to be erased, as well as replaced. But, erased is precisely how I felt – scratched right off his project pad forever. As a man, he had the ability to pick up and start again in a way that I never could – in a way that an older woman cannot. It seemed as if he could puzzle back together for himself all the stereotypical pieces of a complete family - he could just do it all over again - while I had to, once and for all, retire such images and reframe family, reframe complete. I felt, at last, up to the task and ready for a future.

I am not the first in my family to shoulder the work of such radical reframing. With the death of her husband, Ben "Salty" Soliwoda, my mother had had to do it at a much younger age than my own. I am none other than her child, though now, when I visit her, she no longer knows it.

....

Her frame is pure fragility, her stare blank – for the most part that is. Random flames of hostility erupt in her eyes and sporadic displays of fighting spirit inhabit her limbs: both surprising from such a hushed, white haired, elderly soul. When she smiles one of her generous unknowing smiles, however, the face is pure cute – on this mother of mine – just as it has been at every age of her life.

On the outside, the place where she dwells appears as lovely as a mellow wish: sprawling Cape Cod looking architecture nestled on the Lake Erie bay front, boats sailing by, seagulls roaming the lawn's edge. My mother was never a water fan, though. Lake Erie didn't impress or entice her like it did the rest of the family. Drownings are what she spent a lifetime duly noting in the Erie newspaper, the ever-present danger of water. She would have preferred a clear view of a shopping mall, had there been any preference left in her. A few steps inside this sweet wish of a place overtakes the outside promise of freedom and fair weather folly, for the elegant dining room, plush sofas, and personalized rooms are filled with those in the throes of restricting ailments and the harsh winter of their years. My mother sits among a particular grouping of them, lost in the permanent haze of Alzheimer's.

The disease nibbled away first at her mind, and then turned riotously towards devouring her well-maintained and well-dressed body. Her speech fell prey to it, as well. She doesn't care that a scenic lake sits outside the window, one that tourists eagerly flock to, and she minds not what pants are slipped around her waist and what blouse is buttoned up - not one speck of her cares or notices.

Having stayed in Erie, Pa., my sister bore the burden and the consequences of our mother's diminishment on Greengarden Blvd. She watched front and center as she slipped into reclusion and confusion. Karen was stretched thin when having the sense to eat became too much to ask of a woman single-mindedly obsessed with nothing but attending Sunday mass at Blessed Sacrament Church, of a woman who thought that every day was Sunday and that my sister never came to see her. My mother's vanity flickered out for good when she stopped caring about her appearance. She faded away entirely from the remains of her physical identity.

Coming upon my mother clothed in a mish-mash of garments was like a hard slap across the face. She floundered belligerently between an unwelcome awareness and an unconvincing denial that something was dreadfully wrong with her. But the real fight left in Irene Poplaski Soliwoda Siry expressed itself in demanding that she finish out her days exactly where she was: on Greengarden Blvd.

She cherished the blonde colored bricks dating back to Salty more than life itself. The fight, however, became an impossible one for her to win as every physical and mental part of her began to buckle. As my sister and I edged her out and away from her one and only wish we felt like cold-blooded traitors conspiring against the woman who bore us and loved us. We stood drenched in the waters of betrayal. The god-awful day of the move was the only time that both my sister and I wished our mother's disease had progressed further than it already had, that her mind had vanished without a trace. It hadn't then, but it seems to have now.

For several decades my feelings towards my mother consistently circled around the notion of protection: mine for her. They are different now. When I visit her I am overwrought with the simplest realities of a child's love: she is my mommy, I am losing her, I cannot protect her. I hold her elbow and the pale veiny hand attached when we walk up and down the hallway outside her room; I am struck by how warm her clenched hand is, as if I never knew it before. I kiss her soft and confused face more than I ever have, more like I should have. If only we could have. I brush the back of her hair to cover the spot where her cowlick twirls about exposing the pinkness of her scalp, just like I do mine every morning. So much more swirls about us and between us – I knowing, she not. How on earth will I bear losing what little is left of her?

Perhaps it's my own age, one in which nostalgia occupies greater space than it used to, but I experience Erie, Pa. differently, as well. It strikes me with sentiment, rather than despair – it does not suffocate my fully adult self. Scorching memories will always abide, but ones of belonging, as well. It was the home of my immigrant grandparents, my parents, myself. Now when I visit, I often make a point of driving through the eastside neighborhood, pausing in front of Grandma and Grandpa Poplaski's old house, then Grandma and Grandpa Soliwoda-Smieciuich's old house. The neighborhoods and the houses reveal two things: they are different and the same – like so many of my memories.

On summertime visits I cruise around the Lake Erie peninsula taking in beaches familiarly patched with blankets of young and old tanning bodies, the smells of suntan lotion and charcoal grilled hot dogs, the screeches of children and gulls. Heading south from the peninsula I make a turn onto Greengarden Blvd., driving past Blessed Sacrament School and Church on my right, and the continuous strip of green boulevard I once thought so extravagant on my left. The car barely registers the hill I thought of as being so hard to climb on foot at school day's end, it easily cruises to the top offering up a view of Teresa's Delicatessen, still defining the corner.

Progressing with a child's eyes, I slowly roll past the driveway upon which my dad tumbled me about with cases of beer bottles in the back of his delivery truck: reverse…forward…reverse…forward. What giddy and rollicking pleasure could be had without cracking open a single beer! I've come to find Salty more on the Greengarden Blvd. driveway than at Calvary Cemetery, despite its belonging, along with the blonde brick house, to someone else. From there I aim the car in the direction of my sister's house: Aunt Karen's house as we call it. My kids and I annually disrupt her turf with our boister and traditional mess, as does my brother's family. Karen is very close to being the only breathing member of the family left rooted in the ground of our birth. She, her pets, and her meticulous house provide what I can't seem to stop myself from expecting from Erie, Pa.: a home in the very place I felt so utterly compelled to run from.

My eyes have been permanently trained to soak in the abundance of magnificent old trees growing in the city of my birth, their towering trunks so thick and sturdy, their branches and leaves billowing out green tents of shade in one season, riotous color in another, and naked tentacled limbs in yet another. More than one perfectly bent tree trunk has been known to wink a seductive memory my way, bringing a wistful smile to my lips – a smile fully earned.

EPILOGUE

I started writing my life stories in 2007. Two years later, well more than half a ream of typed in paper spilled out before me. The pile collected dust on my desktop corner for a couple more years until I rustled up the pages, adding and subtracting galore for another long and finicky stretch of narrating time. Then, one day, it appeared as if a taut skin had grown and stitched itself around the entire body of it. It felt like a hand in a tight leather glove patiently resting on a steering wheel had guided a hundred thousand words plus to their final destination. It assembled itself like a finely sculpted body revealing its essence. One day the whole of it felt complete. I was done with it. The story was told. I was certain.

Then, 2011 arrived screaming for an epilogue.

The few years prior to the arrival of 2011 my life had snuggled up onto a solid bed of contentment. So much had improved, calmed, satisfied. I'd found a partner. First I'd journeyed through life with Jesus, then Bob stepped in to march a long and winding trail of ups and downs alongside me, then I walked solo, and then Joan and I crossed paths and recreated home together.

I didn't turn to a woman because of any nagging dissatisfaction or lack of interest in men, it happened because gender no longer seemed to be the primary qualifier for the companionship I sought - my search ran more in the unisex-category of *personhood*.

I discovered the reward of that personhood in Joan. But, then again, perhaps the switch over was inevitable for Bob would have been a formidable act for any other man to follow. He still had his claws around my entire notion of manhood and how manhood related to me. Did another man even *exist* who would willingly step into the ring with that unsettled, half-baked bulk of confusion?

For all my wishing to belong, my life had never been one of status quo, but nonetheless, breaking with status quo so decisively as to partner with a woman was anything but an easy bite to swallow - for Joan as well, I should add. It was more like chomping down on a concrete cornerstone of society and suffering the raw digestive consequences daily. I feared stereotypical assumptions of same sex relationships, resurrecting then battling my own inscribed thoughts of shame of guilt. I had no idea how to *think* of myself in my new state of being; in my eyes all existing labels fell upon me in a misfit. Couldn't I just call myself *me* and be done with it?

Generously and frequently I padded my therapist's coffers while wrestling with the question of what mattered most in my current stage of life. Well, I should have known the answer to that one: what mattered most was *mattering* - the same old primary ingredient as before. In forming our relationship Joan and I mined an abundance of mattering together, a treasure's worth of thick and luscious mattering. That's why the relationship feels so honey-coated and stands so tall, even while staring into cold multi-faced perceptions of it being so wrong. I'm simply not willing to spend another precious minute of my life living in fear of the branding perceptions of others. I've learned from the damaging futility of such fear and I've *finally* dumped that garbage overboard once and for all.

Back to screaming 2011.

At the end of January my sister phoned saying that I should fly home to Erie, Pa. asap. My mother had failed so dramatically since I'd put the last period on the last word of this book that there are barely words left to describe the scant remains of her physical state of being. I arrived to find so much less of her, the skin-covered bones resting in the same bed she had occupied for the past several years, her mouth gaping open, a wisp of breath inhaling and exhaling from the dark dry hole of it. Iris, the overly fed resident black lab, was sprawled alongside her bed, the place - of all places - the dog chose to call home. Iris had chosen to attach herself to, and devoutly watch over, the one resident in the entire place who probably disliked dogs the most. Nudging the dog out of my way, I sat on the edge of my mother's bed, staring at the brittle remains of her. For the next week or so I sat like that, though sometimes I stretched myself out alongside her smallness, cradling tiny clumps of her. Each night I took Iris out for a walk before trying to sleep in my assigned bed down the hall. After a few nights down the hall, I abandoned my bed and took to sleeping in my mom's room on a pile of cushions arranged on the floor right alongside her. Territorially, I claimed the final stretch of vigil keeping as mine alone - I wanted my mother to myself. Karen had spent years' worth of visits enduring and monitoring my mother's decline. She conceded the end to me. I was ready to force it, if need be.

Each morning I tuned in my mom's vintage TV to the classic movie channel in the hope that she could still hear conversation and music from a time she seemed to have remembered and cherished the most. But, when Super Bowl Sunday arrived, I gave her no choice but to indulge me, and I switched the channel to the game - she disliked sports as much as she disliked dogs. It was a selfish move on my part, but almost the entire Alzheimer's unit was gathered within hearing distance down the hall for a full-blown Super Bowl party - whether they knew it or not - with popcorn, pizza, and all, so I succumbed to the festivities and partied with my horizontal, unknowing companion.

My brother Tim and his wife Diane drove from Delaware to bestow their personal goodbyes upon our mother's frame. This time my brother and I cried freely in front of each other. This time it was impossible not to. A wet healing soaked the core of us and shortened the space between us. The woman who had made us family was stretched out before us, our mother. Tim and Diane had to return to Delaware, but they knew beyond a doubt that they would be back in no time at all.

The hospice nurse arrived early one morning and examined my mother with no more than a glance - all that was needed. She told me that death was imminent, so I hovered even closer to my mother, watching and listening for the knock on the door. I was expecting a defining grimace to envelope her ashen face or a gurgle to emit from her parched throat, some pronounced exclamation point of death, some certifiable statement issued. But her last breath came and went so quietly that I nearly missed it. And her face stayed the same. I stared at her, not believing that it had come and gone. "Mom?… Mom?…are you there?...are you still there?" I must have repeated that question 20 times in between disbelieving sobs. I fell across her chest - I would have crushed it had she been living - and asked the question to her over and over again. She did not respond. My mother was gone. She left Erie, Pa. and me on February 8, 2011.

....

I returned to St. Louis a parentless adult child, faced with the sobering fact that life's ending would now move on to coddle my generation of the family. My mother's death at age 87 was not a tragedy by any measure, but her physical absence assaulted me regardless. To cope I drew upon a lesson learned from Bob and threw myself into the blessed distraction of work. My latest venture was rehabbing houses, of all things. I found myself mustering up genuine enthusiasm for restoring houses in need of salvation - a type of enthusiasm Bob had *always* exhibited for buildings, but I had never fully comprehended. Somewhere along our way his excitement must have seeded itself in me for now I displayed the fruitfulness of it – tiny fruit compared to his.

Through the remainder of winter, the entirety of spring, and into the blistering hot days of August, I went about the business of transforming distressed dwellings into welcoming abodes. The work of redemption, the facelift of a second chance, resonated with me. One of those blistering hot August days my cell phone rang at 6 a.m. - a call far too bright and early for me to believe in it. I woke to the persistence of it, but didn't bother to answer. Surely it was a wrong number. But the caller rang again, so I rolled over and picked up: *"This is Max's neighbor…Max has been shot… shot more than once…the medics are working on him…they're taking him to St. Louis University Hospital."*

Shot more than once…*my son??? MY MAX???* The deafening questions burst inside my head. Joan and I tossed on clothes and dashed to the emergency room, arriving only minutes behind the ambulance. After a handful of long and agonizing minutes, a doctor approached requesting that we remain calm, as he escorted us into the ER room. He explained that Max appeared to have four or more wounds from a semi-automatic AK47, and that they were preparing him for exploratory surgery to assess the extent of the damage. I could have just a brief moment with him; he was hanging on to consciousness. As I moved towards my son he turned his head in my direction, his lovely blue eyes: *"They shot me Mom…"* I choked out every motherly assurance I could muster as they whisked him off down the corridor and into surgery. *"Love you…."* his voice trailed behind the gurney.

I am ever so grateful to the doctor who, at that insanely vulnerable moment of my life, led me to believe that Max would be *okay* - though I don't think he *actually* said that. I think I was simply incapable of hearing anything other than that, so somehow I heard it, somehow I made those words ring in my ears. After all, I had seen my son, I had talked to him, of course he would be all right! *He was alive! ALIVE!*

I tried to call Max's dad, but no answer. I called Daisy and remarkably for the early morning hour, she did answer, wailing loudly at the sound of "Max" and "shot" coming together in such horrific union. She thought that her dad was likely already out on his bulldozer, working on his latest and greatest endeavor at a place he called Cementland. She offered to drive out there to find him and tell him the news on the hot muggy morning of August 13, 2011.

When Bob finally phoned me I told him the little I could of the multiple wounds to Max's abdomen, thighs, and arm. His voice sounded stricken and his being walled off from taking any comfort whatsoever in the "he'll be alright" la-la talk that I had bubble wrapped myself in. By the time he arrived at the hospital Max's exploratory surgery was over - only the first of many surgeries as it turned out - and he was nearly ready to be transported to the intensive care unit. Bob and I sat beside each other in the ICU waiting area, both of us stiff and quiet until he took my hand and broke into deep convulsing sobs.

Oddly, I didn't know what to do. His sobbing was extreme, but I sat numb to it. We'd been, what some might call, "estranged" over the nine years since our divorce, though not entirely for there had been periodic contact - not particularly pleasant contact. It seemed as if he had, for reasons I could never fully fathom, totally voided any and all of the good of us and framed me entirely in the enemy camp of his memory. It brought me tremendous sorrow over the years, but I had finally come to grips with the terms of it for I could not fix it – I could not relocate myself in his memory. Daisy suddenly entered the waiting room, rescuing me from the numbing dilemma of the moment. I turned my attention to comforting her, for I knew how to comfort her.

Upon entering the ICU room, my bubble wrap instantly fell to my feet. Max was on a ventilator. There were wires and cords and tubes going everywhere and machines blocking the bed. There were bags of clear and red and odious liquids going in and coming out of him. There were bandages and tape all over him, his hands were wrapped and bound to the bed, his face was tinged gray-yellow, sweaty and puffy.... how could this be my son?

The tragedy that landed Max in the ICU occurred at his house, one of the houses I had rehabbed for his personal use. Max's roommate had arranged a rendezvous at the house at the crack of dawn with two men he had never met; an exchange was to occur, something not yet qualifying as legal as far as I know.

The roommate waited on the back porch to conduct his business, but when the men arrived with an AK47 in hand it became dramatically clear that they had come for more than the pre-arranged exchange. They forced their way into the kitchen as Max slept in the adjoining bedroom - along with his dogs, Stella and Sydney. At the threatening commotion the dogs, both pit bulls, and Max emerged from the room simultaneously, apparently startling the two intruders. One of the men abruptly began firing his AK47 at Max and the dogs while Max's roommate made a run for it out the front door. The two men charged out the back with nothing in hand other than the decimating havoc they had wrought. Neighbors heard the commotion, one calling the police and another, a fireman, dashing to Max's immediate aid. The police pursued the intruders and managed to capture one while the other escaped. The neighbor, the fireman, more than likely saved Max's life. A fireman.

Within the next few days - of what turned out to be my son's four-week stay in the hospital - I came to realize just how serious his injuries were, just how close we came to losing him, and just how lucky we were. It took seven surgeries, seven painful ordeals, before Max was deemed ready to come home with a battlefield forever mapping his body and a prognosis for full recovery.

The prognosis was better than we could have ever hoped for given the life-threatening attack, yet I'd never allowed myself to hope for less. I never visited the land of less for I knew that once there I would be gobbled up whole by the terror of the place. But it was clear to me that Bob had skirted the territory in his own search for understanding, forgiving, and healing. He and Max had been riding some rough waves in their relationship of late. Bob was clearly terrified and distraught over the possibility of not having the chance to right things with his first-born, his Maxie Boy. His encounter with the fear of permanent loss changed him. I thought it could never happen, but Bob changed.

For 28 days I camped at my son's bedside, departing at night when

ICU rules forced me out, despite my sly efforts at non-compliance. Bob appeared 26 of those days, if I recall correctly, often around lunchtime so that he could offer Max something better than hospital fare and eat alongside him. It seemed unthinkable, but Bob was visiting in the middle of the day, the middle of his *workday*, rain *or* shine - a hardcore change indeed. Typically, I left the room when he arrived to give the two of them the alone time that I felt they needed and wanted, but, inevitably, we wound up spending some time together alongside Max's bed. Seeing the same balsamic vinegar and olive oil glistening on their lips and spotting their fingertips was like witnessing personal intimacy. When Daisy entered the room the big belly of time seemed to creak and groan and readjust its face to reveal a long ago portrait of four. At first our togetherness was laced with awkwardness and reserve, but as the hospital days progressed we began to joke and tease in a familiar language, a language that tasted of home.

Max's horrendous ordeal brokered a cure for what had long been diagnosed as incurable among us. Healing my son and shining a light on a once-upon-a-time family was more than I could have ever hoped for from four weeks of hospital togetherness. But, as it turned out, the hospital cafeteria had yet more to serve up.

Bob and I were together in Max's room one morning when I decided to run down to the cafeteria to get a cup of coffee. He jumped up like a jack in a box, asking if he could tag along. Off we went, Bob tailing me like a gigantic child in tow. I got my coffee and he got his Gatorade. I was set to head right back to Max, but Bob asked if we could sit for a minute. I tensed instinctively, but reached to pull out a chair from around one of the many cafeteria tables spread before us and sat down. Without hesitation he gathered my limp hand in both of his large callused ones, leaned over the table, focused his eyes dead center on mine, and said: *"I'm ready to apologize now. I'm ready to say I'm sorry for my part. I'm sorry for hurting you. I don't want to hurt you anymore."* His look was so fiercely intent that the sting of it turned my head away, just as my tears crested from the hot news of the words I had waited year after year after year to hear. The long awaited words tumbled out with little fanfare, just a quiet ring of sincerity and the scent of promise resonating from them. With those few words we reconciled: BaBa and YaYa reconciled.

Max moved in with Joan and me when he left the hospital. He had some serious convalescing to do, as well as weeks of physical therapy to endure. Bob parked his dented red truck and entered the house for the first time in years. On his first visit I gave him a home tour, pointing out all that was new and all that was the same in the place we had shared for close to 20 years.

His visits to Max continued, one time bringing along his two young sons while his wife was out of town. We descended downstairs for playtime, he and I resurrecting our infamous Ping-Pong competition with familiar gusto - as if the balls had never stopped bouncing - while his young boys chased after our wild artillery of shots. We appeared to be documenting our words of reconciliation with action. Nonetheless, I held parts of me in reserve for I had endured too long a history of broken promises to yet feel secure in his latest one. Bob no longer possessed his formidable power over me for I felt strongly in possession of myself, but I feared more hurt. Perhaps that's contradictory - perhaps my fear still equated to his power. Anyway...I *felt* in control. Time would have to attest to the change in him before I swallowed it for keeps. Our new relationship needed watering, the steady watering of time.

....

Max's progress appeared to be for keeps. After only three weeks at home his mending patterned a schedule of slow and steady improvement. And Daisy was back to her scheduled routine of working with her dad at Cementland, doing whatever grubby physical work he instructed her to do at the 57-acre site of his latest and greatest creation.

Bob actually purchased the old cement-manufacturing site before we were divorced, and he'd been working on it for the 10-year period since, pouring an abundance of time, money, and heart into it. It's impossibly hard to calculate, but he appeared to be more madly in love with this project than he had ever been with *any* other project - maybe because he suspected that this one might actually be the last of his mega-scale-architectural-landscape-sculptural environments. It would go on forever, according to him. He was in no hurry to be shortchanged of the divine pleasure he experienced there.

Calling his current undertaking "audaciously ambitious" is likely a gross understatement since I haven't witnessed his transformative progress on the monstrous lay of the land for some years. But that will change when he I get the personal tour I've been promised. The tour will, no doubt, be riddled with wildly gesticulating hands and arms, a non-stop spewing of mumbled enthusiasms, down and dirty explorations, and a degree of danger - A Bob Deluxe Special!

An 8 a.m. call on a Monday in September forever erased the possibility of that tour. I answered the call promptly for 8 a.m. was a reasonable time for the phone to ring – unlike the 6 a.m. call in August. The oddity of the call was in that it was Daisy on the line so early. She was at Cementland bright and early for she'd promised her dad that she would arrive early everyday that week in exchange for a cash bonus - the magic green motivator. Daisy went searching for her dad as soon as she got there to provide him with the visual proof he needed to pay up. She visually scoured the hillsides searching for sight of the bulldozer he would likely be sitting on so bright and early. But Ricky, one of Bob's longtime and trustworthy crew members, rushed up to stop her in her tracks. Daisy spotted a flurry of commotion on a hillside a distance away, but Ricky began distracting her eyes by filling her ears with some on-the-spot-improvised-baloney-story about her dad having been in a serious accident off on a small country road somewhere. No one had *really* expected Daisy to show up so early. All Ricky wanted was get her out of there.

As Daisy fed me this befuddling blurb of news over the phone, I asked her to pass the phone to Ricky. "Bob's been in an accident…it's bad," he uttered in a voice unlike his steady reliable one. "It's bad…it's bad," he kept saying. "*What* are you talking about?" I asked with a high-pitched question mark. His next words sounded at the very moment I heard Daisy release a blood-curdling scream: *"Bob's dead, he's dead…he flipped his bulldozer on a slope, and he's dead."*

Ricky hung up abruptly because the police insisted on questioning him then and there. He was the first to find Bob's body slumped to the side in a dozer that had obviously flipped - nobody knew for certain how many times - and landed upright. The tumble inflicted fatal blows to Bob's head - a head that had endured bruise after thump after bump over decades of risky maneuvers for the sake of his work, a head that had seemed every bit as sturdy as a bowling ball.

The Monday morning news choked off my air…my heart ticked madly…my legs went rubbery. Breathless. Breathless. Suffocating.

Max was downstairs, blissful in the sleep of his recovery. I descended the steps in an aged manner and stared at the closed door to his room. The knock I was about to execute felt as if the thud of it would collapse the entire house. "Oh, Mom…let me sleep more," is how he groggily

greeted my entrance. I sat on the side of his bed. "I can't Max," I said in a
sorry whimper. I felt a hundred years old. At the feeble tone of my voice
questions rapid fired out of him as he sat up to face me: *"What is it? What's
wrong? Is it dad?"* "Yes, it's your dad." *"Is he dead?"* "Yes, he's dead Max...he
flipped his bulldozer." **"NO!"** he **screamed, "NO! NOT NOW!"** as he leapt
out of bed, then recoiled from the physical pain of it. He stomped around
in a kind of madness tossing about everything within his reach, all the
while screaming and crying at the top of his bruised lungs: **"NO! NO!
NO! NOT NOW!"**

My mind jerked back to Daisy with a start: *Daisy!!!* God, I had to get
to my daughter, Bob's daughter! Max and I willed our bodies into the car
and headed for Cementland, a 15-to-20-minute drive north along the
Mississippi River. Pulling into a lot heaped with a vast tonnage of scrap
metal possibility, we came upon Daisy being comforted by two more crew
members. They released her from their embrace and she shuffled slowly
towards us, moving at the speed of the age I felt.

Our three bodies twisted into a fleshy bundle - a limp knot of speechless
grief. We unraveled and navigated our way around the salvage mounds,
maneuvering through the skeleton of a giant warehouse structure,
continuing along the curves of man-made canals, until we reached the rest
of the work crew, along with Bob's two brothers, all standing immobilized
a short distance from where the bulldozer tilted precariously at the foot
of a steep hill.

Police and dark suited men swarmed the area and cautioned us back
from the dozer and the body slumped within. We could get no closer.
No one seemed to know for certain exactly when the accident occurred,
if it happened early Monday morning, or on Sunday, or even Saturday
evening, for Bob took pleasure in working alone on weekends whenever
he could. The only thing that appeared 100 percent certain was that Bob
departed this earth while shaping it.

The stunned and silenced lot of us stood for what seemed like hours
waiting for Bob's body to be disengaged from the yellow cage of steel.
Through blurry vision I scanned the familiar but lost looking faces of
Kurt, Ricky, Bobbie, Mary, Steve...people who had worked with Bob for
ages, enduring the agony and the ecstasy of his mercurial leadership. I felt
a motherly urge to address them: *"Thank you for all you did for Bob...thank
you."* That was the best I could muster, and most definitely the least. And
there were younger faces in the crowd, people who had come after my

time. They, too, deserved thanks, for Bob was rarely easy on the young ones. And there were his buddies still en route to the site: Gary, Bruce, Scott… I felt compelled to bless them all equally right then and there. I wanted to fall on my knees and bless them.

Still keeping the small crowd of us at bay, when Bob's body was finally brought down on a gurney, the coroner requested that one family member, and one family member alone, step forward to formally identify the body before they transferred it into the waiting van. Max insisted on being the one. While he stoically advanced to execute his duty as first born, I raised such a full-blown emotional ruckus at the thought of Daisy and I not being permitted to see Bob, that the authoritative congress of dark suits and police conceded to giving us 30 seconds to glimpse his face, once they'd gurneyed him into the van feet first. Daisy and I squished in close to the van doors to see what little we could from such a restricted and upside down position. From our twisted perspective the worst of Bob's head wound was obscured, but enough damage remained visible to physically confirm, along with the cold dark blue of his lips, that the unthinkable had happened: superman was dead.

Physical confirmation or not, day and night rained down utter disbelief that Chainsaw, Bob, BaBa, was forever gone from this earth - the place where he had embedded so many indelibly beautiful and riotous footprints. Having blatantly defied death on so many occasions, an army of us had been brainwashed into believing that he was invincible, that he would break the rule of death just like he had broken soooooooo many other rules day after day, decade after decade. Mostly though, his absence was inconceivable because he had so much *more* work to do, so much *more* that required *him* for completion, so much still to be defined. Stealing that work from him, from the commanding grip of his hands and manic mind, was almost more painful to bear than having him stolen from us. My grief didn't know which way to turn.

The following weeks I battled through a familiar barrage of the merciless blows inflicted by sudden death. I watched in anguish as my children fell into the abyss of a fatherless pit, swallowed up whole by the shock and suffocating void of it. I felt pathetically helpless - just as my mother must have felt - to rescue them from the bruising and heartbreaking trauma that I prayed they would never have to experience, not that way anyway - not suddenly. I knew this sorry territory well. I could not rescue them, but I would try with all my might to help them rescue themselves.

....

What can you say about timing like that? An August shooting and a September death - back-to-back months of emotional and physical annihilation. The son lives and the father dies, or *so* the father dies - an exchange, perhaps? A price? A bargain? A coincidence? Had Bob cut a deal? No, I don't think so. I believe that what happened to Bob was one of the very few uncomplicated things in his life: an accident on his bulldozer. But was it an accident that Max was saved by a fireman? Maybe Salty can answer that one.

SALTWATER

ACKNOWLEDGEMENTS

For years of persistent and astute literary guidance, I am deeply grateful and indebted to my dear friend Gillian Noero. To my sister, Karen Soliwoda, I offer life long appreciation for her sustained interest in my writing and for the bestowal of her family blessing. And to Dick Weiss whose curiosity and assistance nudged me the final distance towards publication, I extend great thanks.

Without Joan Newman, my partner, at my side my writing days would have been long and lonely ones. For her companionship, support, grammatical corrections, and love I am ever grateful.

I honor the memory of my parents, Irene and Ben, and my Soliwoda/ Poplaski heritage, as well as my stepfather Robert Siry. I treasure the past, present, and future of my children Max and Daisy. And lastly, my life would have been far less without decades of Bob Cassilly's life spilling into mine.

ABOUT THE AUTHOR

G ail Soliwoda Cassilly grew up in Erie, Pennsylvania. At nineteen she joined a missionary order of nuns and spent a decade living and working in the U.S., Europe, and Africa. Upon completing her M.F.A. degree, she settled in St. Louis, Missouri and established her reputation as a teacher and sculptor. She is most notably recognized for co-founding the nationally acclaimed City Museum, along with her former husband Robert Cassilly. She has a son and daughter.